UNSTOPPABLE

"Siggi was someone who would look at the Himalayan mountains and say, 'I can climb that.'"

—Rodgin Cohen, Esq., senior chair, Sullivan & Cromwell

"Siggi understood a truth that often escapes experts in the world of finance: Human nature is the greatest determinant of market trends. For someone with so little education, and no formal business background, his achievements after liberation are as breathtaking as his survival itself. A fascinating read, deeply moving and illuminating."

—Nouriel Roubini, professor of economics and international finance, Stern School of Business, New York University

"Hard work, intuition, and faith helped guide Siggi through the horrors of Auschwitz to the upper echelons of the business world. Though he never escaped the trauma of his memories, his experiences will now educate and inspire others."

—Marc Leder, co-CEO, Sun Capital

"Siggi's life story is a David and Goliath saga that reminds us what one individual can do—a unique, mesmerizing biography."

—Michael Berenbaum, former president, Survivors of the Shoah Visual History Foundation, former chair, US Holocaust Memorial Museum

"This book details the incredible story of Siggi Wilzig, a man who defied the odds and survived the hell of Nazi death camps and built a legacy in America. It teaches us hope and provides inspiration in times of trouble."

—Dani Dayan, former consul general of Israel in New York

"A powerful and moving narrative . . . Siggi was a towering Jew, a role model for the ages . . . a staggering success story and an amazing American."

—Rabbi Abraham Cooper, associate dean, global director, Ed Snider Social Action Institute, Simon Wiesenthal Center

"This book is a wake-up call to the threat of Holocaust denial and a gripping, powerful account of one of the most successful entrepreneurs and philanthropists in America—an extraordinary life."

—Harley Lippman, former chair, board of trustees, the American Jewish Congress, founder/CEO, Genesis 10

"After his liberation from Nazi death camp Mauthausen, Siggi Wilzig worked for the US Army Counter Intelligence Corps and collected evidence which I used to bring war criminals to justice. As a liberator of various concentration camps, and a US prosecutor at the Nuremberg Trials, I can confirm the authenticity of the horrors Siggi described. His survival and success after coming to America will be an inspiration to all readers."

—Benjamin B. Ferencz, chief prosecutor, Nuremberg, Einsatzgruppen Trial

"A tower of strength, a strong warrior who believed in helping people. Humanity needs men like Siggi B. Wilzig in order to stay human."

—Congressman Frank J. Guarini

"A story of struggle and triumph . . . his legacy will be forever remembered."

—Senior Senator Robert Menendez

"He taught all of us that you don't have to be a victim of circumstances. May we one day inhabit a world where more people live by his example."

—Congressman Donald M. Payne

"Given his lack of any formal education, Siggi's business acumen was incredible, and his life was a testament to human endurance—heroic and unparalleled."

—Marc Bell, managing partner, Marc Bell Capital

"Siggi had the heart of a boxing champion. He took on all comers, dodged lethal blows, came back again and again, and refused to quit. You've got to read this story. It's a knockout."

—Yuri Foreman, World Boxing Association super welterweight titleholder (2009-10)

ABOUT THE AUTHOR

Joshua M. Greene is a Holocaust scholar whose biographies have sold more than a half-million copies worldwide. Greene is a popular lecturer who has spoken at the Pentagon and before the Judge Advocate General's College, and his documentaries on Holocaust history have aired on PBS and Discovery. Greene has appeared in several national media outlets, including NPR's *Fresh Air* with Terry Gross, FOX News, and CNN.

ALSO BY JOSHUA M. GREENE

The Dressmaker's Daughter: The Biography of Edith Lowy

My Sister's Keeper: The Biography of Renee Hartman

Witness: Voices from the Holocaust

Justice at Dachau: The Trials of an American Prosecutor

Here Comes the Sun: The Spiritual and Musical Journey of George Harrison

Gita Wisdom: Krishna's Teachings on the Yoga of Love

Swami in a Strange Land: How Krishna Came to the West

Hidden: A True Story of the Holocaust

My Survival: A Girl on Schindler's List

UNSTOPPABLE

UNSTOPPABLE

SIGGI B. WILZIG'S

ASTONISHING JOURNEY

FROM AUSCHWITZ SURVIVOR AND

PENNILESS IMMIGRANT

TO WALL STREET LEGEND

JOSHUA M. GREENE

FOREWORD BY DEBORAH E. LIPSTADT

INSIGHT
EDITIONS

SAN RAFAEL • LOS ANGELES • LONDON

INSIGHT
EDITIONS

PO Box 3088
San Rafael, CA 94912
www.insighteditions.com

Find us on Facebook: www.facebook.com/InsightEditions
Follow us on Twitter: @insighteditions

Library of Congress Cataloging-in-Publication Data available.

Trade Edition ISBN: 978-1-64722-215-4
Export Edition ISBN: 978-1-64722-436-3

Publisher: Raoul Goff
VP of Licensing and Partnerships: Vanessa Lopez
VP of Creative: Chrissy Kwasnik
VP of Manufacturing: Alix Nicholaeff
Cover Designer: Jonathan Bush
Interior Designer: Andrea Lau
Editorial Assistant: Maya Alpert
Managing Editor: Lauren LePera
Senior Production Manager: Greg Steffen
Project Manager: Pat Walsh
Foreign Rights: Chandler Crawford

REPLANTED PAPER

Manufactured in China by Insight Editions

10 9 8 7 6 5 4 3 2 1

TABLE OF CONTENTS

UNSTOPPABLE

FOREWORD

I have been teaching about the Holocaust for over forty years and frequently invite Holocaust survivors to speak to my students. Among them have been a Jew who grew up in Germany and witnessed the rise of the Third Reich, a Jew who ended up in a ghetto and described the terrible hardships of life in that hellhole, a survivor of death camp Auschwitz-Birkenau who described the world's largest killing field, and someone who survived in hiding who explained the terrible psychological trauma of being separated from family and forced to adopt a new identity. No matter how intellectually stimulating and challenging my lectures are, presentations by survivors are what my students remember best. Many of my students have never met a survivor before, and it is always an awe-inspiring experience for them.

This book comes at a particularly critical time as, sadly, those who can speak most convincingly about the Holocaust are all but gone. That is why videotaped interviews, memoirs, and biographies of survivors, such as this one of Siggi Wilzig, are so important. All those who survived Auschwitz as Siggi did and who witnessed people being tortured, beaten, and murdered have an important history to relate; yet this book does something

that many other memoirs and biographies fail to do, and that adds to its significance. Namely, it includes the subject's post-Holocaust experiences. What was it like for Siggi to rebuild his life? How did he manage? What was it like to raise children whose relatives had nearly all been murdered in concentration camps? Where did he find the confidence to achieve what he did? How did he learn to experience joy again? Was he able to still believe in God?

What happened to Siggi after liberation is an important part of the miracle of his survival. Not everyone who came out of that dark time had the wherewithal to start anew, having lost everything and everyone. Siggi rose from the ashes, never gave up, and always moved forward. To be sure, like many other survivors, Siggi suffered from emotional scars and foibles. He was, after all, human. Yet he also emerged with the intent of leaving his mark on this world, with a love of life, with the desire to make a difference, and he did all that in an extraordinary fashion.

Still, he carried with him an enduring concern that the antisemitism at the root of the Holocaust was back with a vengeance. He was enraged, as every decent person should be, at the offenses of Holocaust deniers. He worried that, due to their propaganda, people would forget the past and fall prey to the hatred that was its foundation stone. Sadly, today we see that Siggi's fears were not unfounded.

This biography brings the reader into the totality of its subject's extraordinary life and leaves us marveling at the remarkable accomplishments of this man.

Deborah E. Lipstadt, Ph.D.

INTRODUCTION

There will likely never again be a businessman like Siggi B. Wilzig, the only survivor of Nazi concentration camps Auschwitz and Mauthausen to come to America, poor and uneducated, and rise from cleaning sweatshop toilets to becoming CEO of a New York Stock Exchange–listed oil company and a multibillion-dollar commercial bank. That he did so in two of postwar America's most antisemitic industries makes his achievements even more astonishing.

Most takeovers of publicly traded companies are led by American-born, Ivy League–educated men from affluent families with master's degrees in business. Siggi was an unskilled laborer armed with only a grammar-school education, a foreigner who arrived from Europe with $240 in his pocket and made his first dollar in America shoveling snow.

Everyone interviewed for this book agreed on one point: no one had ever known anyone even remotely like him. While all acknowledged the miracle of his having survived years of suffering during the Holocaust, what interviewees emphasized was how he overcame that tragic history to become a powerful force in American business. He stood less than five and a half feet tall, yet people described him as a towering figure who

had no fear of formidable opponents. One former colleague compared his achievements to those of David, the diminutive warrior whose agility and precision brought down the giant Goliath to become King of Israel, and suggested Siggi's triumph over his antisemitic enemies was no less astonishing than that of his biblical counterpart.

Judging by recordings of Siggi's public talks, he also possessed King David's inspired voice. Siggi exercised an oratory ability described by more than one former associate as "Shakespearean." When, for instance, he was invited to be the first Holocaust survivor to address the officers and cadets of the United States Military Academy at West Point, as reported in the *New York Times*, his talk was "vivid" and "personal" and conveyed the horrors of Auschwitz with such eloquence that students and seasoned veterans wept. His voice, clear and precise despite a noticeable German accent, rose and fell with the emotion of the moment. He knew when to lift a finger for emphasis, when to pause, when to grip the sides of a podium, and when to lean toward listeners for greater intimacy. Siggi spoke the way he lived—with all his being, attentive to detail, focused on educating his audience—and listeners departed from these encounters inspired as deeply by the man as by his message.

Customers, friends, and business associates described him with the kind of enthusiasm reserved for world leaders, with superlatives such as "unforgettable," "a volcano," and "a genius," while others called him "an irresistible force of nature" and "the most brilliant man I've ever met." No one failed to mention the one descriptive they knew meant more to him than all others combined: Holocaust survivor.

While creating an accurate account of Siggi's Holocaust experiences was daunting, the greater challenge was piecing together his metamorphosis after liberation into a memorable figure in postwar American business. Every associate, competitor, and employee interviewed had a favorite Siggi story to share, and each astonishing, frequently hilarious, occasionally shocking story contributed to the portrait of a complex man for whom the value of life was found in dreaming impossible dreams and fighting unbeatable foes.

Siggi was fearless; no opponent was too big. When, for instance, the Board of Governors of the Federal Reserve—the central banking system of the US government—coerced him into divesting either his oil and gas company or his bank, Siggi sued: the first person in history to sue the Federal Reserve. It was a war he could not win, but what made the fight memorable was his passion for righteous battle. To this day, a half-century later, that landmark case is still studied in law schools.

There is much about Siggi's life that was exclusive to those who emerged from Hitler's camps. Yet in this immigrant-survivor's unstoppable effort to overcome a bitter past and build a brighter future, we find a message that is universal, inspiring, and quintessentially human.

Vows

On the morning of December 12, 1947, in one of the coldest winters America had ever known, passengers on the ocean liner SS *Marine Fletcher* crowded the deck to gape at the Statue of Liberty extending her torch of freedom three hundred feet into the sky, her face turned toward incoming ships. "*In America, life is golden,*" they sang with arms linked, "*flowers are more beautiful and life is so much better. . . .*" It had taken the 36,600-ton steamer thirteen days to make the journey from Bremerhaven, Germany.

Twenty-one-year-old Siegbert Wilzig had been nauseous, vomiting, and losing weight for most of the two-week ocean journey. Hearing the cheers, he climbed weakly to the top deck and took a deep breath. The fresh air was a relief after the bad smells of so many people cramped together on the deck below. Winter had thrown a silver net of snow and clouds behind the Statue of Liberty; no buildings obstructed his view, and Lady Liberty's oxidized green body glowed in the morning haze. The *Marine Fletcher*'s engines pulsed, and the deck trembled beneath his feet. Statistics compiled after liberation indicated that nearly all Jews deported to Auschwitz died within four months of arrival. But here he was, alive and in America after having spent nearly two years in that concentration camp.

Steamships were too big to dock at Ellis Island, so harbor lights guided the *Marine Fletcher* to anchor a mile away by the Verrazzano Narrows. Ferries arrived portside, where the crew received passengers clutching weathered suitcases and shuttled them to Ellis Island for immigration processing.

Siegbert was young, but he knew from his years in concentration camps that appearances could mean the difference between life and death. With a little money earned after liberation he had purchased a fashionable fedora, winter coat, and dress pants, and he managed to enter the processing room looking dignified despite the grueling journey across the Atlantic. Windows in the one-story arrival hall were closed against the winter chill. Three-winged metal fans screwed to the wooden walls kept fetid air circulating. Paintings of American presidents behind glass enclosures decorated the processing hall. Siegbert stopped long enough to study his reflection and comb his thick black hair, which rose up from his scalp like a lion's mane, into an obedient shape that added an inch or so to his diminutive height.

In his passport, immigration officials noted the government special status stamp, which he had earned working for the US Counter Intelligence Corps, and waved him through. Siegbert—who later changed his name to Siggi Bert Wilzig, which he considered less European and easier to pronounce—scanned the crowd waiting behind a wooden barrier that separated America from the rest of the world. There on the other side was his older sister, Jenny, who of all the Wilzig siblings most resembled their late beloved mother. Seeing his sister revived memories of spring 1936 when he, Jenny, and the rest of their family had fled attacks by antisemites in their West Prussian village of Krojanke, Germany.[1] After dark, the Wilzigs climbed into an open wagon and made their way to Berlin, where cousins arranged rooms for them in a three-story apartment building at Georgenkirchplatz 20 near the public square called Alexanderplatz.

Once his family was settled in their new home, Siegbert borrowed his brother Erwin's bicycle and conducted reconnaissance around Berlin.

By listening in on conversations in cafés, he learned that some people were managing to escape Europe by securing exit visas. Siegbert visited a dozen consulates, looking for back entrances and open windows in his mission to steal the necessary documents. At one consulate, he watched a woman in the last stages of pregnancy push her way past police lines and run inside. Consulates were safe zones—not subject to German law—and a child born there was eligible for emigration. This woman was desperate to save her child's life, even if it meant giving birth in the washroom of a government building.

Over the next several weeks, Siegbert risked his life scaling embassy walls, breaking into offices, and gathering up rubber stamps. With the stolen tools, he forged three visas. He offered two to his parents, but his mother, Sophie, declined. "I was born here," she told him, "and I will die here." Siegbert gave her visa to his older brother, Joe, who had been a prisoner in concentration camp Dachau but managed to get released. Siegbert figured Joe was already a marked man and needed to get out of Germany quickly. In his youth, Joe had been a boxer, and some letters in the Wilzig archive suggest Siegbert may have written on the visa form that it was being issued for "sports competitions."

His sister Jenny was pregnant, and Siegbert insisted that she and her husband, also named Joe, accept the two remaining visas. On June 10, 1940, as Hitler's forces were marching into France, Belgium, and Holland, Jenny and Joe left Germany and settled in Shanghai, China. From Shanghai they later made their way to the Dominican Republic, where they were among eight hundred Jews who set up provisional homes in the northern town of Sosúa and eked out a living as dairy farmers.

Somewhere amid the English language books and magazines for sale in Sosúa's tin-roofed shops, Jenny found a copy of the US Yellow Pages. She bought it for three dollars and searched for names of jewelry businesses, calculating that jewelers would have enough money to provide an affidavit of support for her and her husband. Under "Jewelers, Rhode Island," she found the Jewish name Silverman and sent a letter explaining

their situation. In the following weeks, they received a favorable reply from Mr. Silverman, who provided the necessary paperwork, and soon Jenny and Joe departed for the United States.

Now reunited on American shores, Jenny told Siegbert the tragic news that her five-year-old daughter, Margit, had died of smallpox in Shanghai before the journey to the Dominican Republic. Siegbert remembered watching hundreds of other children die, forced into gas chambers, their dead bodies later thrown into crematoria fires, and made a mental inventory of his family.[2] He was alive. Jenny and her husband were alive. Their brothers, Joseph and Erwin, had survived. Everyone else was gone, including his four other siblings and their children. In years to come, he would calculate that fifty-nine family members had perished.

In a secret pocket of his suitcase, Siegbert had hidden two hundred and forty dollars. He dug into the pocket and pushed forty of the precious dollars into Jenny's hands, telling her to buy a bus ticket, visit Mr. Silverman in Rhode Island, and offer thanks in person to the man who had helped her reach America. Jenny tried to turn down the gift, saying she had money of her own. Siegbert insisted she take the forty dollars and visit her benefactor. Offering appreciation was what polite people did, particularly Jews who were lucky enough to make it to America thanks to someone's good graces.

In the two years since she and Joe had arrived in America, Jenny had found work in a sweatshop on Lorimer Street in Williamsburg, a refugee-crowded section of Brooklyn. In the assembly line of bowtie manufacturing, Jenny was a "turner." She took silk ties with one side open and inserted a metal pointer, like a car antenna, under the seam and turned the bowties inside out. Once the sewing was done, she used the metal rod to turn it right-side out again, which hid the stitching. That was her job, six days a week, twelve hours a day.

Also waiting at the immigration gate to greet Siegbert was a representative from the Hebrew Immigrant Aid Society (HIAS), recognizable by

a white enamel badge in the buttonhole of her jacket and a navy-blue armband. HIAS had been around since 1881, but none of its efforts at resettling Jewish immigrants came close to what it faced in the aftermath of World War II. There were approximately 150,000 refugees who had managed to escape the Final Solution—the Nazi plan to exterminate the Jewish people—and make it to America, all needing a place to live. The HIAS official explained they had arranged for Siegbert to have a free room at Hotel Marseilles in Harlem for the first few months. His sister Jenny had invited him to stay with her, but the prospect of a space of his own appealed to him more than sharing his sister's modest apartment. This was his entrance into America, and he would make it on his own terms. He kissed his sister goodbye and promised to call her once he was settled.

He walked out of the immigration building into the worst snowstorm in recent history and boarded a ferry that soon arrived on the Manhattan side. The snowstorm had become so intense that HIAS volunteers used sleds to move suitcases from the dock to waiting buses. Siegbert boarded a Greyhound bus and got off an hour later at 103rd Street and Broadway, where he entered the lobby of Hotel Marseilles. Since the stock market crash of 1929, the eleven-story Beaux Arts hotel, built of brick and limestone and crowned with a sloping mansard roof, had lost much of its charm. The forty-year-old building was now a dilapidated halfway house for refugees.

Gazing around the lobby he saw meeting areas, a recreation space, a medical examination room, and a kosher dining hall, meaning that the food served there respected Jewish dietary laws. Conversations were taking place in a dozen languages. He approached a bulletin board and read announcements inviting immigrants to receive free English lessons and attend screenings of films that would orient them to life in America. In one corner of the lobby a large map of the United States hung beneath a sign that read THIS IS HOW AMERICA LOOKS. Tacked to the wall were photographs of city scenes with ribbons stretching to the cities' locations on the map. He

watched arrivals line up in front of a table where volunteers distributed suits and dresses. Then the arrivals were escorted to their rooms. For many, it was the first time in years that they held a key to their own quarters.[3]

Siegbert looked out from his window, down onto pedestrians heading home through blinding snow. Amazement over being in America was quickly giving way to harsh realities.

"What now?" he wondered. He had nothing: no resources and no credentials. He spoke with a thick German accent, had only a grade-school education, stood five feet five and one-half inches short, and years of torture and starvation were still fresh in his mind. Yet here he was, still breathing, staring out the window at snow-covered New York streets. By comparison with the past, everything here was a paradise. The bus ride to Harlem from Ellis Island had been paradise. The neighborhood grocery stores, high-rise apartment buildings, and beer trucks were paradise. His smelly room in an overcrowded hotel with cockroaches scurrying across the scuffed hardwood floor, the heavy snowfall outside his window, the two hundred remaining dollars in his pocket—which would soon disappear if he didn't find work—it was all paradise.

On the street below his window, weary pedestrians fought driving winds and six-foot-high snowdrifts, evoking for Siegbert harsh memories of other blinding storms, when starving men and women trudged forward on death marches wearing nothing more than thin prisoner uniforms. Traffic in the New York streets snarled and drivers honked their horns, impatient to get to wherever they were going. Even to a twenty-one-year-old newcomer like Siegbert, it was clear that Americans, who never knew the inside of a concentration camp, were alive in every sense, moving purposefully toward some vision of tomorrow. He liked that. He would do that, too: grasp opportunities and not allow the darkness of the past to rob him of a bright future.

In that seminal moment of his new life, Siegbert made three promises to himself. First, he would never go hungry again. Second, he would

marry a Jewish woman, have children, and help rebuild the Jewish people. Third, he would preserve Holocaust memory and speak up whenever he witnessed injustice. He had no illusions about such vows. He knew better than to think he could change the world. Antisemitism would never go away and Jews would always be persecuted. That was just business as usual. Still, the Almighty had saved him, and now his job was to grab whatever scraps remained from the rubble of his life and cobble them back together into an edifice of yet-to-be-determined size and shape.

Staring down from the window of his room in Hotel Marseilles, Siegbert remembered a promise he had made after liberation. His best friend in Auschwitz had been a young man six years his senior named Lothar Nartelski. Siegbert had promised Lothar he would visit his parents once he reached America. Lothar had a sad history. He was born with one leg slightly shorter than the other. When he walked, he hobbled, which was sufficient in 1932 to disqualify him for an exit visa with his parents since most nations refused to accept refugees who were physically hampered or could not work. Lothar's parents had no choice: if they were ever going to save their child, they had to leave Germany and arrange some other way to secure a visa for him. The Nartelskis left Lothar in the care of a sympathetic family, wept in fear for his future, then hurriedly boarded a boat for America. Sometime after arriving in New York, the Nartelskis changed their name to Nartel and moved into a home in the Bronx, a few subways stops from Hotel Marseilles.

HIAS officials in the hotel lobby explained to Siegbert how the New York subway system worked. He buttoned his overcoat against the cold, walked to the nearby subway entrance, put a nickel in the wooden turnstile, boarded the next train, and made his way to the end of the line, Van Cortlandt Park. He found the Nartels' home and knocked, and Jacob Nartel's wife, Katie, opened the door. The Nartels knew about Siegbert from letters their son had sent home, and when Siegbert introduced himself, Katie screamed.

"Oh my God! Jacob! It's Siegbert! He's here!"

"In those days people still opened their door to strangers," Siggi recalled for an interviewer. "The Nartels had a small place, a three-room apartment that was typical German-Jewish, sparkling clean. Lothar's father, Jacob, sold neckties. He sold everywhere, including barbershops and shoe stores, three ties here, five there, a dozen somewhere else. They were in shock seeing me, but what a fantastic dinner they gave me! They wanted to know everything—what happened, how their son survived, how I survived."

Siegbert had not yet told anyone his story. What could the Nartels or anybody else possibly understand of concentration camps, of lice and filth, of torture and starvation and piles of dead bodies? The gap of understanding between those who had been there and those who had not was insurmountable. People in the 1940s were accustomed to movies about the war—Hollywood had been working that angle for years—but movies had a beginning and a middle and an end. There was no "end" for people who had survived the Holocaust. Still, Siegbert had made a promise to Lothar, whose visa had not yet come through, that he would find Lothar's parents and tell them what happened, and here they were. They were entitled to know.

So, as he would do many years later for Steven Spielberg's Shoah Foundation—a preeminent archive of survivor testimony—and as he would do in dozens of lectures for other organizations during his lifetime, he swallowed the pain and told them the story.[4]

Chopped Jew Meat

Siegbert Wilzig was born on March 11, 1926, the second youngest of eight children born to Sophie Sommerfeld and Isidore Wilzig, who lived in the town of Krojanke in West Prussia, Germany. Both of Siegbert's parents had been educated in the local secular primary schools. Isidore was a good-looking man with a sense of humor, a ready smile, and an interest in newspapers. His wife, Sophie, preferred books. By the time Siegbert was five years old, his mother had made her expectations of him clear: he was to do well in school and always keep kosher.

Like other Jewish families in Krojanke, the Wilzigs would sooner go hungry than eat non-kosher food or do business on the Sabbath. If, for instance, a customer knocked on the local jeweler's door Friday after sundown when the Sabbath started, the jeweler would not answer, no matter how slow business had been for him that week.

In addition to attending regular school, Siegbert took classes twice a week at a nearby *cheder*, or religious school, where the local rabbi instructed children in the basics of Judaism and the Hebrew language.

Siegbert's hometown lay at the easternmost extreme of German territory, about ten miles from a strip of land called the Polish Corridor.

The Corridor had been carved out of Germany at the end of World War I by order of the Treaty of Versailles—an amputation of fully 13 percent of Germany's territory. This loss of German land to Poland created a contempt for Poles among Krojanke's Jews and non-Jews alike. The people of Krojanke also blamed the Poles for their town's growing poverty, since the border change had led to a loss of trade. The town's 3,500 citizens worked at the few remaining industries, namely clothing manufacturers, dye works, breweries, pottery workshops, and brick and tile factories. Siegbert's father, Isidore, bought and sold scrap metal and pelts and made a modest living in a town whose real estate value was among the lowest in Germany.

Even at an early age, Siegbert operated with remarkable self-assurance. When he was six and just starting school, Christian boys from the village yelled in his face, "Go to Palestine, *du kleine Jude Schweinehund*! You little Jew bastard!" He stared up into their faces and yelled back, "You Christians—you can go to *Rome*!" then took off, fleeing down dirt roads, veering between houses and barber shops and racing into the forest before they could catch up with him.

On workdays, he jogged alongside his father Isidore's wooden wagon on trips to neighboring farms. It galled him when ignorant, hateful farmers mocked his father and forced him to pay higher prices for their scrap metal and pelts because he was a Jew. One day, Siegbert and his father stopped at a farm about five miles from town. Outside a weathered wooden barn, a farmer stood watching them. At his feet were sheepskins bundled up and ready for market. While Isidore negotiated with the farmer over a price for the skins, Siegbert wandered closer to the barn and looked through an open window. He saw the farmer's sons slaughtering pigs, sawing the carcasses into pieces and feeding the limbs and organs into a waist-high meat grinder. Siegbert made the mistake of walking into the barn for a closer look. The farmer's sons looked up, grabbed him,

lifted him up by his feet, and dangled him above the grinder's serrated blade. "Now we make chopped Jew meat," they laughed. When they finally dropped him to the ground, Siegbert ran screaming from the barn.

From then on, Siegbert avoided young people and kept company with adults. When school let out, he headed for the shops and haunts of Krojanke where men and women socialized, conducted business, and talked about grown-up matters. He studied their card games and learned to judge by their faces and gestures who held the good hands and who did not. His mother taught him her own insights into adult living, such as "never borrow money from a poor man," and she nicknamed him "one who sniffs around the pot" for his grown-up curiosity. Village kids weren't as kind. They called him "trough-sniffer"—pig—for sticking his nose into adult matters.

Despite the hardships, many Jews, including the Wilzigs, took great pride in their German ancestry. There had been Wilzigs in Germany for more than six generations, and like other Jews in the region, Siegbert's father, Isidore, had been a soldier during World War I and thought of himself as a German first and a Jew second. That changed with Hitler's rise to power in 1932. Rabbi Leo Baeck, addressing a gathering of Jewish organizations in 1933, declared, "The one-thousand-year history of German Jewry is at an end."[5] In the small towns and villages of Germany, Jews could no longer ignore the growing Nazi menace.

By 1936, it was impossible for Jews to do business in Krojanke. The Jew-haters were spreading rumors that this one or that one had made anti-Nazi remarks, and such fictionalized reports were sufficient grounds for the municipality to take over a Jew's business. The Wilzigs fled to Berlin, as rumor had it that Jews still had a chance to make a living in the German capital. The Olympic Games would soon take place there, and with press in attendance and the world watching, Berliners, no matter how much they hated Jews, would have to be on their best behavior.

At first, the Wilzigs did indeed flourish after arriving in Berlin, doing business as clothing merchants. Siegbert attended classes in an elementary school with an enrollment of 1,500 Jewish children. After that, he took two years of trade school. Things changed when the German government began restricting all aspects of Jewish public and private life. By 1936, Jewish children were no longer allowed to attend school, and Siegbert's schooling came to an abrupt end. Jewish businesses were shuttered or taken over, and Jewish men were sent to work in forced labor factories.

By 1938, the German army had conscripted most men capable of handling weapons. That left a workforce inadequate to meet the production needs of the German army. The police rounded up whoever remained, mainly the young and the old, put them to work as slave laborers in factories, and imposed severe consequences for not showing up or for failing to do a good job.

In 1943, sixteen-year-old Siegbert was in the middle of his night shift at the Weber Lamp Factory when an officer walked in and arrested him. The officer wore a brown wool jacket with wooden buttons, the standard uniform of regular local police, not the black clothes with shiny brass buttons worn by the SS, Hitler's secret police. In Siegbert's experience, most regular police weren't registered Nazis, and for all he knew this guy was just a normal policeman doing his job. Besides, Siegbert calculated, if this guy was an SS officer, he would be taking Siegbert to the police station in a car. They were traveling by public trolley, past dark buildings and empty streets.

"I don't want to shoot you," the policeman said. "But if you run away, I'll have to."

"Yeah, word of honor," Siegbert said. "Whatever you gotta do with me, you gotta do. I'm not going to embarrass you. You don't have to shoot me. I'll just sit here next to you," and then he held out his greasy hand and the policeman shook it. Siegbert's hands were dirty from the day's labor. The Weber Lamp Factory didn't make lamps anymore; the company had

been converted to manufacture munitions to support the German war effort.

For the past two years, Siegbert had been working twelve-hour shifts, six days a week. Half the month he worked a daytime shift, the other half at night, mostly making aluminum mine casings to be shipped to German Field Marshal Erwin Rommel's army in Africa.[6] Siegbert's job was to mount mine casings onto a motorized wheel that turned like a vertical lathe. As the casing turned, Siegbert pressed a hard steel chisel against the casing's metal wall to make grooves for a cover. The chisel spit out sharp curly shavings and sometimes, hoping to slow down production, he dropped a handful of metal shavings into the hole where oil lubricated the lathe and occasionally that was enough to burn out the motor. He had to be very careful. If any of the non-Jewish workers saw him do it, they'd report him.

Siegbert wondered if maybe that's why he was now under arrest. An attractive German Christian woman working next to him surely knew what he was up to. He hoped it wasn't she who had reported him, since she left him bits of bread from time to time in a paper bag and he wanted to believe she was flirting with him, a sixteen-year-old's fantasy of an affair with a woman twice his age. Before starting at the Weber factory, he had known a beautiful girl named Marian, whose family lived in a fancy Berlin suburb called Charlottenburg. Once a month on Sunday afternoons, Siegbert and Marian would spend intimate time together in the corner of a local Jewish cemetery where no one could find them. Then he thought about this other girl who worked near him in the Weber factory, a girl who always looked at him with adoring eyes and always wore a dark green overcoat—but this was no time to be thinking about girls.

The officer bent down and whispered in his ear, "You have a record."

What record? Siegbert wondered. Having a record with the local police was sufficient excuse for a Jew to get deported from Berlin in 1943. Then he remembered that five years earlier, at age eleven, he got caught

coming out of a movie house. Jews were forbidden to enter places of public entertainment.

In those days, Shirley Temple films drew huge crowds to theaters across Europe. Germans in particular couldn't get enough of the blond-haired, blue-eyed American child wonder. German toymakers sold collectible Shirley Temple dolls. The Ross Verlag tobacco company offered Shirley Temple "bonus cards" in each pack of Zuban cigarettes. Siegbert had no interest in Shirley Temple, but before each screening, movie houses ran newsreels, and they were worth seeing. Newsreels showed what was happening in the rest of the world, and the more he could learn about the world, the better his chances of survival.

Siegbert found a method for getting into the movies. Instead of sewing a yellow Star of David onto his jacket as the law required of all Jews, he used a pin so that he could remove the cloth star before purchasing a ticket. After the movie, he reattached the star before leaving the theater. This one time, police were stationed outside the theater and saw him make the change. An officer called him over, examined the star, and pricked his finger on the pin. Even though Siegbert was too young to be detained for long and was sent home, the incident earned him a police record.

Now he was again under arrest, sitting in a trolley, imagining how the Nazis were going to kill him, and wondering whether he would be sent away in one of those cattle cars people spoke about in whispers. Some years before, when police had begun rounding up Jews, officers entered his family's apartment. They saw his father Isidore Wilzig's World War I medal hanging on the living room wall and left without saying a word; war heroes, even Jewish ones, deserved a little consideration. But that was before *Kristallnacht*, the "night of broken glass" in November 1938, when Nazis destroyed Jewish storefront windows, burned synagogues, and arrested 30,000 Jewish men, including Siegbert's oldest brother, Joe, and sent them to concentration camps. Wherever Siegbert was being taken now, he knew this time his father's war record would not do him any good.

The trolley came to a stop in front of the dilapidated tenement building where the Wilzig family had lived since coming to Berlin. Residents of his building were assembling on the street with whatever they could carry: food, blankets, sheets, pots, professional tools, and personal necessities. The policeman took him by the arm and told him to stand with one of the crowds awaiting deportation.

"Take also your typewriters!" an SS officer yelled to the growing crowds. "Take the heads of your sewing machines! You're being resettled in a safe place where there will be work for everybody!"

Siegbert knew better than to believe anything the Nazis said and feared the worst.

In one of the crowds awaiting deportation, Siegbert saw his father and mother standing with his older brother, Willie, and next to them stood his oldest sister, Martha, with her husband and their seven-year-old son. Siegbert's other brothers, Louis and Martin, were also there in another group waiting to board. Everyone held suitcases and bags of food. Police herded them into open-back trucks. Siegbert climbed into one of the trucks and watched as his family members climbed into other trucks. The caravan of vehicles set out.

Twenty minutes later, the trucks arrived at a tree-lined field where on weekends in the warm weather Siegbert used to watch wealthy Berliners ride horses. A train track bordered the field. SS pushed people out of the trucks and ordered them to line up along the tracks, yelling out that trains would soon arrive to take them to their place of resettlement. The crowd was immense and Siegbert lost sight of his family. In the distance he saw the girl in the dark green overcoat, looking alone and lost, and farther down the line he saw pretty Marian from the wealthy Charlottenburg family standing with her parents. Marian waved to him, urging him to join them. Siegbert waved back, but after considering a moment he hurried over to the girl in the dark green coat instead. She came from a

poor family like his, he reminded himself, and all she ever wanted was to hold his hand. He felt proud of that, choosing her over the rich, beautiful Marian.

"I don't care what happens to me now," the girl in the dark green overcoat whispered to him.

"I wasn't a prince," Siggi told the Nartels, "nor was I Albert Einstein, but she looked up to me like I was both. She didn't know where her family was. She had no one, and she knew I wouldn't leave her."

The crowd of people caught in the roundup waited three days in the field for the train to arrive. Siegbert and the girl in the green coat finished whatever food they had stored in their pockets. On the third day, a train pulled up to the loading platform. Guards shoved people into the cattle cars—eighty, ninety, more than a hundred in each—and shoved a piece of bread into each person's hand. No one knew how long the trip would be. How many days was one slice of bread supposed to last? Siegbert and the girl in the dark green coat were pushed into one of the cattle cars, pressed tightly against each other, and the train departed. Through wooden slits they saw signs: DIRECTION KRAKOW.

The train moved slowly. One day became two, then three. There was no water. With more than a hundred people crowded into cattle cars too small for half that number, most were forced to stand during the four-day journey. Only a thin band of light penetrated the wooden slats in the walls. The train made no stops. People relieved themselves in a bucket, which quickly overflowed, and the filthy contents spread across the wooden floor. Siegbert watched several of the older people die, some perhaps from hunger, others perhaps from lack of air in the windowless cattle car. People moaned in pain and fear. Siegbert and the girl in the dark green overcoat held each other close.

After four days, the transport arrived at a railroad siding in Poland. It was night. The doors opened with a crash, and harsh reflector lamps lit up the scene. Uniformed guards shouted out commands in German for everyone to line up on the long platform, and anyone who moved too slowly was beaten on the spot.

"Unless you were there," Siggi commented in later years, "you can't imagine how horrifying a nightmare it was."

Siegbert overheard other prisoners say the name of this place: Auschwitz-Birkenau.

Auschwitz

In their accounts after liberation, survivors remembered arriving at the unloading platform at Birkenau.[7] Some described a nauseating smell; others recalled flames shooting into the night sky that came from bodies burning in the camp's crematorium ovens. Some prisoners remembered the sounds of barking dogs, while others recalled hearing violins. The Nazis, they later discovered, created orchestras using prisoner musicians and forced them to play while fellow prisoners were marched to work. In his 2002 video testimony for the Shoah Foundation, Siggi described his first impressions: guards in crisp uniforms, brandishing whips and sticks and yelling for everyone to get out and put their belongings in a pile.

A dozen men and women from his boxcar refused to let go of their luggage. The guards punched, kicked, and beat them with lengths of rigid rubber hose while yelling, "*Raus! Raus! Antreten!*" Prisoners who did not speak German failed to understand the order "*Out! Out! Line up!*" and guards beat them for disobeying.

It snowed the night Siegbert's train arrived at Auschwitz, and a cold wind blew across the Birkenau station platform. While trying to

climb down from the high cattle cars, some of the older people lost their balance and fell to the ground. Trucks arriving to transport the prisoners inside the camp rolled over them, crushing their bloodied bodies into the mud. Prisoners in striped uniforms ran up, threw the dead bodies onto pushcarts, and wheeled them away. Siegbert searched among the faces but saw no one he knew. Where were his father and mother? Where were his siblings? A guard in a thick winter coat came up to him.

"How old are you?" he snapped.

"Eighteen," Siegbert lied.

"What profession?"

"Master toolmaker," he lied again.

The guard pushed Siegbert onto a line of prisoners on the left, then pushed the girl in the green coat to a line on the right. Siegbert did not know that the line on the right was for prisoners selected to be killed, or that almost all children under eighteen were sent to the right, along with the younger children, the elderly, and the sick. Nor did he know that anyone without useful skills was also sent to the right, to be killed. Where did the impulse come from to lie, claiming he was eighteen and a "master toolmaker"? True, he did have some toolmaking training in trade school, but he never completed his schooling and never worked a day in his life as a toolmaker. The mystery of that impulse, which surely saved him from the gas chamber, would plague him for the rest of his life.

Siegbert saw family members in the right-hand line, including his sister Martha's husband, holding the hand of their young son. They saw Siegbert and motioned for him to join them.

"I didn't go," he recalled a half-century later. "Who knows why, maybe because like other teenagers in West Prussia I was brought up to obey commands from officials. Whatever the reason, I stayed in the line on the left."

Siegbert pointed to the line of people on the right. "Where are they taking them?" he asked a prisoner who was stacking suitcases.

The man looked at him with a sad face, raised an emaciated finger in the air and turned it in circles, imitating smoke from the crematorium fires. Siegbert, fresh off the transport, had no idea what the gesture meant.

"As a Jew growing up in Germany in those years," Siggi told an interviewer, "you expected to be beaten and mistreated. But a gas chamber? A crematorium? Now that you didn't expect. The stench and the smoke from the chimneys—and what they did to the children! *What they did to the children!* I can still hear the screaming of children who were ripped away from their parents. The memories don't stop. To this day, I argue with the Almighty that if the cries of children would leave my ears, I would go more often to synagogue. Flames shooting up from the crematoria, the horrible smell—it was unbelievable."

Siegbert again scanned the line to the right and caught a glimpse of the girl in the dark green overcoat. As if seeing her for the first time, he thought, "She looks so young, so innocent." He watched snow fall on the loading platform as guards marched her off with the others. A moment later, she was gone.

Siegbert, along with thirty other prisoners whom guards deemed fit for work, were pushed into a truck that quickly drove off into the night. Less than twenty minutes later, the truck stopped inside Buna-Monowitz, the Auschwitz subcamp that housed factories for slave labor. The smell of synthetic rubber reached him from nearby buildings.

"The minute we got there, we went through a so-called shower of freezing water," he described. "After, they made us dress quickly in striped uniforms and caps and broken-down shoes with wooden soles. Then they shaved our heads and forced us to run to another building maybe a hundred yards away, to get prisoner numbers tattooed on our arms. Some of the people fell from running in the mud, but you learned not to look back because if a guard caught you, you'd get a beating. Mud was everywhere, everything was puddles, and the people who fell and were lying in the

mud and dirt didn't even look like people. They looked like bunches of rags."

Once inside the building, Siggi stood before a prisoner wearing a white jacket over a striped shirt and pants. The man plunged a needle into Siegbert's left arm and blood oozed out as he tattooed the number 104732 into his flesh.[8]

As he walked away, Siegbert tried unsuccessfully to suck out the ink as *kapos*, prisoners assigned by the SS to supervise forced labor, marched him and others from his transport to the barracks. He dropped exhausted onto a hardwood bunk covered with a thin layer of straw. Through the wooden barrack walls, he heard people screaming and guns going off. Later he learned these were prisoners shot while trying to escape. Others, he also later discovered, stripped of all hope of ever escaping, chose to commit suicide by throwing themselves on the electrified barbed-wire fence surrounding the camp.

At three or four o'clock in the morning—no one knew the time, but the sky was pitch black—a guard stormed through the barracks, yelling for prisoners to line up outside. Once they were in line, he yelled, "*Muetzen auf! Muetzen ab!*" Siegbert spoke fluent German and recognized the words and the bravado. He had known bullies like this in Krojanke. They wanted respect from Jews, so he snapped to attention, clicked his heels, whipped off his cap, saluted sharply, and barked, "*Jawohl, Herr Kommandant!*" "Yes, Commander, sir!" It was a clever move on Siegbert's part to psychologically win the guard over by elevating him from his lowly post to head of the camp. The man smiled.

Some of the new arrivals spoke no German. They did not know "*Muetzen auf! Muetzen ab!*" meant "Cap off! Cap on!"[9] and did not remove their caps.

"For ignoring his order, that guard beat three of them," Siggi recalled, "as a warning to the other prisoners what would happen to them if they didn't respond to orders. That was the greeting we got on the first

day, and that guard did that with every transport that came in. For any reason, if someone's hand didn't go up fast enough, or high enough, or it didn't go up at all, he took a rubber hose with copper wire inside it and smashed them. He had this other technique for inflicting pain. If you didn't obey his commands fast enough, he hit you with his fist and followed through with his elbow. If the first blow didn't kill you, the second one could.

"He did the same thing if prisoners didn't straighten out their bunk bed to his liking," Siegbert continued. "It was just a handful of straw soaking with stool and urine, thrown on top of hardwood planks with a piece of paper for a blanket, and there was no way you could straighten out something foul like that. But the guards were sadists who looked for any reason to kill, especially that one guard with such brutal techniques. He took great pleasure in beating the heck out of any prisoner who wore glasses or looked like an intellectual or an educated fellow. The Nazis opened the prisons of Germany and brought hardened criminals into the camps and made them masters over kids like me and over priests and lawyers and teachers and anyone else they decided was an enemy.[10]

"You know," Siggi described for his interviewer, "because I could outwit the guards, I always felt superior to them. I hated them. I hated their brutality, their inhuman behavior. I felt stronger, more intelligent, and I had confidence in myself from childhood. As a child, I considered myself a very smart young fellow. So even though they had the guns and did all the killing, I felt superior. It was obviously a touch of arrogance, and some of it was justified and some not justified, but even in that totally hopeless condition I looked down on all of them."

Between 1933 and 1945, Nazi Germany established approximately 42,000 camps of various types for the imprisonment of Jews and other "enemies of the Reich" from across Europe: concentration camps, labor camps, prisoner-of-war camps, transit camps, and killing centers called

extermination camps or death camps.[11] Auschwitz was not only the largest concentration camp but also the largest killing center.

To facilitate the growing number of inmates, the Germans uprooted the local population from eighteen square miles of land. After evacuating residents from six villages in the surrounding area, Auschwitz comprised nearly 10,000 acres. Two miles from the main camp was Auschwitz-Birkenau, where deportation trains rolled in day and night. Between 1.1 and 1.3 million people were murdered in Auschwitz, including Sinti and Roma ("Gypsies"), Soviet prisoners of war, political prisoners, and "antisocials." Nine out of every ten people murdered in Auschwitz were Jews.

Initially, the murder of men, women, and children arriving at Auschwitz took place in makeshift gas chambers, which quickly proved insufficient to handle the growing number of victims. In early 1943, four large and efficient crematoria were erected in Birkenau, each with a built-in gas chamber. The new gas chambers were massive, capable of holding as many as two thousand victims at a time in each chamber. By the end of February, when Siegbert arrived by transport, manual executions in Auschwitz had been replaced by assembly lines that were "processing" more than four thousand victims a day.

From more than one million Jews deported to Auschwitz during its five years of operation, about 200,000 were chosen for labor, led into the camp, and registered as prisoners. Postwar records indicate there were about 3,800 people who arrived in Auschwitz on Siegbert's transport. He was one of six hundred who survived that first selection, during which camp officials decided who was fit for slave labor and who was not and should consequently be murdered. He would survive a dozen more selections over the next twenty-three months, including two at the hands of the infamous Dr. Mengele.[12]

In Buna-Monowitz, Siegbert was one of approximately 80,000 slave laborers working for the German armaments industry. The day began at

4:30 a.m. when prisoners were forced to run from their barracks to the *Appelplatz*, or roll-call square, where they stood for hours at attention regardless of weather, until the prisoner count was completed. Anyone who was too weak to remain standing was taken away to be killed.

The next order of the day was work details. Prisoners were marched to places of forced labor both inside and outside the camp, sometimes as far as six miles away. A workday lasted twelve hours or more, and no rest was allowed. Siegbert was assigned to dig drainage ditches, lay cables, and haul stones to pave the way for roads.[13] Supplies arrived by truck, and guards supervised as Siegbert struggled to unload hundred-pound bags of cement and long metal reinforcement bars. Three prisoners were needed to carry each of the heavy bars. Whenever possible, Siegbert positioned himself in the middle of the bar, earning a little respite for his shoulders by letting taller men at the ends bear the bulk of the weight. When guards put him at the front or back, the rough metal bars rubbed through his flimsy clothing and turned his shoulders raw and bloody. Siegbert waited until guards weren't looking, then ripped off corners from the paper cement bags and used them as padding for his shoulders.

"If the guards caught me ripping these bags, they would have beaten me," he described. "But the pain in my shoulders was excruciating, so I figured why not take the risk? The work was brutal and it would have killed me sooner or later, so I had to figure out a way to get myself reassigned."

One morning, on the march to work, he overheard SS men ordering a group of prisoners to join a bricklaying detail. Siegbert broke ranks, ran up to them, removed his cap, and saluted.

"Bricklaying?" he said, cap in hand. "I had six months' experience as a bricklayer."

He knew it was foolhardy for a prisoner to look an SS officer in the face, even if it was to volunteer for a particular job. After the war, many prisoners would swear to not knowing what their tormentors looked like,

other than that they all wore boots, since they dared not raise their eyes to their faces, let alone speak to them, which was forbidden and cause for the harshest punishments. Falsely claiming to have special skills carried even greater risk of retribution.[14] The guards looked at the impudent half-dead teenager.

"Why waste him?" one guard said to the other with a shrug.

They transferred Siegbert to a bricklaying detail and ordered him to teach the other bricklayers what he knew.

"I have to suppress a smile," he would one day joke with an audience. "I knew as much about bricklaying as you know about belly dancing. But I learned by working with them, and every day I learned a little bit more. So I was teaching one bricklayer whatever I picked up from the others. In Auschwitz, you were either sent to the gas chambers or else the Almighty was on your side and put an idea in your head for how to stay alive one more day."

Bricklaying took place outdoors in the rain and cold, and Siegbert's health quickly deteriorated. "I wanted to get into the Buna prisoner hospital in order to get a better job inside," Siggi described in his testimony. "The hospital doctors there never bothered trying to save the older prisoners—they were just shipped away to the gas chambers. They only let young ones in. But I wasn't very sick, so they wouldn't normally take me either. To get in, I had to have something they needed. I sneaked in there and heard this one prisoner doctor talking to someone in Polish. I spoke some Polish, so I asked him, 'Do you need help? I have experience as a male nurse.' To make a long story short, the man gave me a job. He didn't go through all the steps to test if I knew anything about being a male nurse. He was just impressed that I spoke Polish.

"The first day in the hospital," Siggi recalled, "*kapos* made me load Jewish patients onto a truck. I still have a picture in my mind of Jewish patients cursing me for not lying to the guards, for not telling them 'this

one is healthy' or 'that one is healthy.' The prisoners thought that a male nurse like me had the power to save them. I had no such power. I just loaded them onto a truck. I knew where they were going, but I couldn't bear the idea that I was sending them to their death. So I told myself the truck was taking them to recover at some other hospital or maybe some other camp. Three hours later, the truck came back with their clothing. They were all dead."

In the hospital, eight patients were crammed into bunks meant for half that number and lay on pallets covered with straw saturated with feces, urine, and pus. Patients went unwashed for weeks and their bodies reeked so badly the stench could be smelled far away. The hospital lacked sewage, and prisoners relieved themselves in buckets that quickly overflowed, creating a swamp of human waste. Hospital rooms were consequently infested with fleas and lice. Prisoner doctors had no supplies and dressed wounds with bandages made from scraps of paper and filthy rags. Persons suffering from diarrhea were given a piece of charcoal to swallow, and often the only medicine available was a word of encouragement. So ineffective was the hospital that prisoners referred to it as the crematorium waiting room. Dozens of patients died each day, and at night, outside the hospital, rats gnawed on piles of dead bodies waiting to be carted away.

"Don't think by any stretch of your imagination that this was a real hospital," Siggi cautioned. "Please don't go telling your friends, 'Hey, it couldn't have been so bad. Siggi told me there was a hospital.' This so-called hospital gave a little preferential treatment to Christians, but if you were a Jew you didn't expect to come out alive."

Extermination was the predetermined fate for all Jews, sick or healthy, from the moment they entered Auschwitz; and the few who survived, like Siggi, would forever be haunted by the mystery of their own survival.

One day a doctor took Siegbert to an area of the infirmary where he saw patients on the verge of death. Siegbert looked around and there on one of the lower bunks was his father.

"Let's assume that Auschwitz had close to a hundred thousand people," Siggi explained. "To have found my father in there was more than a minor miracle. He was badly beaten, to a point that . . ." He wept as he recalled the moment, then continued, "I knew that he wouldn't make it. My father's last words were, 'Son, in Berlin you and your mother kept kosher, even when bread and radishes were the only foods you could eat. But here, you will need your strength and you're gonna be alone. Who's gonna take care of you?'

"Don't worry, I have friends," Siegbert reassured him.

"The desk sergeant came the next day with prisoners carrying a big vat of raw grated potatoes," Siggi described for his interviewer. "Imagine that you're starving to death, and here you see grated potatoes like your grandmother used to make pancakes. You would give your right arm for it. The guards stood there and ordered me to feed it to the prisoners, and we gave these dying people ten to fifteen large spoons of these raw potatoes."

Siegbert walked around the room, ladling out portions to the sick prisoners, including his father. One older prisoner shoved the ladle away.

"That older prisoner said to me, 'What are you, *an idiot?*'

"'I'm not an idiot,' I told him, and he says to me, 'Yes, you are. You don't know what's what. Come back tomorrow. You'll see.'

"And the next morning, 80 percent of them were dead with their stomachs bloated. They had been bleeding all night from it. And there was my father, dead. The potatoes were poisoned. You never could figure out how the SS came up with these ideas," Siggi told his interviewer.

"Poisoned potatoes? I think I helped kill my father."[15]

Young Siegbert covered his father with a blanket and walked away before prisoners arrived to cart the bodies to the crematorium. "I wanted to remember him the way he looked in life," he later explained, "not the way he looked in a pile of corpses." He didn't cry when they took his father's body away. Had he shown any emotion, the SS would have thrown him on the wagon and sent him with the dead bodies to be cremated.

Isidore Wilzig, age fifty-seven, died April 8, 1943. They had been in Auschwitz fewer than forty days.

A few weeks later, word reached Siegbert that his mother had been sent to the gas chamber the day she arrived. Siegbert adored his mother, the woman who had imparted lessons of wisdom and who had always given him unqualified love. At least she hadn't been tortured or experimented on, he thought, remembering that in the camps there were fates worse than death.

"The Nazis did these horrible things to prisoners in Block 10," Siggi said. "That was the experimental block—and there I am, pretending to be a doctor's assistant. I couldn't even stand watching a chicken get slaughtered, let alone witnessing all these tortures. One morning, the so-called doctors had me arrange three glasses on a table. This was an experiment supposedly to figure out how to anesthetize wounded soldiers. Into each glass they had me pour a clear liquid from different bottles, like three shots of vodka. Then they picked prisoners and made them drink. The first one drank and slept two or three hours. The second one drank and slept for about eight hours. The third one drank and fell dead to the ground immediately. From one minute to the next, you didn't know what to expect.

"Another day," Siggi continued, "they took me with them looking for people who had a certain kind of a forehead that slanted backward. I can't explain it. They wanted people with that slanted forehead, and they shipped them from Auschwitz in Poland to a town near the French border. After the liberation, I found out that when the American and French troops came in, they found the heads of these people preserved in alcohol. Can you imagine? Sickening!

"Not only were they evil monsters," Siggi said, "but their minds were so twisted that at the same time they were experimenting on us like guinea pigs and murdering us, they were also offering us extra bread if we let them take our blood. According to what some of the prisoners told me, they were using our blood to save German soldiers on the front. This was the same Jewish blood that was supposedly poisoning the 'pure' Aryan race. And one

time, I have to admit, for that extra piece of bread, they got this little guy you're looking at to give his blood. But once I learned they were using our blood to save German soldiers, I never did it again. 'No. I'm not gonna save a Nazi SS man. Keep your damn piece of bread. I'd rather go hungry.'"

There was a boy in Siegbert's barrack who had been his schoolmate in Berlin until the day they shut down all schools for Jews. Siggi described him as a bright kid who came from a divorced family and lived with his mother. His name was Dargenberg Alexander, a tall, gangly boy dubbed by classmates "Teckel," slang for Dachshund. By saving his pennies, Teckel bought jazz records on the Berlin black market. His favorite artists were Duke Ellington and Louis Armstrong, and in happier days Siggi's mother used to sing a duet with him: a song made famous by American artist Sophie Tucker called "Some of These Days." *And when you leave me / I know you'll grieve me / You'll miss your little honey / Some of these days.* In Teckel, Siegbert found a link to his disappearing family.

"He wasn't as religious as my family was," Siggi remembered, "but after my father died in Auschwitz, I was alone, and I felt very close to Teckel. Then Teckel got a high fever. He was in bad shape. I knew from seeing prisoners on the brink of death in the hospital that he wasn't going to survive. We had no medicine. I had nothing to give him."

Siggi described that shortly before Teckel died, someone smuggled in some smelly cheese in a wooden container about half the size of a cigar box, "a poor man's cheese," Siggi called it, "infested with worms. It was like a cookie on the outside," he said, "and white on the inside where the worms turned it all mushy. People who liked it said, 'Oh, worms, that means it's good. It's ripe now.' Yeah, ripe. So anyway, someone brought a box of this cheese to the hospital foreman and Teckel smelled it. He knew he was dying, and he insisted I get him a piece. The thing was, you couldn't eat that cheese without drinking some water."

Tap water in Auschwitz was vile and poisonous.[16] Siggi remembered a drainpipe that collected rainwater, and the morning after a rain, prisoners

would lick the pipe rather than drink from the faucets. But Teckel was dying, and Siegbert could not deny a dying friend. "I knew he didn't have long to live, so I got him water from a faucet and a piece of that smelly cheese. He lived two more days." Siegbert made friends with another prisoner, a Polish Jew named Max, who also worked in the infirmary. "At one point, I was dying from double pneumonia," Siggi recalled. "I was burning up from fever and screaming for water. Max was the only other person in the room at that time. He couldn't bear to hear me scream, so he walked outside." Then a prisoner-orderly came in carrying a ceramic bowl filled with a dark brown liquid and placed the bowl on the top shelf of a closet. After he left, Siegbert climbed slowly onto a chair and took down the bowl. The liquid looked to him like the foul coffee they gave prisoners in the morning. When Max came back in and saw his friend about to drink, he ran over and gave him a shove. The bowl went flying and Siegbert fell to the ground.

"That's Lysol!" Max yelled. "You'll die if you drink that!"

After a few days, Siegbert had regained a bit of strength and was sent back to his duties in the infirmary.

"From then on, I had all the smelly soup and stale bread I wanted," he said. "How was that? Because the *kapos* took food from prisoners who were half dead and couldn't eat anymore and traded it for goods. I never stole food from any prisoner, but I found things to trade with the *kapos* for food or for a little piece of soap to keep myself clean."

Prisoners were devoured by filth. Everything reeked. Vermin burrowed deep into their skin. There were no showers for prisoners, and when it rained Siegbert stood outside and cleaned himself as best he could, anxious to avoid the fate of others: a slow, painful death by decay and the rotting of their own bodies.

————

Talking to the Nartels about his friends in the camp reminded Siggi of someone who had been with him in Block 9, a boy who spoke often about his mother from whom he'd been separated on arrival. One day, the boy happened to look out of the Block 9 window and saw his mother being marched into Block 10—the experimental block. "That's my mother!" he told Siegbert.

"Someone managed to get this boy's mother a note that she should look through the window and see her son," Siggi explained. "Each day he looked at her from his window, and the mother looked at him from her window. It was a sad sight. Then one day the mother stopped coming to the window. The boy kept staring day after day, but I knew she was dead. To the best of my knowledge, no woman ever came out of there alive."

Siegbert couldn't bear to see the boy's pain and made up a story to comfort him.

"You know," he told the boy, "I saw your mother come out of Block 10. I saw her go back to the women's block. She was wearing the same dress she had when she went in. She looked okay, a little thinner, but only a few pounds less."

"That's impossible," the boy said. "I never take my eyes off her window. How is it you saw her and I didn't?"

"You weren't there just then. It was during the lineup."

"Oh," said the boy, relieved, "it was when I had to go to the lineup."

"That's exactly when it was," Siegbert said, "during the lineup. She came out with a dozen other women."

Here was a boy like himself, who would never see his mother again.

"And I see him now," Siggi told his interviewer, "standing by the window, breathing on the glass to clear it so he could look for his mother. Soon after that, the boy went through a selection. He never came back."

———

After eight weeks in the infirmary, Siegbert was ordered to assist a prisoner-doctor in an operation. A boil the size of an apple had formed under a patient's arm, and with no ether or other anesthetic available, the doctor operated on the fully conscious patient. Siegbert was forced to help by holding the man down while the doctor began cutting. The prisoner screamed as blood and pus sprayed from the cut. Siegbert swooned.

"What are you," the doctor yelled, "a nurse or a shoemaker?"

Siggi's time in the hospital had come to an end, and another skill had to be invented if he was to survive. The following day, Siegbert heard SS officers talking about an upcoming transfer of young people from Buna-Monowitz to the Auschwitz main camp for training as carpenters.[17] Siegbert returned to his barrack and asked some of the older inmates whether he should volunteer.

"There's no job training in Auschwitz," they told him, "just gas chambers. You won't survive. Better you run now and grab the electric wire. That will be less painful than what can happen to you in the main camp."

"I couldn't take such talk about not coming out alive," Siggi said. "I didn't want to hear it. Whenever my mind told me I was not going to survive, the Almighty told me to keep going. So I stayed away from the others."

In the hospital, Siegbert had met a prisoner-doctor from Cologne whom he described as "a bit of a philosopher." Siegbert told the doctor what the SS had said about carpenter training in the main camp and asked what he thought.

"I can't tell you what to do," the doctor said. "It could be just as bad over there, or worse."

"I don't think I will survive much longer here in Buna," Siegbert said.

"You're a smart young fellow," the doctor said. "Follow your instincts."

That was advice Siegbert would remember for the rest of his life.

"Choices" inside Auschwitz posed a wrenching dilemma for prisoners. On the one hand, a choice based on dependable information could

save your life. "Don't go near that *kapo*," someone might say, "he's a beater." On the other hand, it was impossible to gauge the truth of such statements. The "right" choice could be just as fatal as any other—"choiceless choice," the option of choosing something bad or something worse.[18] On the day of the transfer, Siegbert made his choice and presented himself to the SS as a volunteer for carpenter training. There were two trucks.

"You pick," the officers told him. One truck would go to Birkenau, the other to the main camp. There was no telling which was which and no way to know what the fate would be of passengers in either truck. In one truck he saw five dead bodies. In the other, a handful of prisoners barely alive. Siegbert climbed in the truck with the dead bodies and the truck rumbled off and arrived at the Auschwitz main camp. Later, he learned that the second truck had taken the half-dead prisoners directly to the gas chambers in Birkenau.

To the left of the gate to the main camp, Siegbert saw a prisoner orchestra playing a popular polka. Siegbert recognized the song. *"Roll out the barrel, we'll have a barrel of fun…"* The truck entered the camp. Through the windows of a block to the right, Siegbert saw young women.

"That was Block 24," he recalled, "a brothel. The women were for the SS. Women who had been in Block 24 for six or eight months were taken away, nobody knew where to, and fresh young girls were brought in to replace them."

Past Block 24 was another building, which Siegbert later learned was the punishment block. "That's where people were hanged," he said. "That's what you saw when you first came into the Auschwitz main camp. An orchestra, a bordello, and the gallows."

In the truck, he overheard SS saying they could use someone with experience to do their laundry. "Oh, I worked in a laundry for years," the seventeen-year-old lied, fabricating yet another explanation for how he had acquired his skills. They gave him the job and for a while he washed laundry until it became clear he knew nothing about it. "Oh, my expertise is not the cleaning part," Siegbert explained to the SS, "it's the *hot water*

part," and for the next several months the SS had him shovel coal into six ovens that heated water for the laundry.

On the day Siggi told his story to Lothar's parents, the blizzard outside their home dumped more than twenty-six inches of snow on New York City, burying cars and sidewalks and making streets impassable. Siggi watched from a window of their living room as a blanket of snow covered Eagle Avenue. Across the street, the sidewalk leading to a drugstore disappeared beneath the blizzard. He had arrived at the Nartels' home on one of the last subways before the mayor shut down service, and Siggi would be there for the night. Katie Nartel prepared dinner while he continued recounting his story.

Prisoners, he explained, were forced to stand naked in the cold, often for hours at a time, while doctors examined them to see who would live and who would die. Some inmates jogged in place to show they still had energy. Some of those selected to die were lined up in a narrow alley that connected Blocks 1 and 2. This was the location of the prisoner laundry where Siegbert was put to work on night shifts. The laundry consisted of a series of tubs and coal ovens[19] housed in a room with two windows that opened onto an alley. It was down this alley that the SS marched prisoners to their death in the gas chambers. One time, he described, he and two other laundry workers waited until the SS were at the far end of the alley, then they reached out through the window and pulled into the laundry room any younger inmates they could grab. One day Siegbert was picked for death and stood in line with others waiting to die in the gas chambers. The guards pushed the line forward, and Siegbert was saved when comrades pulled him through the same window.

Like other jobs, the laundry room assignment did not last long, and soon Siegbert found himself again on a work detail outside in the cold and rain. When it rained in Auschwitz, fog set in, and on one particularly

rainy day, to discourage anyone on Siegbert's work detail from attempting to escape by hiding in the fog, guards took Siegbert and a hundred other prisoners into a nearby barn. One guard in particular was well known to prisoners as a violent drunkard.

"How do you make Hungarian goulash?" he yelled. "Who can tell me?"

A prisoner spoke up, describing tomatoes and other ingredients. The guard stood up, walked over, and smashed his face with the butt of his rifle, sending him reeling. "You forgot the onions," the guard said. Then he turned to the others. "*Who can sing?*" he yelled. "*Who can sing, you Jew bastards?*" They were all hungry and dying and no one felt like singing, but Siegbert calculated that here was a madman who might kill them if they refused to sing. He stood up and put one foot over the other, dancing in quick-time, and sang "*Roll out the barrel, we'll have a barrel of fun . . .*" The guard clapped and kept time with his boot. When Siegbert finished, the guard handed him a slice of stale bread.

"An extra slice of bread to me tasted like a filet mignon dinner," Siggi described, "but what would have happened if he didn't like my singing? You never knew if something you did would save you or kill you."

The SS imposed a policy called *Vernichtung durch Arbeit*, "destruction through work," forcing prisoners to carry out assignments as senseless as they were torturous. Prisoners were made to pick up rocks weighing as much as 100 pounds, run with them from one place to another, carefully stack them, then carry those same rocks back to where they had come from.

"They wanted to kill us from exhaustion," Siggi explained, "or else from starvation. There was no real food. You had a bowl of putrid soup made with rotten carrot peels or rotten potato peels and foul cabbage that stank to heaven." Occasionally, there were opportunities to steal food. One day a master sergeant put Siegbert to work tending four rabbits the officer was fattening for Christmas dinner. "If they die, you die," he threatened. Then he signed a paper that allowed Siegbert to

go to the pigsty in the officers' area to collect food in a bucket for the rabbits.

Siggi knew that the food given to the pigs was better than the food given to the inmates, so from an old piece of tin he fashioned a tray that sat about two inches from the top of the bucket. He entered the pen, scooped up the pigs' food, and filled the bottom of the bucket. That was the food he would eat later. Then he covered it with the tray, added two more inches of food for the rabbits, and started walking out. An SS captain with a whip in his hand stopped him. Siegbert showed his pass. The captain looked at the paper, then at the full bucket. How much can four rabbits eat? He started poking his whip into the bucket. If the SS discovered the false bottom and Siegbert's attempt to steal the pig food, Siegbert would be brutally whipped or shot instantly.

At that moment, an SS woman rode by on her bicycle.

"There was only one attractive SS woman in the camp," Siegbert explained, "and she had this sexy way of wiggling her behind on the saddle of the bicycle, so naturally everybody looked, including that SS man. So, he's watching her, and he waves me on. That SS woman saved my life—twice. That was once. The second time, I got caught with mittens I'd stolen from a warehouse. For that I could get twenty-five lashes with a bullwhip. In my frail condition, that would have surely killed me. A guard was taking down my number for his report, and just then that same blond SS woman rode by on her bicycle. He got distracted looking at her behind moving around while also writing down my number."

The next day during roll call, guards read out the numbers of prisoners sentenced to the punishment block. Siegbert heard his number being called: "One—zero—four—" The numbers were correct—except the last one.

"Thank God for her behind," he thought.

Sometimes when he and Lothar were marched outside the camp, they met Polish civilians who had goods to trade. "I don't want you to get the impression that we were running a department store," Siggi explained,

"but sometimes we were able to make a trade. One day I traded a watch for a piece of silk.[20] I marched back into camp with that silk wrapped around my body under my prisoner uniform. But I knew there would be a search. There was this SS man who stood at the gate and always grabbed this one or that one and checked him for contraband. My thought was that if I bumped into him, he would hit me but probably not go to the trouble of searching my clothes. Where that idea came from, only the Almighty knows."

Siegbert knew this guard, Oswald Kaduk, from previous encounters. Once, Kaduk had forced Siegbert to watch while he beat up Siegbert's friend Lothar. Of all the pitiless men who abused and tortured prisoners in Auschwitz, Kaduk was among the worst. According to Kaduk's testimony in the 1963–65 Frankfurt war crimes trials, he was the son of a blacksmith and had grown up with a need to prove himself a "real" German by demonstrating he could be tough.[21]

"This killer, Kaduk, was the man I made it my business to bump into so he would hit me," Siggi recalled. "We marched into camp, eight across. When I got to Kaduk, I hit him with my shoulder. He gave me a shot in the head with his fist—and sure enough, he didn't search me."

Back in his barrack, Siegbert frantically looked for a place to hide the length of silk cloth. He peered through the keyhole of the door to make sure no guards were approaching and saw an SS officer coming toward the barrack. By the side of the barrack was a vat of boiling hot soup reserved for the SS. Without thinking twice, Siegbert ran out and pushed the cloth into the boiling soup, burning his hands, then raced back inside and hid his scorched hands behind his back.

"When the officer got his soup, he found the silk cloth in it," Siggi described. "That Nazi killer looked around trying to figure out who'd put it there, but when his eyes fell on me, I remained calm. Thank God he didn't look closer. Had he seen my scorched hands he'd know I'd done it. These were the kind of split-second decisions I had to make every day just to stay alive."

"I was a *schlepper*," Siggi explained, using the Yiddish word for a gofer or carrier, "cement bags, rebars, anything they wanted moved I was forced to carry. But even if you were useful to them, they might still pick you for death. You would go through life-and-death selections—left meant you lived another day, right meant you died that day—and what could you do to save your life? Pinch your cheeks to make them bright and healthier looking? You never knew what would help. Being a professor or a lawyer didn't help you. Intelligence didn't help. The prisoners had a saying, 'All the bright ones went up the chimney.' There was no telling who would survive and who would die. We had one *kapo* who beat anyone with red hair. Other *kapos* beat anyone who was very tall or homosexual[22] or had a physical deformity. There was no pattern at all. It was unbelievable.

"I sit sometimes now," he recalled, "and I remember the hunger, and I say to myself, 'It couldn't have been me. I wasn't there. It couldn't have been me.'"

In Auschwitz, hunger was a twisting, gnawing pain that made prisoners dizzy and drove them insane.[23] Inmates were allotted one foul bowl of rancid soup, fewer than 700 calories per day. Bread was like gold, rare and precious. Each day, Siegbert noted his legs growing thinner, his arms becoming more and more like sticks and his pants hanging looser. Hunger became so unbearable that he resorted to eating anything.

"I remember eating mustard," Siegbert said, recalling for the Nartels a summer afternoon in Auschwitz. He had not eaten in several days. There was a fence, and on the other side were the officers' quarters. From a distance, he watched the SS with their families in the yard, having a picnic.

"The children of the SS were eating and dancing, while elsewhere on the campgrounds Jewish children were burning," he described. "The smell was always there, but it depended where the wind came from. Maybe two-thirds of the time you had the smell, and it is a little bit hard to

describe because there is no other smell like this. What comparison do we have? Have you ever smelled people burning? I hadn't, and you don't want to know. But it was there, the real McCoy if you can call it that.

"One of the SS had thrown a paper cup of mustard over the fence," he described. "I was so hungry I ate the whole thing. I got very sick from it, but I ate the mustard.

"Let me tell you something about hunger," he said. "On Sunday afternoons when we had a little time off from the labor details, we would talk for hours about food. The Czechs said that back home when they cooked potatoes, they added plums or bacon. But the Greeks said no, no, you add olives. And after talking about food for an hour, you felt like you actually ate something.[24] That's how hungry we were. You ate whatever you could, and somehow you stayed alive. Mustard for you is just mustard. In Auschwitz, mustard was food."

Everything in Auschwitz took on bizarre and tragic meaning, not just mustard. Something as common as rain, something that would normally nourish life, in Auschwitz meant another kind of death. Rain penetrated everything, soaking clothing, blankets, and the wooden planks of barrack roofs. "What can you do when all you have is one wet, ragged prisoner uniform? You can take it off to dry, but then you might freeze to death. Or you can leave it on, but then you could catch pneumonia and die from that.

"There was no knowing what was right or wrong," he said. "I don't know how I'm here today. We all went through so many difficult horrible things."

One job in Auschwitz favored survival: working in the storage warehouses, which prisoners called "Canada," a country they envisioned as a place of great riches. It was in the Canada warehouses that clothing, shoes, valises, and other items confiscated from arriving prisoners were sorted and stored. Between 1,000 and 1,600 prisoners worked at any one time in the Canada warehouses, sorting through tens of thousands of suitcases and other bag-

gage. Watches, bracelets, cash, fountain pens, safety razors, scissors, pocket flashlights, rings, and other valuables were stored in wooden crates, which were then sealed and shipped to Nazi headquarters in Berlin.

An assignment to the Canada warehouses was highly prized, as it meant working indoors with opportunities to "organize" or steal jewelry, medicine, and other items found in the lining of clothes confiscated by the Nazis. One of the prisoners assigned to Canada was the Nartels' son, Lothar. By this time Siegbert had discovered how important allegiances were to survival, although conditions in Auschwitz did not favor friendships. In a world where fear and suspicion were constant, there was little to foster trust or affection among prisoners. Tempers flared, suspicions festered, and self-preservation outweighed impulses toward generosity or closeness.

Still, while extreme conditions drove some inmates to trust no one, those same conditions forged bonds among others. Finding someone you could trust meant having an ally when scavenging for food or other survival needs. Lothar appreciated Siegbert's skill at solving problems, and Siegbert admired Lothar's calm demeanor and general knowledge. When Lothar was assigned to the Canada warehouses, his first thought was to find a way to bring Siegbert in with him, and he came up with a plan.

"Someone working in the warehouse died," Siggi told the Nartels, "and at the risk of his own life, Lothar gave me the dead prisoner's number and changed the records. That's how he got me in to work with him in the warehouse."

Siegbert and Lothar sorted clothes, shared food, squirreled away jewelry and other valuables inside empty toilet paper rolls for use in the camp's black market, and nurtured a friendship that helped keep them sane.

"By getting me that job, he saved my life," Siegbert told Lothar's parents. "Thank God," they said and wept after hearing about the countless sufferings their son and Siegbert had endured.

Prisoners distinguished between "organizing"—stealing from the Nazis—and stealing from one another. If a prisoner took another prisoner's

food, the prisoner hierarchy judged him as guilty as a murderer. If a man stole another man's bread, he could be beaten to death by his fellow inmates.[25] Organizing or robbing from the Nazis, on the other hand, was considered commendable, and anyone capable of doing so without getting caught was generally respected. Opportunities to organize were greater in Auschwitz than in other camps, as Jews transported to Auschwitz were told they were being resettled and should take valuables or anything useful for starting a new life in the east. On arrival, everything was confiscated.

Anyone caught stealing from the Canada warehouses faced severe consequences, but despite constant surveillance by guards, occasionally opportunities arose to "organize" valuables. With these treasures, inmates bartered with SS men and civilian workers for a range of goods: alcohol, cigarettes, food, soap, a better pair of shoes. The usual value of these goods was nowhere near what prisoners had to pay for them. One survivor reported that in the women's camp the price of an apple was a diamond ring. Inmates used their warehouse booty to buy off guards, obtain better work details, and receive preferential care in the infirmary. The corruption went as high as the camp commandant's office, where enough gold and cash could even rescind orders of punishment and execution.

In one mountainous pile of clothing Siegbert found items marked with the names of his relatives, the Sommerfelds, who had fled Germany for Holland in the late 1930s. "Because of their upbringing," Siggi told his interviewer, "they always marked personal information on their clothing—names, dates of birth, and where they were born—like parents in the United States do for their children going to summer camp. It was a one in a million chance that I would find their clothes in such big piles of clothing."

Nazi soldiers had caught up with the Sommerfelds in Holland and deported them to Auschwitz, and Siegbert had found all that was left of his cousins: a handful of shirts and vests.

It was in the spring of 1944, when Siegbert had been in Auschwitz a full year, that American planes began flying over the camp. By then, the Allies controlled the skies and the US 15th Air Force was flying from southern Italy, pounding Axis industrial complexes in Central and East Central Europe. For the first time, Auschwitz and its rail lines were within striking distance of Allied bombers. Escapees had been delivering detailed reports to Allied government authorities on the camp's geographic layout as well as on the horrors of the gas chambers and crematoria. Based on these reports, the War Refugee Board and other reputable agencies had repeatedly urged the US War Department to bomb Auschwitz and stop the slaughter, but the US military declined, arguing that bombing the concentration camps would divert from the more pressing need of winning the war.

Between July and October 1944, 2,700 bombers flew missions in the vicinity of Auschwitz. On Sunday, August 20, 127 Flying Fortresses, escorted by 100 Mustang fighters, dropped 1,336 five-hundred-pound high-explosive bombs on the factory areas of Auschwitz—fewer than five miles east of the gas chambers—yet no bombs were dropped on the gas chambers themselves, and no effort was made to stop the slaughter of Jews inside the camp.[26]

"Not once," Siggi said, "did they ever try to bomb the crematoria or the gas chambers or the railways that were bringing people to be slaughtered. When they heard planes coming, the Nazis put up these artificial clouds of smoke to hide the ammunition factories. By mistake, the Americans dropped three or four bombs near where we were, and a few of the SS died in the bombing—but only by mistake. No military action was ever officially undertaken to destroy the gas chambers. Other SS knew the end of the war was coming, and you should have seen how they began to act as if they were our best friends. As the bombs exploded, they called out to us, 'Comrades, take shelter here with us.' Yeah, sure, now we were their comrades. Just three hours earlier they would have gladly killed us. But now American forces were winning the war, and the Germans were

going to become prisoners. So now they called us 'comrades,' as if that would get them more favorable treatment. Frankly, we were praying to the heavens that the Americans would bomb us all to smithereens, but Auschwitz was never bombed again, intentionally or unintentionally. The next day it was back to normal: selections and killings."

The battle between Germany and the Soviet Union—the "Eastern Front"—deteriorated into the largest, most brutal engagement in military history. Of the estimated seventy million deaths in World War II, more than thirty million occurred there. By New Year's Day of 1945, most of German East Prussia was under Soviet control and the Third Reich teetered on the edge of defeat.

On January 17, 1945, Stalin's forces entered Warsaw and were within days of penetrating Germany. In preparation for the Soviet invasion, and to avoid eyewitnesses to Nazi crimes from falling into enemy hands, the Nazis evacuated their victims from Auschwitz and other concentration camps and marched them to camps deep inside Germany and Austria. German authorities continued the death marches as late as May, just days before war's end.

The night before the death marches from Auschwitz began, when the other prisoners were asleep, Siegbert, Lothar, and four other men crept out and hid in the mud under the barracks, huddled together in their blankets, watching fires burn in the distance, and debated what to do. Rumors had it the Germans were going to blow up the camp to leave no evidence of their crimes. One man said the "healthy" prisoners—those who could still walk—would be marched out at dawn, God only knew where to. Another man said it was impossible to stay hidden under the barracks. Who knew how long they would survive in the bitter cold? Better, they all agreed, to take their chances on the march rather than freeze to death hiding. They crawled back inside the barracks and waited for morning.

On January 18, 1945, Auschwitz guards lined prisoners up in front of the gates marked ARBEIT MACHT FREI ("Work Will Make You Free"). About 60,000 prisoners[27] were forced from the Auschwitz camp system in Poland and deported to camps Flossenbürg, Sachsenhausen, Gross-Rosen, Buchenwald, Bergen-Belsen, Dachau, and Mauthausen. The prisoners left in columns five across, long processions of miserable human beings forced to walk for their lives through piercing cold and snow. Whoever stopped was shot in the back of the neck. Any prisoners who collapsed from exhaustion were merely abandoned by the guards and left to die. Prisoners heard the rifle fire and a few moments later stumbled by the bodies. Guards grabbed Siegbert and Lothar and ordered them to drag the bodies to the side of the road and bury them in the snow.

During the halt, some prisoners tried to run away. Siegbert watched one prisoner run into the chicken coop of a nearby farm. Hearing the chickens squawk, the farmer came out of his house with a shotgun and shot the prisoner dead as he cowered among the feathers and straw.

Four or five days later, the prisoners and their guards arrived at Gleiwitz, Poland. "I didn't know it then," Siggi described, "but I know now that Gleiwitz was a huge center for trains coming from all over Poland, Germany, and Czechoslovakia. After walking maybe from four o'clock in the morning, we arrived there. We marched by some open cattle trains, and the doors of a train that had just arrived there opened—and I saw a scene there that is something that stays with me every day of my life. We saw people standing there in the cars, with a blanket over their shoulders, like skeletons made of skinny white bones, and they were huddled together. In the cars were piles of corpses, and the guards were ordering these skinny prisoners to throw them out. We were used to seeing dead prisoners each morning who didn't survive the night, and that was already terrible. But the sight of these skeletons in blankets throwing dead bodies from the

cattle cars was a devastating sight. I will never forget it as long as I live. Then the guards put us into one of the open cars, and we went by train through Czechoslovakia.

"The Czechs were good to us," Siggi continued. "They would throw bread or onions or potatoes or whatever they had into the open cars, even with the SS shooting at them from the train. I caught one piece of bread, but of course the other prisoners jumped on me. I split the bread in half and threw one half in the air so they would fight over it. The other piece I kept in my jacket and later I split it with Lothar.

"My legs were in pain from standing for several days, so for one moment I crouched down just to rest, and all of a sudden this guy twice as big as me sits on my head and pins me to the floor. He was sitting on my head and neck, and I was screaming and trying to push his heavy body off of me, but he didn't give a damn. He was exhausted like everybody else and saw something to sit on, and luckily, I was able to squirm out from under him."

Finally, the train arrived at a station, no one knew exactly where. The guards ordered them out of the open cars, and the march began again on foot. Siegbert and Lothar reached into their prisoner jackets, took a pinch of sugar, scooped up a handful of snow, and sprinkled the sugar over it.

"In Auschwitz, only the SS had sugar, and no prisoner could get any under normal circumstances," Siggi explained, "but the night before we left there were rumors about the march and panic set in. Prisoners broke open the door to a supply shed next to the kitchen. Some of them stole shoes, others stole some clothes, and Lothar and I grabbed handfuls of sugar. We had no paper bag or anything, so we put it in the seams of our prisoner uniforms. On the march, we took a handful of snow and sprinkled some sugar on it, and we called it sherbet. I told Lothar, 'If we survive, the greatest meal will be snow with sugar, plus anything else to eat.'"

After a day, Lothar could not walk any farther. He stopped, exhausted, ready to die, and dropped his blanket and the one rusty can of meat they had "organized" before the march. Siegbert saw SS men with rifles approaching from the rear of the line. Before they could shoot Lothar, Siegbert quickly turned around, bent down, and told Lothar to drape his arms around his shoulders. Siegbert struggled to his feet and walked on, stumbling under his friend's weight.

Two men worked their way up the line. Siegbert recognized them as Christian prisoners who had always been impressed by how he got things done.

"Tonight, we're going to run away," they whispered to Siegbert, "and we want you to come with us. You speak better Polish than the Poles. Come with us. We'll escape together. We're not offering this to anybody else, just you."

Siegbert shook his head no and nodded to Lothar riding on his back. "He's my friend and he's lame in one foot. If I leave him, he'll be shot within an hour."

"You have to think about yourself," they told him.

Siegbert shook his head again. "He's my best friend and he saved my life. I can't leave him."

The two men moved up the line.

Two other prisoners then approached from behind. Siegbert remembered them, too. In Auschwitz, he'd watched Lothar teach them how to make cabinets and draperies for SS officers. The ability to create a piece of furniture meant the possibility of receiving preferred treatment from the SS, who were constantly looking for items to furnish their apartments.

"Keep it up, Lothar," they whispered, patting him on the back as they walked ahead.

Siegbert was disgusted by their indifference to Lothar. Lothar had taught them skills that likely saved their lives, but they did nothing to help him now. Was a pat on the back the best they could do for him?

"What I have to say," Siggi told his interviewer, "is that I'm not a hero, but how could those two just walk away? Lothar had helped them to stay alive—just like he'd helped me by getting me into the Canada warehouse—and now that he's in trouble they pass him by and do nothing? They just didn't give a damn. I was furious about that."

The extra weight from carrying Lothar had strained Siegbert's flimsy wooden shoes and weakened the thin laces, and the shoes slipped up and down against his heels. Prisoners were not issued any socks, only a small rag-like piece of cloth that failed to cover their feet, and a splinter from a wooden shoe would easily penetrate the rag and pierce the foot. A splinter could create a wound, which could turn septic and fill with pus, and the body of a starving person had no strength to fight infection. In Auschwitz, Siegbert had seen what a splinter could do: decay a leg so completely that it rotted holes big enough for gauze to go in one side and come out the other. The medical term for this deterioration of tissue was phlegmon, something prisoners referred to as "the black mold." People didn't die only from starvation and torture in Auschwitz; they also rotted to death.

"The shoes were made of cheap material with wooden soles and heels but very flimsy and they had busted into pieces," he described, "and I needed something to hold them together somehow. I was considering pulling out threads from my jacket to tie them together, but the jacket was all rags that you couldn't unravel. There was nothing around us but snow, but then I saw a thin tree. In Auschwitz, you weren't allowed to have a knife or fork, but little by little with a rock you can scrape a spoon till it's sharp. I had that soup spoon, and I crawled over to this little tree and peeled off the bark—strips as thin as my finger—and I kept the strips in my pocket for a while so that the frost would melt. I massaged them a little to warm them up, then I twisted two of them together and tied them around my shoes."

He stood up and walked cautiously. The strips held. Siegbert offered a prayer of thanks, since only the Almighty could have put such an idea in his head that saved his life.

One evening the guards stopped the march and ordered prisoners to sleep in the snow, while they bedded down in a barn warmed by heat from cows and horses. Siegbert and Lothar crawled up to the barn door hoping to catch some of the warmth and huddled together under their one threadbare blanket. By the side of the barn, Siegbert saw vapor rising from a tall pile of straw mixed with horse and cow manure. He remembered reading somewhere as a child that during the First World War, if a soldier had frostbite, the Germans would dig a hole in such piles of straw and manure and put him in it up to his neck, which was supposed to work better than liquor for keeping a body alive.

"You see the steam coming off that dung?" he whispered to Lothar. "The minute it gets dark, we're moving over there."

An hour later, the two friends crawled next to the pile of manure and absorbed whatever warmth it offered. They reached out, picked dandelions, blew off the tops, ate the stems, threw up, and survived one more night on the death march from Auschwitz.

Ten days after their departure from Auschwitz, on January 30, 1945, Siegbert, Lothar, and the remaining prisoners stumbled through the gates of Mauthausen concentration camp in Austria.[28] From nearly 6,000 people who started out on the march, fewer than 1,600 were still alive.

In a narrow alley between a barrack and a fence, Siegbert, Lothar, and other prisoners found a steam pipe and huddled close for warmth. Nearby, a young prisoner stood on two garbage pails and peered inside the barrack window. One of the pails fell over and out rolled the rotted stub of a cabbage. Siegbert picked it up, broke it in half, and gave one

piece to Lothar. They tried to eat it but the core was solid ice, so they used the frozen cabbage as ice packs and held them to their foreheads to reduce the fever they had contracted during the death march.

"Our rest didn't last long," Siggi recalled. "Guards with machine guns ordered us into this cement room with pipes along the ceiling and slammed the doors. That's when I said my final prayers because I was convinced this was a gas chamber and figured, 'This is it, we're not gonna come out.' People were sprawled out on the floor, moaning or screaming in fear. We were lying there, it seemed like forever. Finally, there was a trickle of cold water that came out of the pipes. No poison gas, just water. Nobody can even imagine the relief we felt at that moment.

"Then they chased us out of that shower. We were sick and exhausted, and they forced us to run naked for what seemed like miles, holding our wooden shoes in our hands in the ice-cold night. Then with their guns pointed at our heads, they herded us into a wooden barrack."

Siegbert, Lothar, and some of the other survivors of the death march collapsed on the barrack floor.

"Lothar," Siegbert said in a weak voice, his little remaining strength ebbing away, "when they ask you what you can do, say you're a metalworker or a toolmaker—anything they can use for the war effort. Don't forget."

"Yeah, yeah," Lothar mumbled through a haze of fever, hunger, and exhaustion, "I'll tell them that."

"Over and over and over again, I told him to say that," Siggi recalled in frustration years later. "I told him that's what they needed, metalworkers. If you say you're a metalworker, they're not gonna kill you. He says, 'Yes, yes, yes, I'm gonna say it, I'm gonna say it'—and he doesn't say it! *He doesn't say it!* The Germans shipped him to Ebensee, one of the worst Mauthausen subcamps."

That was how eighteen-year-old Siegbert lost track of his best friend, with no way of knowing if either of them would survive, and if they did, whether they would ever find each other again.

———

The SS put Siegbert to work in the Mauthausen main camp tossing dead bodies into mass graves. A week later, the SS demanded that toolmakers step forward. Siegbert raised his hand and was sent by truck 170 miles away to the town of Melk, to work in a bus factory that had been converted to manufacture armaments.

"The SS treated us a little better there," he recalled, "maybe because it was near Vienna and when we marched to work the civilians could see us."

The better treatment did not last long. In early March 1945, a few days before Siegbert's nineteenth birthday, a *kapo* ordered him to bring him hot water from a stove at the far end of the factory. Siegbert carefully filled a bucket and carried it back without spilling a drop, but the careful delivery was not enough to satisfy the *kapo*.

"You didn't bring the water fast enough," the *kapo* said and then smashed him in the face with a club. Siegbert fell to the ground. One eye swelled and his cheek turned black and blue.

That same day, having learned that Russian soldiers were approaching from the east, the Germans started a second death march. "The Russians were brutal to German prisoners of war," Siggi explained, "and the American soldiers had a reputation for being more humane to their prisoners. So the Germans took us on a second death march, this time from Melk back to Mauthausen. That's where the American forces were rumored to be heading."

Around two thousand people started out, including prisoners from smaller camps, a hundred or more dying each day from disease or malnutrition or a German bullet. After two weeks, Siegbert was the only German-speaking Jew left. "There had been one other," he recalled, "a man with an English-sounding name like Harry Levy or Harry Levine, but one night the SS men took him into a barn and made him take off his shoes and dance until he collapsed. Then they whipped him and made

him get up and dance again. Every time he collapsed, they whipped him, until finally he died."

The march progressed slowly. When Siegbert and the remaining prisoners finally arrived back in Mauthausen, he was shoved into a barracks and onto a bunk with four other men. They all collapsed from exhaustion, and in the morning Siegbert woke to find that one of the men had died in his sleep. The second night, another died, then another, until he was the only one left alive on his bunk. He arranged the dead bodies next to him as though they were asleep, so that when rations were handed out there would be more stale bread for him to eat. The smell of dead bodies filled the room. An SS officer walked in, sniffed the air, and told Siegbert to open a window.

"Then that officer said to us, 'Cleanliness is important. Now I am going into town to get us a horse. Tonight, we will have meat and potatoes.' Why did he do it? He knew already that the Americans were nearby, and he wanted to have witnesses, to cover his ass, pardon me. He was a smart one. If they caught him, he wanted to be able to say, 'Here, take a look. I bought 'em a horse, I bought 'em goods—what do you mean I'm inhuman?' That's the real reason he bought that horse."

Siegbert translated the officer's promise of meat and potatoes from German to Polish for the other prisoners in the barracks, but the news meant nothing to men more dead than alive.

"No one had any feelings left," Siggi said. "But that SS officer really did go to a farm and buy a horse that the farmer slaughtered. Then the farmer's wife combined the horsemeat with potatoes and cooked it into a hash. Of course, I knew better than to eat any of it. Our bodies were so destroyed, no one could digest such food. It was like poison. The prisoners who ate it died."

The next morning Siegbert slowly raised himself up and peered out of the barrack window. The Germans were gone, and in the distance on

a hillside was a soldier in a uniform unlike any he had seen before. As Siegbert watched, American tanks and armored cars crashed through the gates of Mauthausen. Prisoners emerged slowly from the barracks, shuffling slowly forward, and Siegbert stumbled along with them. An American soldier looked at him with a blank expression; none of the liberation troops knew how to react to walking skeletons. He opened his field pack and held out crackers. A few stronger prisoners grabbed them away and Siegbert stumbled empty-handed back into the barrack.[29]

In the last days of the war, the prisoners in Mauthausen had formed an International Committee, which took over the camp as soon as the American liberators arrived on May 5, 1945. The Committee had no qualms about taking justice into their own hands. They policed the camp and executed any guards or SS officers still around. That night, Committee men killed eight *kapos* and six SS.

A group of Polish and Russian prisoners from the Committee came to Siegbert. "We've got that *kapo* who beat you with a hose," they told him. "You should help us kill him."

Siegbert shuffled out the door and into an adjoining barrack where he found the *kapo* bleeding from the beatings he had received. A prisoner handed Siegbert the wooden leg from a broken stool and motioned for him to take a turn.

"I hit him one time," Siggi described, "but I was so weak, what could one hit do? Nothing. What the others did, they did. I can't condemn them, but I don't approve of vengeance or killing, and I never killed anyone."

On that first day of their freedom, prisoners scavenged the camp for food. All they could find were bags of dried animal feed in a warehouse. "They ate that feed with water," Siggi recalled. "Big mistake. The water caused their stomachs to blow up and some of the prisoners died. Even though I only ate a little without water, still I nearly died. I wandered outside and on the road, I found a pack of noodles and I ate them dry. That was my first meal in freedom."

On the day of his liberation, nineteen-year-old Siegbert was skin and bones and weighed less than ninety pounds. He was nearly dead from exhaustion, malnutrition, and pneumonia.

"I cried," he concluded for his interviewer years later. "Not for myself. I cried for those others. Even food couldn't save them from death."[30]

CHAPTER 4

Liberation

The US Army evacuated survivors from Mauthausen and sent some to a Red Cross hospital in Linz, Austria, to recuperate. That was where Siegbert and Lothar were reunited: fate had assigned them to the same hospital. Lothar showed Siegbert a newspaper clipping that featured a photo of himself on the day he was liberated from Ebensee. One of the first American soldiers to enter the Mauthausen subcamp had brought a Kodak camera and took a photo of Lothar, who was thin as a rail and had only a towel to wear. When the soldier returned home, he sold the photo to the *New York Post*, and the newspaper ran it on the front page. That's how Lothar's parents learned their son had survived the Holocaust: by seeing his photo on the front page of a newspaper. He was an adult but looked like a child, emaciated and shrunken. Lothar would carry a copy of the newspaper clipping in his wallet for the rest of his life.

Siegbert and Lothar spent two months recovering in the Red Cross hospital. Once they regained sufficient strength, they went to work for the US Army Counter Intelligence Corps (CIC), operating in Austria and Bavaria, with headquarters in Linz, Austria. They volunteered to

serve without pay as a demonstration of thanks to their liberators and for the chance to capture some of their former Nazi oppressors. Lothar was charged with office work in the CIC headquarters. Siggi's assignment was to gather information concerning the whereabouts of anyone who might stand trial for war crimes. He interviewed townspeople, Linz officials, and survivors in nearby displaced persons camps, and from these discussions he compiled lists of potential Nazi criminals.

Despite his youth and inexperience, the CIC found Siegbert an ideal investigator, since he had a knack for creative problem-solving and spoke fluent German. In Auschwitz, he had also picked up enough vocabulary to speak rudimentary Polish and Russian, and within a year he was speaking passable English as well. The majority of roughly two thousand Nazi criminals convicted in war crimes trials between 1945 and 1949 were arrested in these early postwar months, when many former concentration camp functionaries and party officials were still hiding in nearby forests and towns, and the CIC directors gave twenty-one-year-old Siegbert the authority to make arrests on his own.

"Linz had more Nazi war criminals per square mile than any other place in Europe," Siggi recalled of his time with the CIC, but it was hard to figure out who was and who wasn't.[31] "I was afraid of nothing, but after surviving Auschwitz, capturing Nazi war criminals was not exactly the way I wanted to die. So I got permission to form an armed backup team and chose three non-Jews: two American officers and a Russian."

Siegbert's team was given a jeep and sent out the door. "Let's go hunt some Nazis," Siegbert told his crew.

By this time, German locals had good reason to cooperate with the Allied forces stationed in their towns. In exchange for solid information about possible war criminals, some transgressions from the past could be overlooked. If someone had been a minor functionary in the local Nazi government, or if rumors held that so-and-so had only been a supplier of

food or supplies to the concentration camps, US Army authorities would go easy on them in exchange for help with the investigation of a higher-ranking Nazi criminal.

A local resident had approached the CIC team with a possible lead. There was a well-to-do couple, the man said, who lived in a posh upstairs apartment on the main street. They might be hiding some history the CIC team would want to know about. "He's a celebrity around here," the contact said. "Some kind of bicycle racing champion."

Flashing their US Army credentials in the landlord's face got the team access to the apartment and the four officers conducted a room-by-room search.

"It was a luxury duplex apartment," Siggi described, "expensive furniture. Not everybody could afford to live in such a place. Why would this guy get such a luxury apartment? He must be somebody. We spent two hours going through the apartment. The most interesting thing we found was a collection of eighteen stopwatches, which meant our source was correct: the man was at least a semi-professional athlete. And if that was the case, then maybe he had some letters that connected him with people high up."

After searching the apartment for two hours in hundred-degree summer heat, Siegbert's team was exhausted. They walked down the stairs and were getting into their jeep when something occurred to him.

"I want to go back to the apartment," he told them.

"Are you crazy?" one of his team said. "We looked at every inch."

"There's one inch we didn't look at," Siegbert said.

"Where?" another investigator asked.

"Never mind," Siegbert told him. "You go. I'll walk back later."

The more expensive apartments in town featured walk-in fireplaces finished in tile. Siegbert remembered seeing ashes in the fireplace of the apartment they had just scoured.

"This is July," he thought. "Who in their right mind builds a fire in July?"

Back in the apartment, he rolled up his sleeves, put his hands in the ashes, and pulled out a handful of half-burned letters and photos. He

conjectured that the tenants had tried to burn them on learning that the CIC was conducting inspections, then left in a hurry. Among the partially burnt documents were notes of congratulation to one Herr Aulbreck for outstanding performance in bicycle races, signed by elite officers of Hitler's inner circle. One of the photos showed a good-looking man wearing an SS uniform—and that's when Siegbert recognized him: a guard from Mauthausen. The discovery warranted revisiting some of the shops in the area. Someone was bound to know something about the whereabouts of Herr Aulbreck.

Siegbert went door to door on both sides of the apartment building. Through the window of a clothing shop he noticed a tailor making changes to a man's jacket. He entered the shop and found a woman with a child, apparently waiting to retrieve the jacket. Siegbert looked closer and noticed the tailor was removing Nazi insignias from the sleeves. Siegbert looked at the woman and recognized her from the photos in the apartment he had just left.

"Where is your husband?" he asked casually.

"Oh, I don't know," the woman replied. "He must have gone to the countryside."

Siggi commented on the moment years later. "If she said he'd fled to Russia, I might have stopped the search. If he had gone to Russia, he was either a prisoner or else dead. But when she said she didn't know where he was, I sat down."

"Madam," he said, "I've been to your apartment. Eighteen stopwatches—is that common in Linz? If I go next door, will I find someone else with eighteen stopwatches? Or fifteen? Or ten?"

"Well," the woman answered, "you may. Would you like me to go with you to visit our neighbors?"

"No, I don't think that's necessary. And I'll tell you why. I found the letters of congratulations for your husband's races, personally signed by some important men. By the way, I also noticed your husband never won first place. He always took second. But second place is not bad," he said with a smile, intimating that sometimes it's better to settle when you

know you can't win. The wife caved in and provided information as to her husband's whereabouts. Over time, she gave up the whereabouts of three other former Nazi officers. Siegbert's team arrested them all and turned them over to the CIC.

Most of the surviving Nazi higher-ups had fled Germany for havens in South America and other parts of the world. A local informant, however, hinted that at least one VIP Nazi was still in the vicinity of Linz and gave Siegbert the name of a nearby village.

To gain intelligence from the people in this village, the CIC arranged for Siegbert and his team to take over a grocery store that had belonged to a former Nazi party member. The foursome knew nothing about groceries, but it was the right move. After only a short time the CIC team became part of the fabric of the villagers' everyday life.

"We won over the townspeople by giving them favors when they shopped with us," Siggi explained. "At that time, you bought food with ration coupons. If my team was generous and gave someone maybe a quarter of a pound more butter than the coupon allowed, they might tell you something you wouldn't hear otherwise."

Customers gossiped about who lived in the area and the undercover CIC team was shocked to learn that in this town of nine hundred people, nearly all had been card-carrying members of the Nazi party. One woman named Kessler was a regular, and after winning her good graces with extra groceries, the team learned that she and her husband had turned bitter toward the Nazi party when the husband lost a leg in what the couple considered a useless military exercise. The team revealed to her their role as agents of the CIC and asked if she had any information that might help them. Frau Kessler whispered that across the street from their farmhouse in the nearby town of Wolfshausen lived a high-ranking Nazi.

Not much was known about Hans Goebbels other than that he was the younger brother of Joseph Goebbels, the late Reich Minister of Propaganda and one of Hitler's most ardent supporters. In the First World War, Hans had been an artilleryman. He joined the Nazi party in 1929 and rose to various ranks including local propaganda leader and served during the Nazi occupation of France. One other detail was known, and it proved crucial to the team's efforts to find him. Like his infamous older brother, Hans had a clubfoot: a congenital malformation that twisted one of his feet.

Siegbert and his team took turns staking out the farmhouse. They casually drove by at all hours of day and night, but they never found anyone home. They continued surveillance during heavy rains and at odd hours and eventually their diligence paid off. A man finally arrived by car at the farmhouse, matching the description of Hans Goebbels: short, aquiline nose, and a clubfoot. The team rushed up, handcuffed him, and drove him to CIC headquarters for questioning.

Once his identity was confirmed, the CIC turned Hans Goebbels over to the French, who tried him for crimes committed on French territory and sentenced him to life imprisonment in a French internment camp, where he died in 1947.

Having witnessed so many atrocities in the camps, Siggi's faith had been severely challenged, but he insisted that his belief in the Almighty never wavered.

"Is there a God? That was a big question in Auschwitz," Siggi told an interviewer. "Nobody had the answer. Somebody said maybe there never was a God. Someone else said maybe there once was a God but He resigned. Somebody said maybe He's not paying attention to us anymore, maybe He wants us dead. The guards would mock us and had this sadistic trick. There was a line that prisoners were forbidden to cross. The guard would light a cigarette, take a puff and throw the cigarette on the other side of that line. If you smoke, you know what it's like to be deprived of a

cigarette for a long time. Some prisoners would try to get that cigarette, and then the guard would shoot them and report they had tried to escape. One of those SS guards looked at me after he'd killed a smoker and said, '*Wo ist dein Gott jetzt?* Where is your God now?'

"The answer became clear while I was on a particular assignment for the Counter Intelligence Corps," Siggi explained. "I had to take an airplane somewhere. That was my first airplane ride. It was a cloudy, rainy day. The plane took off and it went up into the clouds, and then it got over the clouds—and the sun was shining. I tell you it was a beautiful day above the clouds, and that reminded me again that the Almighty was always there. Some say He died. No, He didn't. The Almighty was talking to me. 'I'm up here,' He was saying. 'Don't despair. Sometimes a dark cloud like Hitler gets between us, but, you know, I'm up here.' In that one split second, I was reminded that He'd never left."

In November 1947, as a thank-you from the CIC for nearly two years of service, twenty-one-year-old Siegbert received free passage on the SS *Marine Fletcher*, departing Bremerhaven, Germany, for New York.[32] On December 12, he arrived in America, looking for work and a new life.

Neckties and Love Lights

Having listened for hours to Siggi's tragic story, Jacob Nartel eagerly made a phone call and arranged Siggi's first job in America. Diagonally across the street from the Nartels' house in the Bronx was a drugstore buried by snow in the blizzard of December 1947, and Siggi was hired to shovel the sidewalk for two dollars a day. By the second day, he had found two kids in the neighborhood to do the shoveling for fifty cents each. A dollar profit, without having to lift a finger. By the end of the month, he'd made his first $20 in America.

His second job came through two brothers with the family name Fried whom he had befriended on the boat from Germany. The older brother found him a job working in a sweatshop in downtown Manhattan that manufactured leather goods. For $28.50 a week, Siggi worked standing up at a long wooden bench with thirty other workers, applying glue to cloth linings and affixing the linings to the insides of leather totes and schoolbags.

"I assure you," he said fifty years later, "today you would have to wear a mask. It stunk to heaven. It was dirty work." Each morning, work-

ers climbed the dark wooden stairs that opened onto a loft running the length of the building and took their places at the bench. At one end of the loft was a glass-enclosed office where the owner, Mr. Schaeffer, watched to see who was working and who wasn't while he talked to customers and contractors on the phone and simultaneously plowed through paperwork. Everyone wore thick shoes to guard against splinters from the rough wood floor. At night, after the crews had gone home, an elderly Black man cleaned the toilets.

"Let me clean the toilets," Siggi told his boss, "and I'll throw in cleaning your office for free." The extra work would mean $1.50 a week more in his pay envelope. Mr. Schaeffer shook his head. "That's not for you," he said. "That's a colored man's job."

"Is there a law?" Siggi responded. "Try me out, then decide whether to keep me on." An idea came to mind. He rolled up his sleeves as though preparing to start that minute and casually revealed the number tattooed on his arm: 104732. Everyone in those early postwar years knew what a concentration camp number meant. Schaeffer must have known that Siggi was looking to pressure him into the extra work, but he would have also noted the young man's willingness to work hard. He gave him the toilet-cleaning job, and that brought Siggi's earnings to $30 a week.

In order to save money, Siggi decided to move in with his sister Jenny. Hoping to earn a better living, he convinced her to introduce him to Mrs. Friedman, her boss at the bowtie factory.

"How much are you earning with Schaeffer?" Mrs. Friedman asked.

"Thirty-six dollars a week," Siggi answered, a 20-percent exaggeration, "and I won't work for less than that."

Mrs. Friedman had problems with her legs, which were always bandaged, but her wits were sharp, and she could recognize a hard worker when she met one. She offered him the $36 as a guarantee against commissions for every dozen bowties he finished. Siggi quit Schaeffer's leath-

er goods sweatshop and began working at Friedman's bowtie sweatshop. Each morning, he walked from Jenny's Brooklyn apartment on Lorimer Street to Friedman's factory and climbed the stairs. Over his spot on the workbench, a rubber hose hung from the ceiling and belched clouds of chemical steam into the room. Siggi sat on a barstool, inhaling the carcinogenic fumes. With one hand he grabbed the hose and waved it back and forth over the ties to soften them. With the other hand he ran a heavy iron over the ties to flatten out creases. The assembly room was stifling from lack of fresh air, and the chemical smells got to everybody. Half in jest, half in earnest, the workers passed the time making jokes about their collective fate while their hands worked automatically on the bowties.

"Who needs this?" one worker said. "It smells disgusting here and I can't breathe."

"What are you complaining about?" another said. "Look at him, that poor boy, what he went through," and they all agreed that Siggi had the saddest story. Siggi minded his own business, ironing ties and breathing through his mouth. He looked around the loft at the rows of ties, wooden benches, and chemical hoses, then at the women behind their wooden tables. "If my mother were alive," he thought, "I wouldn't want her working in a sweatshop like this."

Siggi looked for a better job and found one courtesy of Erwin, his younger brother. In 1942, fifteen-year-old Erwin had run away from the family's Berlin apartment, hoping to make his way to Switzerland. He was captured and transported to the Riga Ghetto in Latvia. On October 13, 1944, the Soviet army liberated the ghetto, and on May 1, 1945, Erwin and a handful of other prisoners were transported by the Swedish Red Cross to Sweden. Through *Aufbau*, a newspaper for German-speaking Jews seeking family members,[33] Erwin made contact with Siegbert and their only other surviving brother, Joe. Siegbert and Joe arranged for Erwin's immigration to America, where he found work with Brooklyn Master Craft Necktie Company, a clothing wholesaler on Court Street in Brooklyn.

Mr. Glaser, Erwin's boss, liked Siggi and hired him as a necktie saleman. Siggi quit Mrs. Friedman's factory and took easily to the life of a salesman, which drew upon all his natural talents and storytelling skills. Most important, every sale earned him a commission. Siggi called his friend Lothar Nartelski, who had changed his name to Larry Nartel after receiving his immigration papers and was living with his parents in the Bronx. Siggi convinced Mr. Glaser to hire Larry, too, as a necktie salesman for Master Craft.

Siggi and Larry pooled their money, bought a 1947 Dodge, and drove off with a trunkful of ties: three lines, one retailing for a dollar each, a second for a dollar fifty, and a third with more workmanship and detail selling for the royal price of two dollars. They drove out of New York, out of range of sweatshops and foul smells, and into God's country. The two friends drove to small towns in Western Pennsylvania, West Virginia, Kentucky, and Ohio, Siggi at the helm, determining where they would go, whom they would talk to, perfecting their pitch, and discovering America.

Siggi controlled the road trip, down to details of their personal hygiene. If Larry's breath smelled bad, Siggi reached into his pocket and handed him a peppermint Life Saver. "Go brush your teeth," he told Larry. "You stink from the mouth. It'll kill the deal." They drove through coal-mining towns of Appalachia, the domain of labor leader John L. Lewis, who won high wages for his union members while steamrolling over opponents that included the United States government. Lewis had called for a nationwide strike just days before Siggi and Larry's Dodge pulled into his part of the country. Due to the strike most people in Appalachia weren't earning enough money for food, let alone fancy ties. Their first week on the road Siggi and Larry made less than $100, barely enough to pay for gas and food.

With a few calls back to New York, Siggi added sports shirts for men and quilted robes for women to their lines. Nothing helped. Not only were sales slow but Siggi and Larry both spoke with a German accent,

and once storeowners surmised the men were European Jews, they made it clear they had no interest in buying from them. By the summer of 1949 it seemed like life on the road had played itself out, and Siggi and Larry found themselves at the home of Larry's brother, Werner, in Flint, Michigan.

"There's this company I know," Werner said, "National Pictures, which has nothing to do with pictures. And they're local, not national. Anyway, the company sends salespeople out hawking things door to door from a catalog. You don't have to do it full-time. Just tell 'em you're moving here, and they'll break you in gradually. You'll probably be selling blankets or else these little lights that sit on top of televisions."

National had fifty employees who earned $75 a week plus commissions, a fortune in those days, but salesmen had to numb themselves to what they did.

"They sold 95 percent to poor people who could have bought the products cheaper in stores," Siggi described, "but they couldn't afford to pay all at once. We sold them a lamp or bedspread or linens or whatever and they paid a dollar or two a week on layaway. We made it convenient for them to shop from home, but first we had to get a foot in the door. You couldn't carry around a refrigerator or a rocking chair or a bed—you needed a door-opener. So we sold this one item that looked like a flowerpot with wires in it. Inside was a one-watt bulb that we were supposed to tell them was good for their eyes when they watched television, which was a lie. Because it was so dim, we called it a love light. It cost National Pictures all of three dollars and we sold it for $12.95. We also had to tell them it was made by disabled veterans, which was another lie. Then, after they bought a love light, you could sell them a sewing machine or a larger item from the catalog."

One night Siggi and Larry were walking back to their car on Michigan Avenue, Detroit's red-light district. The sun had set, and it looked like

Christmas in the middle of August, little red-colored bulbs flashing from glass storefronts up and down the avenue. Twenty-four-year-old Siggi had never before seen women in thin robes posing behind display windows. Maybe they would buy a love light. He walked up to a scantily clad Black woman in an open window.

"I want to show you something," he said, reaching into his bag.

"I want to show you something better," she said, striking a sexy pose.

Siggi looked up and down the street and marveled at the interracial nature of business on Michigan Avenue, where people mingled easily as though discrimination didn't exist. He was in awe. As a child, before coming to America, the only Black person he'd ever seen was in the Berlin circus, a giant weightlifter who, from Siggi's diminutive point of view, stood ten feet tall. Black people were more or less a mystery to him.

The next day, Mr. Fox, National Pictures' regional manager, drove them to their first drop-off point. "I'll show you how to sell," he said. He walked them up to the first house on the street and knocked on the door. A heavyset Black woman answered the door, and next to her was her pretty sixteen-year-old daughter. "Well, what do we got to eat today?" Fox called out and then whacked them both on the behind. Mr. Fox turned to the two young salesman and said, "That's how you do it!"

Siggi was disgusted by his boss's vulgar behavior. "I'd rather die than have to sell like that," he told Fox, thus ending his and Larry's careers as salesmen for National Pictures.

Siggi would always be grateful to Larry for having saved his life in Auschwitz, but their business partnership was proving useless. The two friends parted ways and Siggi returned to his sister's apartment in Passaic, New Jersey. He kept in touch with Larry by phone, but the time had come for Siggi to move forward on his own.

His next residence was an apartment three blocks away from his sister that consisted of a kitchenette and a small second room. A metal bathtub took up most of the kitchen. When Siggi covered the bathtub with

a wooden board, it doubled as the apartment's one table. The toilet was in the hall one flight up. He paid $26.50 a month in rent and spent an additional five dollars to purchase a secondhand single bed and wooden clothes closet.

One day, he'd look back on the tiny space and describe it as "a not-so-efficient efficiency," a generous description of miserable living quarters.

Forced to Elope

That same year, 1950, businessman Jerome Sisselman moved his family into a large, comfortable house in Newark, New Jersey. It took his daughter Naomi only two semesters to become "Citizen of the Year" at Weequahic High School, much to the chagrin of classmates who had been in the Newark school system much longer. Among her other achievements, Naomi maintained a straight A average and mastered Hebrew well enough to tutor children at the local synagogue.

Jerome and his wife, Lorraine, were both born in the US in 1903. Jerome had done well in New Jersey real estate and would eventually own an industrial park, various large cemeteries (both Christian and Jewish), and hundreds of acres in the Meadowlands area only a half hour from New York City. Lorraine suffered from melancholy[34] and became periodically catatonic, staring into space and speaking to no one. Sometimes Naomi brought her mother back to her senses by getting her to cook. Lorraine excelled at *lokshen kugel*, Yiddish for egg noodle pudding; *kishkes*, stuffed beef intestines; *latkes*, potato pancakes; and other calorie-rich Jewish delicacies that kept Naomi rather hefty through high school.

The Sisselmans were Orthodox Jews who worried that their children

might assimilate and marry outside the Jewish faith and kept a vigilant watch over their choice of friends. Jerome founded the Orthodox Jewish school Yeshiva of Newark and didn't believe girls needed a secular college education. "It's a waste," he told Naomi. "Just get married." Naomi made her father a deal. If she finished in the top ten at Weequahic High School, he would let her go to college. She finished ninth and enrolled herself at Montclair State Teachers College in Montclair, New Jersey.

The college campus was a short bus ride from Clifton, where Naomi's older sister Harriet lived with her husband and children. One summer day in 1953, Harriet had chores to run and asked Naomi to babysit. Before leaving her house, Harriet handed Naomi a list of things to buy from Morris Weiner, the local fruit and vegetable vendor. Later that day, Naomi saw Morris approaching their house in his food truck. She waited for him to get out of the truck and then showed him the shopping list. Morris, who thought he knew everyone in the neighborhood, was surprised by this new face. He looked her up and down.

"You look like a *kalleh moid*," he said, using the Yiddish expression for a girl of marriageable age. "Can I give your number to a handsome young man I know? He's also one of my customers." His was a full-service fruit and vegetable business.

"One thing you should know," he said. "The young man is a refugee."

Naomi shrugged her shoulders. "Is he Jewish?" she asked.

Morris nodded yes.

"So?" she said. "Why would I care what country he's from?"

As long as he was Jewish, she was sure her parents would be fine with her dating him. So she agreed to the introduction.

Morris then spoke to Siggi, who lived in Passaic, the next town over. Morris told him how beautiful Naomi was and gave him two phone numbers: Naomi's, and the number of a young woman who worked as a legal secretary. Once Siggi and Naomi knew each other better, Siggi teased her by saying he kept the other number "just in case."

On their first date, Siggi joked that he didn't own a five-thousand-dollar car, so he came to pick her up in a forty-thousand-dollar bus. Naomi appreciated a man with a sense of humor.

"We liked each other immediately," she recalled. "He had been in America six years and said what he admired about me was that I reminded him of European women. He found American women frivolous. I was down-to-earth and mature. He liked that."

They were an unlikely pair. Naomi was wealthy, educated, and came from a big family. Siggi was poor, had been forced out of school at age fourteen, and lost most of his family in the Holocaust. But Naomi found him exotic, sensual, and independent, someone who could understand her independent nature and who, at least at the time, was not constrained by the strict rules of Orthodox Judaism that had dominated her childhood. She also learned her beau was entrepreneurial and had recently started a business with another refugee, Irving Kempler, manufacturing change purses which they sold to pocketbook and handbag factories. She assumed her parents would be impressed by such an ambitious young man.

Her parents were shocked. The thought of their daughter dating a refugee—a man with no money or education and a dubious history—was intolerable. Maybe this person had gone crazy from beatings in the camp. Maybe he had been subjected to horrible medical experiments and was unable to have children. Naomi's aunt and uncle made matters worse, claiming they knew friends of the Wilzig family in Germany who were sure that Siggi was married before and had left his wife. The rumors weren't true, but they reinforced the Sisselmans' judgment that Siggi was not good enough for their daughter.

Six months after his first date with Naomi, Siggi invited her parents to join them at the movies and on the drive home asked if he could marry their daughter. "No!" they both replied, and Naomi's mother announced that Siggi was now barred from ever entering their house again.

A few days later, Siggi told Naomi, "Our only hope is to elope."

Naomi agreed, and after a series of mishaps—lost blood tests, a missing witness—they stood in a Passaic, New Jersey, courtroom before the

only judge available on New Year's Eve, 1953. Siggi reached into his pocket and pulled out a yarmulke, the skullcap worn by religious Jews.

"This is a civil ceremony," the judge commented.

Siggi waved an instructive finger. "I'm getting married, I'm Jewish, and I'm wearing a yarmulke."

The ceremony took only a few minutes, then Naomi called her father and told him she and Siggi had just gotten married. Jerome was livid.

"This is how I raised a daughter?" he yelled over the phone. "To disrespect her parents and ignore our Jewish traditions?"

"You forced me," Naomi replied. "You wouldn't agree to let us do what couples in love normally do."

"Are you pregnant?" Jerome demanded.

"No, I'm not pregnant," Naomi answered. "We're not even going to live together until we have a *chuppah*," referring to the cloth canopy under which a Jewish couple stands during a traditional Jewish wedding ceremony. Siggi and Naomi hadn't touched each other yet. They both wanted a religious ceremony first, to cement their bond.

Naomi waited silently while her father railed on the phone. Siggi stood by her side, helpless to intervene. Eventually, Jerome's tirade ended. "Come home," he told Naomi. "I'll work it out with your mother."

Things, however, did not progress well. Three weeks later, Siggi showed up at the Sisselman home to attend the sweet sixteen party of Naomi's younger sister, Rachel. He rang the bell. When Naomi's mother, Lorraine, opened the door and saw him, she lunged at Siggi and smacked him in the face.

"Get out!" she yelled. "You're not welcome!"

A guest, Rabbi Greenstein, grabbed her arm. "Mrs. Sisselman, what are you doing!" he said. "This man is a Holocaust survivor. You should welcome him."

"I don't care!" Lorraine screamed. "Get him out of my house!"

Naomi's sister, Sonia, intervened. "Ma, leave them alone. They're married already." The revelation came as a shock to Lorraine Sisselman.

"You're a whore!" she yelled at Naomi and ordered her out of the house.

Naomi moved in with her sister Harriet. One evening, nearly two months later, the phone rang. It was her father.

"Can you go to the *mikveh*?" he asked, referring to the ritual bath that precedes a Jewish woman's marriage. "You're getting married next week."

The reception took place on March 14, 1954, in the Little Hungary Restaurant on Houston Street in downtown Manhattan. For $12.95 per person, the restaurant provided kosher food, plastic flowers, an accordionist, and a photographer. It was an awkward affair, since Naomi's aunts and uncles refused to talk with Siggi, his sister Jenny, his brother Erwin, or any of Siggi's other immigrant relations sitting on their side of the room. Naomi's mother bristled. Family members, accustomed to Lorraine's volatility, calmed her down. Isn't it better, they asked her, to gain a son than lose a daughter? Eventually, she capitulated. The Sisselman house had six bedrooms. Siggi and Naomi were given the attic.

Now that they were married, Siggi felt comfortable talking with Naomi about his past. He showed her photos that his sister, Jenny, had salvaged from their life in Krojanke. In one photo, six-year-old Siegbert stood holding a cardboard cone as tall as himself, filled with fruits and candy. It was the custom in those days for parents to present such cones to their children on entering their first year of school.

Those were during the happy days of childhood. Siggi's other childhood stories were not so pleasant. He described for Naomi that he used to play with the two Christian kids from the Kronau family next door. They teased him for being Jewish, and in 1936, when Frau Kronau realized that Jews including the Wilzigs would soon be rounded up and sent away, she started "borrowing" money from Siggi's mother. Both women knew what could happen if Siggi's mother refused to give her the loan. In those days, if a non-Jew complained about a Jew to the Gestapo for whatever reason,

no matter how trumped up, it could lead to arrest or worse. Frau Kronau knew that Sophie Wilzig would not dare insist on repayment, and she continued "borrowing" regularly.

"My mother had no choice but to give her the money," Siggi told Naomi, "so she asked for something in return. The Kronau family had a farm, about eighty miles outside Berlin. My mother asked Frau Kronau that, if it gets worse for the Jews, would she please take her two youngest children—me and my brother Erwin—and hide us at their farm. Frau Kronau said nothing about hiding us, but I'll tell you what she *did* say. 'The police are going to get you anyhow. It's just a matter of time. Leave the back door to your place open, so that I can get your fur coat. Why should we let the police take it?' So help me God, I swear that's what she said.

"We had another neighbor," Siggi continued, "a Polish farmer by the name of Strucka. For a while, before going to Berlin, my whole family was hiding at his place. One day he took my father to his barn and showed him an ax he used for killing pigs. Strucka said, 'If you want, before they catch you, torture you, and murder you, I'll take your family one by one and chop off their heads. They won't feel it.' My father said, 'That's not such a good idea.'

"This is very important to understand," Siggi said. "Strucka wasn't an evil man. To him, it was a favor he was offering. In those days, it was hard to tell the difference between the good people and the evil people."

Siggi told Naomi another story from his childhood. "My mother had a sister named Betty who lived on a farm," he said. "She lived with her husband, her other sisters, and their husbands. Now and then, my brothers and sisters and I would stay in two rooms she reserved for visitors."

During the night of November 9, 1938, Nazi thugs went on a rampage. Throughout Germany and Austria, they destroyed almost two hundred synagogues, ransacked more than eight thousand Jewish shops, smashed windows, and sent tens of thousands of Jews to concentration camps. The tragedy came to be known as *Kristallnacht*, "The Night of Broken Glass."

The following day, Siggi's Aunt Betty and her family learned the SS were headed their way to arrest all Jewish men. Betty's husband and brothers-in-law ran into the fields and hid in haystacks. That night, the SS showed up and demanded to be told where the men had gone. Betty refused to say.

"One of the SS men found a thick oak club in Aunt Betty's house," Siggi told Naomi. "Maybe it was something her husband used when he took cattle to market. The officer took that club and smashed her on the head. He hit her so hard it made a gash in her head two fingers wide, but she still refused to give away the hiding place. When they searched the property, they found the men hiding in the haystacks and sent them to concentration camp Sachsenhausen. A neighbor took pity on Betty and patched her up. He hid her under some blankets and that night he smuggled her away in a horse and wagon to a town on the outskirts of Berlin."

In Berlin, Betty found the building where the Wilzigs were staying. Siggi and his mother were putting up draperies when Betty arrived. Siegbert turned and looked at the strange woman standing in their doorway. "Can I help you?" he said. He had seen her on a visit earlier that same year, but this woman's face was so black and blue and her eyes so swollen that he didn't recognize his own aunt.

"That was the kind of terrifying life we had," Siggi told Naomi, who sat in shock listening to her husband's account of his childhood.

Naomi told Siggi how proud she was of him for building a new life in America and that he could count on her support. He embraced her and promised they would have a good life together, but there would be one condition: he wanted none of her family's money. His achievements would be his own. Naomi agreed and dropped out of college to become a bookkeeper to supplement their income and in time proved herself to be a vivacious, romantic partner dedicated to keeping their home clean and their kitchen strictly kosher. She comforted him when nightmares disturbed his sleep, and for the first time since Larry Nartel saved his life in Auschwitz, Siggi had a best friend.

Naomi gave birth to their first child in 1956 and named him Ivan. Following the Ashkenazic Jewish custom of naming offspring in Hebrew after deceased relatives, Naomi and Siggi gave their son the Hebrew name Yitzhak in honor of Siggi's murdered father, Isidore, whose Hebrew name was Yitzhak. Naomi and Siggi's future children, Sherry and Alan, as well as their future grandchildren, would also be named in Hebrew in honor of family members who perished in the Holocaust or in honor of survivors who had passed away—a custom that implied a responsibility for the children to live a righteous life on behalf of the deceased, to learn about the Holocaust, and to keep alive the name and memory of those who perished.[35]

For a survivor—and for Siggi in particular, whose family had been decimated—of all possible *nachus*, the Yiddish word for happiness and fulfillment, the greatest of all was having a healthy Jewish boy to carry on the Wilzig name.

In the early 1950s, fifty-seven antisemitic groups openly operated in the US and were publishing hate sheets, such as *The American Nationalist*, *The Cross and the Flag*, *Thunderbolt*, *The Defender*, and *Common Sense*, which had a weekly circulation of 90,000.[36] "The Jews are at the very root of all troubles, all conflicts, all revolts of the modern world," stated *The Jewish Problem*, published by the Huron Church News in 1957.[37] The bias was not always so obvious. When ads for resorts included the notice "church nearby," the coded message being telegraphed was that Jewish guests were not welcome.

This was not mere snobbery but a deep-seated animosity toward people who, so the sentiment ran, were products of a degenerate, non-Christian history. Catholics were still taught in catechism that the Jews had killed Christ, and signs reading No Jews or Dogs Allowed were posted in several public buildings of the rural south. Antisemitism kept Jewish businessmen out of higher circles of power and Jewish families from living in the country's choicer neighborhoods. Michigan's prosper-

ous Grosse Point Property Owners Association, to take one of the more obvious cases of housing discrimination, employed private detectives to investigate prospective buyers: Jewish homebuyers received polite but firm rejection letters.

The more insidious, nuanced version of antisemitism acknowledged Jews while limiting their full participation in law, medicine, oil and gas production, commercial banking, and other industries. As a point of reference, well into the 1960s Jews constituted only about 1 percent of high-level executives in finance, heavy industry, communications, trans-portation, and public utilities.[38] Only six of the one thousand people em-ployed by Philadelphia's largest banks were Jewish, and none were in se-nior management.[39] Despite the 1965 declaration by the Vatican that Jews were no longer to be held responsible for the crucifixion of Jesus[40]—and notwithstanding campaigns by Jewish organizations to end discrimina-tion in business and social organizations—the more prestigious New York clubs such as the Links, the Knickerbocker, and the New York Athletic Club continued to exclude Jews from membership.

Antisemites were everywhere, ready to take any steps necessary to keep an ambitious refugee like Siggi in his place.

"Make the Damn Deal"

By the 1950s, postwar America pulsed with the energy of entrepreneurship. Frustrated by years of rationing, Americans were ambitious and hungry for all that peace had to offer. Among those looking to make best use of postwar America's opportunities were Ernie Wachtel and his wife Rose, the Wilzigs' future best friends. Ernie and Rose lived in a suburban section of Newark, New Jersey, with a large Jewish population, several synagogues, and, most importantly for their children's future, Weequahic High School. Luckily, the Wachtels had fled Austria in 1938, before things took a turn for the worse. For them, as for other newcomers looking to live the American dream, a good education was the one tool essential for success.

Ernie used his earnings as a window decorator to purchase a three-story brick home just blocks from the school so his children could walk to class and make their dreams come true. Homes in the section of Newark where the Wachtels lived featured front and backyards but little space between one house and the next. The Wachtels' bedroom window faced a two-story house owned by an elderly couple who had recently rented out their upstairs floor to a family of three. One summer day, Ernie heard loud

high-pitched singing coming from his neighbors' second-floor window. "Shut up already!" he yelled from his own window after a particularly lengthy passage. Eventually, the Wachtels met their new neighbors, the Wilzigs. "One thing led to another," Ernie recalled, and notwithstanding Siggi's penchant for singing in the shower, they became friends.

The friendship strengthened in 1958 when Rose and Naomi both gave birth to daughters in the same month. Naomi and Siggi gave their daughter the English name Sherry and the Hebrew name Tziporah, after Siggi's murdered mother, Sophie (in Hebrew, Tziporah). Sherry was premature at birth and weighed only three pounds. Effective neonatology would not become standard until the 1980s, and most hospitals at the time offered only rudimentary premature birth care. Siggi's little girl was small and vulnerable, and doctors gave her only a fifty-fifty chance of survival. She lived, but because Siggi had seen so many children die in the camps, he would forever worry about her health and safety.

By now Siggi had moved into another career, this time selling fancy leather-bound loose-leaf binders. He drove up and down the East Coast, city to city, college to college, a Jewish version of Willy Loman from *Death of a Salesman*, his shoulders aching and his knuckles bloodied from carrying heavy sample cases. Naomi's father objected to Siggi's routine, since life on the road as a traveling salesman meant spending most of each month away from his young family. Partially to placate his father-in-law and partially to escape the exhaustion of travel, Siggi took a sales job with Nieswand and Son, manufacturers of custom-built furniture in nearby Hillside, New Jersey. The company's showroom on Montgomery Street featured samples of tables, chairs, couches, and dressers and a small office in the back for Mr. Nieswand.

"Take a vacation," Siggi told his boss after only a short time on the job. Nieswand hadn't been out of his office for years but trusted his energetic, fast-talking salesman, so he left for Europe. By the time Nieswand returned three weeks later, Siggi had boosted sales dramatically. Nieswand

made him sales manager and went back on vacation. Within three years, Siggi tripled the business and Nieswand promoted him to general manager.

"Siggi told me a story about his days as general manager," remembered Bob Margulies, who became one of Siggi's legal advisers in the 1980s. "It's a story I use when teaching business strategies to college students. If a salesperson in the showroom was moving too slowly with a customer, Siggi would stand nearby and pretend to clean an ashtray. That was his signal: 'Clean it up. Make the damn deal.'"

Jerome Sisselman, Siggi's father-in-law, owned two cemeteries in Clifton, New Jersey: King Solomon Memorial Park for Jewish customers and Cresthaven Memorial Park for non-Jewish customers. Both cemeteries sold burial plots as well as bronze plaques and granite headstones. In 1963, new legislation dictated cemeteries could no longer sell plots, plaques, and headstones to the same customer. The ruling was passed after publication of *The American Way of Death* by author and activist Jessica Mitford. The book exposed funeral directors who exploited the vulnerability of grieving families by selling them burial services and supplies at usurious prices. Mitford's book was widely read and prompted the government to step in. As a consequence of the legislation, Sisselman was forced to separate his business into two: the cemetery on one hand, and the memorial headstone business on the other.

"Leave it to me," Siggi told him.

Siggi quit his job with Nieswand and within a week he opened Bronze and Granite Memorials for his father-in-law in a building at the rear of the King Solomon Memorial Park. Technically, it was a different company, but anyone coming for an appointment to buy a burial plot at King Solomon had to first drive by the doors of Bronze and Granite. Just as he had done with the furniture business, it took Siggi only a few weeks to create robust sales.

In his spare time, he studied the stock market, and with money earned from selling bronze plaques and granite headstones, he purchased modest

quantities of stock. One of his investments was in Wilshire Oil Company of Texas, a Canadian-owned company trading on the American Stock Exchange. Wilshire seemed like a safe bet, a small company whose stocks sold at an affordable price.

When Naomi found out her husband was purchasing shares of Wilshire on a regular basis, she chided him. "More stock? We can barely pay the bills and you're buying more stock?"

Siggi made excuses, but he didn't stop buying.

Later that year, Siggi and Naomi attended a farewell party for a local dignitary. The Jewish press had dubbed Harry Z. Shreiner "the globetrotting Rabbi" for his peripatetic career, first serving as rabbi to the Jewish-American community in Paris in the mid-1950s and then in Korea. After a brief respite back home, he was now about to fly out to serve as rabbi to troops in Vietnam. Congregants put together a farewell dinner and the Wilzigs attended, along with the city's social elite. "Siggi had no interest in ordinary social parties," commented neighbor Ernie Wachtel, "but he liked to rub shoulders with the upper echelon."

Among the guests at Shreiner's farewell dinner was a businessman named Sol Diamond, a tall, urbane seventy-eight-year-old who was one of Newark's most prominent entrepreneurs. In the 1920s, Diamond had been a member of the New York Stock Exchange and after retiring he parlayed his familiarity with the market to become a major shareholder in mining companies and other businesses. One of his more unusual companies was the Diamond Boning Corporation, located in North Arlington, New Jersey. The company fabricated metal strips or "bones" that helped brassieres and corsets keep their shape. Since the mid-1940s, the leader in women's undergarments was Frederick's of Hollywood, which supplied lingerie for Bettie Page and other pinup models of the day. Diamond was one of Frederick's main suppliers.

Nonetheless, he was discreet about his business successes, refrained from bragging, dressed without ostentation, and drove a twenty-year-old

Cadillac. "It still runs," he told business associates. "Why change it?" One associate described him as "a low-key multimillionaire who didn't try to get on TV or radio or in papers. He just accumulated stocks."

Apart from managing his eclectic portfolio, the lean, gray-haired Diamond was a staunch supporter of progressive causes. In 1956, he canceled plans to build a furniture manufacturing plant in Montgomery, Alabama, to protest the incarceration of Martin Luther King Jr. and other civil rights activists for staging a bus boycott. Relocating his new factory was, in Diamond's mind, a small gesture for a worthy cause.

Diamond stood well over six feet tall. When five-foot-five-and-a-half-inch Siggi B. Wilzig met anyone as towering as Diamond, he had a standard greeting. He would reach up, shake his hand, and say, "I used to be tall like you, six-two, but I joined Montgomery's Eighth Army[41] during the war, and they had me carrying heavy backpacks in one-hundred-and-twenty-degree heat. That made me shrink down to five foot five," and he hunched over to demonstrate what it looked like to carry a fully-loaded field pack.

"Siggi always had a joke in his pocket to warm people up," Ernie Wachtel remembered. "He never was in the British army and he never was six foot two, but that wasn't the point. He made people laugh and they liked him."

Siggi and Sol Diamond swapped stories and in the course of the evening discovered they both owned stock in Wilshire Oil Company of Texas. Diamond sensed a sharp mind behind the corny one-liners and confided to Siggi that he was concerned over Wilshire's failure to realize its potential. The company had a number of deals cooking that could lead to a substantial increase in revenues, provided the right person was at the helm. Those opportunities included acquisition of oil and gas-rich properties in Utah and Kansas, production of asphalt and petroleum byproducts in Oklahoma, purchase of new wells in the Texas Panhandle and New Mexico, and negotiations for seventy more properties around the country.

But the company's problems were mounting. New wells had fallen short of projected yields, engineers were bewildered by a recently devel-

oped form of extraction using pressurized water, and the board had ac-
quired new drilling land without the required title papers. The company
was in trouble and needed fresh energy and a charismatic leader. He could
lead the takeover himself, Diamond said, but he was approaching eighty
and didn't want to risk a heart attack like the one his brother had suffered
conducting a similar takeover battle elsewhere. Might Siggi consider
leading the charge?

Siggi was excited by the offer. His options in business so far had only
been sales, which limited his income. Heading up an oil company would
put him in the big leagues where serious money could be made. He knew
nothing about natural resources, business finance, or how to take over a
company, but he had no hesitation accepting Sol Diamond's offer. The
two men spent the rest of the party in a corner, formulating ideas and dis-
cussing strategies while Diamond puffed away on a cigar. Over the next
several weeks, after finishing his day at Bronze and Granite Memorials,
Siggi drove to Diamond's home in Nutley, New Jersey, where they passed
the evening mapping out plans. Occasionally, they would meet at the
New Jersey offices of the brokerage firm Edwards and Hanley to watch
the tickertape and debate tactics.

"In Siggi, Diamond saw a real go-getter who would hike to the ends
of the earth if need be," said Irving Watchman, the stockbroker who han-
dled their transactions at Edwards and Hanley. "Sol said he would back
Siggi financially and cover the lawyers' fees and other expenses if Siggi
would take up the task of overturning the man who was then president of
Wilshire, a guy named Robert Reed. Siggi welcomed the challenge and
the opportunity to show the world that he knew more about business than
people gave him credit for."

Siggi drove home elated by these meetings with Diamond. He dic-
tated their analysis of Wilshire's annual reports to his wife, Naomi, not-
ing where the board failed to follow a particular protocol or when they
had been delinquent in their annual filings. Naomi typed the notes into

letters that they sent to the Wilshire board in Oklahoma City and its legal representatives at the firm of Sullivan and Cromwell in New York City. So critical were the letters that they troubled Wilshire's board members and their lawyers.

Meanwhile, with as much money as their middle-class income would allow, Siggi continued to purchase shares in Wilshire.

"I didn't see how this was going to change our life," Naomi said, remembering other stocks her husband had bought and other career moves he had made. "But that's how it turned out."

CHAPTER 8

Siggi and Goliath

The all-powerful American oil industry began in June 1870 when one of the earliest players in the industry, John D. Rockefeller, formed Standard Oil, which quickly became the largest refiner and shipper of oil and kerosene in the country. By the end of the 1870s, Rockefeller's company had developed more than three hundred oil-based products such as tar, paint, Vaseline petroleum jelly, and chewing gum, and Standard was refining more than 90 percent of all US crude.

Rockefeller's business practices triggered intense controversy. The company had no hesitation attacking competitors, underselling to their customers, and offering undisclosed rebates to railroad firms that gave priority service to Standard products. Journalists and politicians attacked Rockefeller for his cutthroat methods, and by 1880, according to the *New York World*, Standard Oil was "the most cruel, impudent, pitiless, and grasping monopoly that ever fastened upon a country." Two years later, Rockefeller formed Standard Oil Trust: a monolithic umbrella entity that housed more than forty Rockefeller companies. The Trust quickly became the richest, biggest, and most feared business in the world.

The man behind this financial juggernaut, John D. Rockefeller, was a faithful congregant of the Erie Street Baptist Mission Church, where he taught Sunday school. Religion was a guiding force throughout his life, and oil, Rockefeller believed, had a divine purpose. The underground riches were there, he said, to help establish God's Kingdom on earth. Oil was "the bountiful gift of the great Creator" and a "blessing ... to mankind." Rockefeller even found spiritual inspiration in the mechanics of extraction and refining. "The whole process," he said, "seems a miracle." Rockefeller was not alone in his assessment of oil as a gift from God for perpetuating His plan in the world. "The fact is," wrote *New York Times* reporter William Wright in 1865, "in Petrolia, the church universally believed in is an engine house, with a derrick for its tower, a well for its Bible, and a two-inch tube for its preacher, with mouth rotund, 'bringing forth things new and old,' in the shape of two hundred barrels per day of crude oil."[42]

The partnership of religion and oil solidified after World War I when Baptist oil barons funded Christian institutions such as Baylor University to foster commitment to scripture and God. "The professor who teaches geology," pledged Baylor's president, Samuel Palmer Brooks, "will know not only something about the age of rocks but also something about the Rock of Ages."[43] One of Baylor's graduates, Sid Richardson, became a millionaire in the oil industry and a major supporter of Evangelist Billy Graham. Richardson and other oil-wealthy families such as the Hunts and the LeTourneaus financed Graham's films *Mr. Texas* in 1951 and *Oiltown, U.S.A.* in 1953. Both films told stories of fallen businessmen who found salvation in a union of Christ and capitalism. By 1960, Graham's organization, World Wide Pictures, claimed that, thanks to these two films, millions of moviegoers had accepted Jesus as their savior.

Other revivalists from the Southwest such as Oral Roberts and Charles Fuller used their oil profits to fund ministries. Oral Roberts, a pioneering televangelist, used donations to found Oral Roberts University in 1965. Fuller spent his oil money building Fuller Theological Seminary, which became the hub of the "new evangelical" movement. As if to announce its purpose, Fuller named his company Providential Oil.

Richardson, the Hunts, and the LeTourneaus were a few of the many gentiles who dominated America's oil industry in its formative years, and they guarded their hegemony fiercely. "It was an old-boys' network, pure and simple," said Bruce Wells, executive director of the American Oil and Gas Historical Society in Washington, DC.

In 1879, competitors of John D. Rockefeller's Standard Oil succeeded in breaking up Standard's monopoly on oil delivery by building the Tidewater Pipeline. Rockefeller's competitors paid huge sums for workers to lay wrought-iron pipes six inches in diameter and eighteen feet long, work done mostly at night to avoid detection by Standard's spies. By May of that year, the pipeline extended 110 miles from the oil regions of Pennsylvania eastward through the Allegheny Mountains to a connection with the Reading Railroad. The first shipment of non-Standard oil reached Bayonne, New Jersey, on June 3. When workers turned on the valve, the Tidewater Pipeline delivered 250 gallons of oil an hour, destroying Rockefeller's stranglehold on delivery and opening the door to independent oil producers.

By age thirty-five, all that Texas-born George L. Machris had achieved was a modest business manufacturing cigar boxes, and he could only dream of being a part of the action in oil and gas. Meanwhile, between 1900 and 1910, the registration of gasoline-powered cars jumped from eight thousand to nearly one million. Sensing their moment, George and his older brother, Victor, a garage owner, began selling gasoline door to door. They parlayed their profits into one of the first chains of gasoline stations in the southland. By 1914, they had built up sufficient capital to found Wilshire Oil Company of Texas, which produced and refined on small tracts of land in Texas, New Mexico, Wyoming, and California. The company made good money, and in 1952 Machris retired to his home in Palm Springs, California. He died later that year of a heart attack. Two years after, his widow, Elsinore, remarried another Texas oilman and sold most of her holdings in Wilshire.

The new owner of Wilshire Oil Company of Texas was Britalta Petroleums, a Canadian firm established in 1948. Britalta's president, Robert L. Reed, was a hardworking oilman who saw good potential in the Wilshire acquisition. Still, business in Canada absorbed his attention and he had little time to oversee activity in the States. As a consequence, Wilshire's production of oil and gas lagged. Among other cost-saving measures, the Wilshire board had recently closed the company's Midland, Texas, office and several employees had been dismissed.

Wilshire's operations were further complicated by a labyrinthine succession of mergers and acquisitions that had taken place after George Machris's retirement. By the late 1950s, accounts were in disarray and no one had a clear idea of what properties Wilshire did or did not own. Even company officers, determined to set things right, found themselves bewildered by the company's complex history.[44]

Wilshire's future teetered on a precarious fulcrum of slipshod bookkeeping and absentee management. The company's investment strategy had also proved itself risky. In early 1958, the board approved the purchase of an 11,000-acre property in Eddy County, New Mexico. A thirty-one-day flowing test yielded only eight barrels of oil. The board deemed it incapable of more and shut down the well. Two months later, a second well was tested on the Eddy County property. It, too, failed to indicate potential for commercial production of oil or gas and was abandoned. In its annual report for 1958, Britalta had nothing good to report about their US subsidiary. "To date," President Robert L. Reed wrote, "no substantial commercial production can be reported," a situation that did not change for the next six years.

To take control of Wilshire Oil Company of Texas, Siggi needed to purchase large amounts of company stock. He didn't have the money to do so on his own, so for years he aggressively solicited family, friends, and acquaintances, enrolling everyone he could to purchase shares of Wilshire

and join his investor group.

He visited his best friends, the Wachtels, and sat with them in their kitchen where Rose always had coffee, kosher cake, and a bowl of nuts ready for guests. Siggi laid out his proposal. If they joined him in purchasing Wilshire stock, eventually they could take control of the company, run it right, and generate substantial earnings for shareholders. The way Siggi explained it, the plan made perfect sense, and the Wachtels brought out their checkbook. That was Siggi's gift: an ability to convince anyone of anything. People were mesmerized by his sales pitch.

"You couldn't refuse Siggi," said Ernie Wachtel. "He attracted people like bees to honey. Everybody was glued to his words, and they swallowed everything he served up. I ended up buying some stock at seven dollars a share and so did my father. Much later, my son-in-law and his brother also invested heavily, and we all made quite a profit. We were convinced by Siggi's salesmanship. Otherwise, we wouldn't have bought the stock. Whoever heard of Wilshire Oil Company of Texas?"

"In the beginning," remembered Siggi's brother-in-law Milton Donnenberg, who also bought some stock, "Siggi was a little lamb who got along with everybody. As his knowledge about the business world increased, he grew more and more assertive. And the more business he did, the more his speech improved. His talking became almost Shakespearean, and you couldn't help but listen."

By the winter of 1964, Siggi and his small group of investors had finally acquired enough stock that he was now in a position to address the Wilshire board in person and assess their response to his takeover bid. He packed an overnight bag, drove to LaGuardia Airport, and boarded an Eastern Airlines flight to Oklahoma City, Oklahoma, the location of Wilshire's main office.

His flight landed at Will Rogers World Airport and Siggi quickly collected his bag and traveled by taxi seven miles to downtown Okla-

homa City. The offices of Wilshire Oil Company of Texas occupied one floor of the Petroleum Club Building. With nearly 17 percent of the company's stock, Siggi's small group of investors posed a potential threat to the Wilshire board, but how he handled the next hour could determine the future of his campaign to take over the company.

Before meeting the Wilshire board, he asked a receptionist to point him toward the restroom, where he straightened his tie, washed his face and hands, and ran his fingers over his head to fluff his coiffure slightly higher. People sometimes commented that Siggi looked like Tyrone Power, the handsome swashbuckling Hollywood film star, and Siggi encouraged the comparison by ensuring that his hair was coiffed as high as possible.[45] When he finished, the receptionist escorted him to a conference room where board members stood mingling and talking among themselves. This was the American oil industry of the 1960s, and it went without saying that Wilshire board members were all old, white, non-Jewish men. Siggi was a Jewish David in an industry dominated by Christian Goliaths, and it was clear that his foray into oil and gas would not be well received. He entered the boardroom and shook their hands. Introductions were brief.

"Gentleman," he said, "I will not keep you long." His message was clear and precise. He and his investment group—a fancy term for the dozen or so family and friends whom he had enlisted to buy stock—were not going to be shoved aside, but neither were they hostile. The board had nothing to fear. His objective in meeting with them was to convey his intentions to help grow Wilshire to their financial benefit and his own. If they had doubts about his abilities as an outsider to their industry, they had only to look at the track record of his dear friend and partner, Sol Diamond, whose history on Wall Street and in a variety of businesses should serve as reassurance that the Wilzig-Diamond coalition came with credentials and skills to help move the company to a new chapter in its history and to greater profits than ever before.

Siggi chose his moment carefully. He removed his jacket and rolled up his sleeve. Board members looked at one another in disbelief. What

kind of a game was this? Then, revealing the number tattooed on his arm, he launched into a description of what he had been through in Auschwitz.

"Gentlemen," he concluded, "you are looking at a man who had the foxlike instincts to survive history's darkest hour, a man who has no fear of adversity and who cannot be intimidated by overwhelming odds. The Almighty has given me a second chance at life, along with the skills to make great fortunes. My partners and I looked forward to doing business with you."

He put on his jacket, said his goodbyes, and left.

A sympathetic insider later described for Siggi what happened after he left the room. Board members shook their heads, laughed nervously, and talked about Wilzig's complete lack of experience running an oil company. One of the directors asked, "Who the hell is this little Jew bastard?"[46]

Such slurs only fueled Siggi's drive to succeed. He had not survived Auschwitz just to let a roomful of antisemites push him off the road to success in America.

 †

Siggi returned to New Jersey and once again went knocking on the doors of family, friends, and business associates. Within a few months, his group had acquired enough additional shares that the Wilshire board could no longer ignore him. Sullivan and Cromwell attorney Bob McDonald placed a call to Siggi on behalf of the firm's client, Wilshire Oil, and made him an offer: in exchange for reassurances that the raid was over, the Wilzig-Diamond coalition would get two seats on the board of directors.

It was a start.

Not long before, Siggi had been a novice selling neckties and trinkets. Now he was penetrating one of America's most antisemitic industries. In the 1960s, only one Jew held a position of authority in the oil and gas industry: Leon Hess, who had built the world's largest oil refinery on St. Croix in the US Virgin Islands. In 1963, his company, Hess Oil and Chemical, had gone public. In their one meeting that year, Hess advised

Siggi to not bother getting into the oil drilling business. "They don't like Jews," Hess said. "They'll do everything they can to stop you."

It may have been, Siggi calculated, that Hess didn't want to encourage a potential competitor, especially a shrewd and aggressive competitor like himself—but, he reasoned, if oil was good enough for Hess, why not for him?

"It took several years," he described. "Who has a name like Siggi and talks about buying an oil company? You'd have to be *meshuga*"—Yiddish for crazy—"or else a genius with the Almighty behind you. The people on the Wilshire board said I would never get the stock. Well, I got it anyhow. I bought 5 percent, then another 5 percent, then another."

By the end of 1964, Siggi and his investor group had increased their ownership of Wilshire stock to nearly 20 percent, putting them in a strong negotiating position with the Wilshire board. Per Securities and Exchange Commission (SEC) regulations, they dutifully registered with the SEC, effectively announcing their plans to the general public and sending a clear signal to the Wilshire board that they were not content with only a minority stake.[47] Feeling threatened by the Wilzig group's possible takeover plans, the Wilshire board tried to pacify them by increasing their presence on the board from two seats to four.

Siggi studied the company's current methods, drafted radical plans for overhauling its operations, and submitted his recommendations to the board. The board was impressed. Sensing that Siggi might prove to be more of an asset than a threat, they showed his plans to Bob McDonald, one of their advisors at Sullivan and Cromwell. McDonald was a highly respected banking lawyer and tax expert who had been a leading draftsman of the Internal Revenue Code of 1954. McDonald studied Siggi's proposals and compared them with what the old Wilshire board was doing. Siggi's plans were riskier, but the alternative, he concluded, was to allow Wilshire to continue sinking in its own torpor.

"Let him run with it," McDonald told the board.

Run with it Siggi did, implementing new projects and increasing the number of wells. He made every attempt to look like "an operator," oil

industry jargon for an executive who personally supervised the drilling and ongoing production of oil and gas, but how often he actually visited production sites is unclear. Operators were the ones who got their name in the papers and Siggi played the part with panache. For example, he bought large swaths of one-dollar-an-acre undeveloped land—"goat pastures"—just to impress investors with how much property the company held.

"Several times, he brought home test tubes full of oil," recalled son Ivan, "and showed me how pure the oil was from wells Wilshire had recently struck. The samples were golden and translucent. I was surprised because I'd expected oil to be pitch-black like in the movies. I'm not sure how many times he actually visited the wells, but I'm sure he would have gone to impress employees that he was a team player, a hardworking guy like them, not afraid to get his hands dirty."

That first year, Siggi also moved forward with development of eleven exploratory wells. A well was "spudded" or drilled and the results monitored. If the well yielded a satisfactory quantity of oil or gas at a reasonable depth, Wilshire's engineers would recommend that the company invest. Siggi's decision to invest was based as much on his assessment of the engineers themselves as their reports.

"Dad didn't even take Geology 101," commented Sherry Wilzig, who would one day head the company. "It was his evaluation of people's abilities and character that determined the merits of a deal. He spent as much time studying the potential partners in a deal as he did the deal itself."

In 1965, Wilshire's president, Robert L. Reed, died suddenly of a heart attack and the board looked at its options. Rather than elevating one of their own officers, the board elected Siggi as Wilshire's new president and chief executive officer. Soon after, the board also elected him as their chairman. It was a remarkably fast rise for Siggi, one that had begun just three years after meeting Sol Diamond and only one year after Siggi's first meeting with the Wilshire board.

"Someone told me I wouldn't be happy at Wilshire," Siggi told a reporter, "that I'd be a mongrel. There would be three things against me. I was a Jew, I was a refugee, and I was a stranger to their industry. When the board forgot past differences and agreed to elect me, it was one of the greatest moments of my life."[48]

Soon after his appointment as Wilshire's new president, chairman, and CEO, Siggi hosted his first annual stockholders' meeting. Several hundred stockholders, stockbrokers, and potential investors arrived from California, Florida, Texas, and across the Northeast and gathered at a conference room Siggi had rented in one of the area's more upscale hotels. They heaped their plates with sandwiches and salads and other delicacies from Greenspan's, New Jersey's legendary kosher delicatessen. His eldest son, Ivan, remembered attending stockholders' meetings as a child and marveling at men sporting ten-gallon hats and wondering where all these cowboys had come from.

Then the standing-room-only crowd listened as geologists and petroleum engineers described, with charts and photos, where Wilshire was currently drilling, what they were drilling for, and when they expected to find it. Both before and after the formal part of the meeting, Siggi worked the room, shaking hands and making sure everyone felt they were part of the action.

His message to stockholders was positive and exciting: the engineers were optimistic about Wilshire's future, the company had great potential, and while not yet profitable, Wilshire owned leases on multiple properties ripe for development. New technologies were coming online, opportunities in the oil industry abounded, and now, with the right people at the helm, the future would be prosperous. Stockholders picked up on a not-too-subtle subtext: the old board members had dragged the company down, men in their senior years who lacked the drive and fresh vision to turn potentials into realities.

"Their average age was between eighty and dead," Siggi once commented.

When thirty-nine-year-old Siggi B. Wilzig became president of Wilshire in 1965, the company was showing a net loss of nearly a half-million dollars for the first nine months, on gross income of $1.3 million. Despite the temptation to make up the shortfall by selling off properties ripe for development, Siggi convinced shareholders to wait and give his new team a chance to grow the company. Like a racehorse pointing his nose at a gap in the field and bursting through to take the lead, Siggi grabbed the moment and ran, leading Wilshire to higher revenues than the company had ever known. By 1966, the remaining opposition board members were obliged to admit that their odd-speaking, odd-behaving Jewish president possessed remarkable skills.

"Your management's determination to hold and develop properties is a natural result of the Company's new philosophy," he wrote in his first President's Letter to Shareholders in 1966. "Our plans for the future are ambitious."

Siggi's first act as Wilshire's new president was to cut operating expenses. He then persuaded the board they should diversify the company's holdings so that profits would not depend solely on the gamble of new oil and gas wells. With their support, in 1966 he purchased two companies: Brooklyn Tire and Oil Corporation, a franchised supplier of tires, batteries, and refined petroleum products; and Eastern Radio Corporation, a distributor that sold and shipped electronic components from nine centers across the northeast. Car parts were a natural complement to an oil and gas company, and owning Brooklyn Tire enabled Wilshire to sell its own brand of products. Owning Eastern Radio also made good business sense, since nearly every American industry depended on electronics. Eastern Radio distributed capacitors, transistors, and microchips, components essential to the manufacture of everything from radios and televisions to airplanes and missiles. Siggi narrowed Eastern's suppliers down

to the nation's best manufacturers: Texas Instruments, Hewlett-Packard, and RCA.

"Ours is the least glamorous aspect of the electronics industry," he told a reporter, referring to the mechanical functions of packing and shipping parts, "but it has none of the risks of the manufacturing or research operations. What it does have is all the opportunities for expansion, provided you have the best product and the cash to support growth."

In 1967, the purchase of these two companies, Brooklyn Tire and Eastern Radio, enabled Wilshire to issue, for the first time in the company's history, a stock dividend of 4 percent.

Ultimately, however, Brooklyn Tire turned out to be a disappointment. The factory was located in a derelict neighborhood, frequent warehouse thefts cut into profits, and eventually the tire company was sold. Still, by the end of 1968, under Siggi's guidance Wilshire's revenues spiked to nearly $8 million with a net income of a half-million dollars. In 1969, he purchased a second electronics distribution company, Electrical Supply Corps., in Cambridge, Massachusetts, and Wilshire's revenues continued to rise. Gas sales were up, new wells were being drilled, and for a second time the board declared a 4 percent stock dividend.

It was not long before most major oil companies knew about Wilshire's growth, since the company was participating in the drilling of new wells with Amerada Hess, Standard Oil, Phillips Petroleum, and other big players in the industry. Even the billionaire Koch brothers did business with Wilshire, distributing Wilshire's oil nationwide. Shareholders were ecstatic.

In the 1970 annual report, Wilshire posted even higher revenues: nearly $9 million, with a net income of $700,000. In Siggi's mind, it was not enough. "Although these gains are very gratifying," he wrote to shareholders, "your management is not satisfied, since the growth potential of the Company has not yet been realized." Siggi's energy and ambitions

knew no bounds, but if Wilshire was going to keep growing, the company would need a steady stream of cash.

"Why not buy a bank?" suggested Bob McDonald at Sullivan and Cromwell. "Banks have lots of cash."

The Cash Cow

Every day, Siggi combed the newspapers looking for a bank to take over so that he would have the cash to grow Wilshire Oil Company of Texas. "What I really need," he confided to his office manager, Lisa Roach, "is a WASP bank."

"What's a WASP bank?" she asked.

"A WASP bank is a bank where most of the customers are White Anglo-Saxon Protestants. They put all their money into the bank and they never take it out. Jews? They put their money in, take their money out, put it in, take it out . . ."

While a WASP bank might have been his ideal, any healthy bank ripe for a takeover would do. An article about the Trust Company of New Jersey (TCNJ), a mid-level commercial bank listed on NASDAQ, drew his attention. He obtained copies of the bank's annual reports and found that the bank had a profile similar to Wilshire's: great potential but run by an old-school board lacking vision.

Siggi's legal advisor, Bob McDonald, cautioned him that just as there were few Jews in the oil industry, there were just as few in commercial

banking, and TCNJ's board would not take kindly to him elbowing his way into their business. The prejudice would likely be even greater than what Siggi had encountered at Wilshire. Siggi waved off McDonald's concerns. Antisemitism had never stopped him before, and he wasn't about to let it stop him now.

Commercial banks originated in the Middle Ages and are the oldest and most powerful financial institutions in the world. To this day, among other services, commercial banks receive deposits, make loans, provide credit for building businesses, and play a key role in development of a nation's economy. In the 1960s, when Siggi first grew interested in entering the banking field, there were approximately 12,000 US commercial banks, whose assets represented a full third of the dollar assets of all US financial institutions combined. Except for a handful of commercial banks founded by Jews, there was little room for Jews in commercial banking.

"Probably no industry in the country," noted Senator William Proxmire as late as 1974, when he was chairman of the Senate Banking Committee, "has more consistently and cruelly rejected Jews from positions of power and influence than commercial banking."[49] Not until the 1980s, when banks discovered they had to compete in international markets, did they alter their recruitment policies. An American Jewish Committee survey of the twenty-five largest banks in the United States in the 1970s found only one Jew among 377 commercial bank officers in senior management positions, thirty-eight Jews among 3,027 middle-level managers, and twenty-six Jews among 491 lower officers. "The notion that Jews control the banks and newspapers in this country," wrote Stephen Isaacs, author of *Jews and American Politics*, "is among the most enduring of myths."[50]

In the Trust Company of New Jersey, Siggi found a glaring example of a Jew-free bank. Its founder, William C. Heppenheimer, was born in New York City on March 27, 1860. His German immigrant parents moved to Jersey City when he was four years old. He studied law at Co-

lumbia and Harvard Universities and was admitted to the New York and New Jersey bars. Heppenheimer aligned himself with the Democratic Party, supported Jersey City bosses, and earned the title "General" for his service in the National Guard. He displayed little of the antisemitism which typified the banking industry, but the same could not be said of the German aristocrats on his board.

In March 1896, Heppenheimer and three associates secured a certificate of authority from the Commissioner of Banking and Insurance to incorporate the People's Safe Deposit and Trust Company of Jersey City. The bank opened in April and shared space with an insurance firm in a three-story wooden building on Central Avenue. A teller's "wicket" or window was installed, and an inexpensive everyday office safe served as the depository for cash and books. The bank did well, and the board opened two additional branches in neighboring New Jersey cities.

In 1899, when Heppenheimer and associates announced plans for a branch in Hoboken, they hit a wall. Hoboken was home to the Hudson City Savings Bank, and the federal government had recently passed legislation preventing banks from operating branches in towns where a competing bank had its headquarters. Heppenheimer and his team were savvy businessmen who knew how to circumvent restrictions, so instead of calling their Hoboken office a "branch," they created a new and different institution: the Trust Company of New Jersey.

Trusts differed from banks in their respective functions. A trust's primary function, then and now, was to manage its customers' investment portfolios. A bank was not expected to have trust-style management experience. The federal government took precautions to guard against commercial banks offering trust-style services, and there were penalties for banks that attempted to expand beyond their core services such as deposits, savings, and loans.

Still, there had always been a gray zone where trust companies and banks intersected, and by registering their business as a trust company and offering trust services, Heppenheimer and his colleagues were effectively able to circumvent the government restrictions and open a branch

in Hoboken. Then they opened additional branches in New Jersey: the Bergen and Lafayette Trust Company in 1902, the Greenville Banking and Trust Company in 1909, and the Carteret Trust Company in 1911.

By 1912, Heppenheimer's expanding enterprise required more offices. Management acquired land at the corner of Central Avenue and Bower Street in Jersey City, built an impressive Greek Revival–style edifice with marble columns and floors, and opened for business the following year. By then, the New Jersey legislature had realized the ineffectiveness of its anti-branch restrictions and revised the legislation to allow trust companies to consolidate and convert to commercial banks. Heppenheimer's group quickly pooled their various institutions under the umbrella of the Trust Company of New Jersey (TCNJ), became a commercial bank, and designated the Hoboken branch with its imposing Greek façade as the main office.

By 1920, TCNJ was New Jersey's fastest growing commercial bank and soon Heppenheimer needed even larger headquarters. That year, directors began construction of an eleven-story triangular monolith built in Italian Renaissance style with Botticino marble, located on Journal Square in Jersey City at the corner of Bergen and Sip Avenues. Teller windows, balustrades, and curved staircases were fashioned from mahogany with inlaid bronze detailing. Completion of construction and inaugural ceremonies took place in 1927.

By May 1945—the month that the 11th Armored Division of the US Third Army liberated Siegbert B. Wilzig from concentration camp Mauthausen—TCNJ had expanded to eleven locations, employed 283 officers and staff, and boasted deposits in excess of $100 million. By 1946, the company was managing nearly 100,000 savings accounts. One of every seven residents of Hudson County banked with TCNJ. That same year, the company president, Joseph G. Parr, announced that TCNJ had at last been elected to membership in the Federal Reserve System, a government seal of approval attesting to the bank's financial stability,

dependable management, and capital sufficient to meet the needs of its community.

Like Wilshire's board prior to Siggi's takeover, no Jew had ever served on the board of TCNJ. A plaque mounted in the bank lobby listed the names of its board of directors: Armbruster, De Groff, Mehl, Schlemm, Schmidt, Schroeder, and Schumann. "Over a seventy-year period," Siggi told an interviewer, "I don't believe they hired a Jew even to be a teller. Do you want to know how German it was there? On June 14, 1940, when two officers in the bank heard that Nazis had occupied Paris, they played Nazi songs and danced in the main branch. That's how German it was."[51]

The more Siggi learned about the nation's complex tax codes, the more he saw one great benefit in Wilshire taking over the Trust Company of New Jersey. If Wilshire acquired 80 percent or more of the bank's stock, Wilshire and TCNJ could file a consolidated tax return. At that point, the bank would have the right to "upstream" to Wilshire tax moneys otherwise due to the government. Instead of writing a check to the IRS for taxes owed on the bank's earnings, TCNJ could legitimately write a check for that amount to Wilshire.

This upstreaming of tax money was perfectly legal and would provide Wilshire with abundant cash to finance its growth.[52] The bank would become what Siggi affectionately called his "cash cow," supplying Wilshire with large, steady streams of development money for opening new wells, expanding into new territories, becoming more profitable and therefore less vulnerable to a hostile takeover. The arrangement would be a potential goldmine. To drill new wells and expand, other oil companies had to constantly raise money from outside investors in complex limited partnership agreements. The process was time-consuming and risky: any of those outside investors might sue if the oil company did not perform to their expectations. By receiving funding from their own subsidiary, Wilshire could effectively avoid such risks. There was also a profit motive: no outside investors meant not having to share profits.

It would take years for Siggi to acquire enough TCNJ stock to consolidate the two companies for tax purposes, but the benefits of doing so were irresistible. A takeover of TCNJ consequently became Siggi's number-one priority.

"Siggi approached the TCNJ takeover in an unusual way," said Edward Davin, former TCNJ executive vice president. "He made a tender offer directly to shareholders rather than going through the board of directors." Tender offers are invitations, usually announced in newspaper advertisements, by a prospective buyer to all stockholders of a publicly traded corporation to sell or "tender" their stock at a specified price during a specified time. In those days, in a tender offer the bidder contacted shareholders directly and did not need to consult with directors of the company, who may or may not have endorsed the proposal.

Don Brenner, who had been an assistant to Leon Hess of Hess Oil and Chemical, joined TCNJ's board in 1968. "When Siggi was looking to get control of the bank," Brenner said, "there wasn't a lot of stock out there. Most of it was held by maybe a dozen people. Siggi picked up little bits whenever they came on the market. The board began noticing and asked, 'Who is this guy Wilzig who's buying our stock?' Most of the directors on the board in those days were old Nazi types, big tall German WASPs, none of them under seventy years old, totally close-knit. So they got worried about a takeover—and by a Jew! My father was the single largest stockholder at the time. He and a couple other board members decided to freeze Siggi out."

When Brenner's father died in January 1968, Siggi visited the man's home to offer condolences. Don had inherited his father's shares, and Siggi calculated that the young man would listen to an argument if it made sense.

"This bank is a disaster," Siggi told him. "It has no drive-through service and the branches are very old. Yes, it's making a little money. But the

other members of your board have no interest in investing in modernizing the branches. Their only interest is in collecting dividends. They have only thirteen branches and no plans to grow. You're not going to survive."

Siggi counted on Brenner's youth to move his allegiances away from the board and sell him his stock. For good measure, Siggi rolled up his sleeve and showed Brenner his prisoner number. But before he could give his pitch about no one intimidating him again, Brenner pushed his arm away.

"The Nazis didn't beat you down. I get that. But don't try beating *me* down. If I go with you, it's because I want to." Siggi was not accustomed to people talking back to him, but he could tell when things were going his way and so he waited. Brenner nodded.

"Okay. I'll throw my stock in with you. But there are people who will kick me off the board if they find out. Let's keep it quiet."

"When they found out," Brenner recalled, "nobody on the board was happy with me. I didn't care. Siggi was right. The bank was going to fall apart."

Ed Davin was TCNJ's comptroller in those years, but he was still a young man with ambitions of his own. "The Trust Company was an old-school bank," he said, "and even though the board was treating me well, until I met Siggi I was thinking of moving on to a more progressive company somewhere else." The first week Siggi showed up at TCNJ offices, he entered Davin's office, introduced himself, and said, "I know a lot about you. I know you're a hard worker and I don't want you to be concerned about your future. I'm going to take over the bank, but it will only affect your future in a positive way." He made it clear that he would be loyal to Davin if Davin remained loyal to him.

Other officers made the mistake of feigning their allegiance. No one knew for certain if Siggi would succeed in taking over the bank, and some of the staff tried to hedge their bets by cuddling up to him and badmouthing the people in charge.

"He was smart enough to see through that," Davin said. "Siggi knew that if they were capable of badmouthing people who were still working in the office, they were likely to badmouth him, too, after he took over."

By October 1969, Wilshire's ownership of TCNJ voting shares had grown to 25 percent.[53] That year, Siggi made TCNJ shareholders an offer: two and a half shares of Wilshire common stock in exchange for each share of the bank. That brought in an additional 18 percent and raised Wilshire's ownership to 43 percent—within striking distance of becoming the majority shareholder. By 1970 Wilshire had acquired more than 50 percent of the bank's stock. Wilshire now had voting control over a commercial bank.

A financial writer for the *Newark News* wrote, "The dynamic Clifton resident, who concedes he is a prime example of this-could-happen-only-in-America, has big plans for expansion of the seventy-five-year-old Jersey City bank."

The contrast between Siggi and Otto Weinert could not have been more striking. In the 1920s, the TCNJ had been the second-largest bank in the state; by 1967, it had slipped to twenty-first. TCNJ President Otto F. Weinert Jr. was a veteran banker but of the old-school variety, content with the status quo. Siggi used his growing influence to circumvent Weinert and convince the board to modernize and overhaul the company's thirteen branches. "We saw a fine established institution that wasn't keeping up with the times," Siggi explained tactfully to reporters, "and wanted to realize the full potential of its proximity to New York and Wall Street," carefully avoiding any overt criticism of Weinert's passive approach to business. The article that appeared in the *Newark News* mentioned that "there originally was opposition from some directors to his bid to take over the bank." What the article did not report was that the "opposition" was whispering the same slurs Siggi had endured when taking over Wilshire Oil Company of Texas. "Behind my back," he confided to one journalist, "half the Bank board called me 'the little Jew bastard.'"

Nonetheless, the TCNJ board came to the same conclusion that the Wilshire board had reached: this Siggi character had a natural ability to run a business, despite his lack of formal training and despite his being a Jew. The board realized that putting him in charge might mean they would get to retire and earn better dividends than they had seen in years. Here was a man driven to make the bank grow, someone who understood that the duty of business was to increase profits for its shareholders. On January 1, 1971, the directors elected him chairman of the board and in May of that year they added the title chief executive officer.

"Despite their antisemitic insults," Siggi told a reporter, "once in power I didn't fire anyone for it."

At age forty-four, Siggi was now the youngest chairman and CEO of any major bank in the state.

Siggi understood that he was gate-crashing an entrenched, non-Jewish industry and that it would be prudent to avoid waving red flags. As soon as depositors learned of his takeover of the bank, the Jew-haters among them might take their business elsewhere. Steps were needed to protect his rising fortunes, and he appointed Tom Lynch as the bank's president. Lynch, an Irish Catholic, had served as law partner of the late New Jersey governor A. Harry Moore. Lynch was also vice president of the Chamber of Commerce of Jersey City where the bank was located. Putting such a distinguished Catholic at the helm would not only pacify bank customers who were suspicious of Jews, but it would also buy Siggi time to get to know the employees, earn people's confidence, and learn how to run the bank.

Siggi's goal had always been for Wilshire to gain complete control of TCNJ, and in December 1971 he instructed his legal advisers at Sullivan and Cromwell to draft papers requesting permission from the Federal Reserve for Wilshire to acquire the bank's outstanding shares.

The timing could not have been worse.

———

From 1950 to 1969, as Germany and Japan recovered from World War II, America's share of the world's economic output dropped, adding to an already bleak economic landscape created by the war in Vietnam. Public debt grew, unemployment rose, and by 1969 the price of gold had fallen to half its 1960 level. The value of the dollar plunged, prices of food skyrocketed, and pressure mounted for President Nixon to fix the economy before chronic inflation set in.

On the afternoon of Friday, August 13, 1971, Nixon met secretly with high-ranking White House and Treasury advisors including Federal Reserve Chairman Arthur Burns, incoming Treasury Secretary John Connally, and then-undersecretary for international monetary affairs Paul Volcker. They debated what Nixon should do. By the end of the day, the president had made up his mind.

"The time has come," Nixon told the American people via television broadcast from the White House, "for decisive action, action that will break the vicious circle of spiraling prices and costs." He then announced his decision to suspend the convertibility of the dollar into gold, to freeze all prices and wages throughout the United States for the next three months, and to impose an import surcharge of 10 percent on all foreign goods.

"I am relying on the voluntary cooperation of all Americans," he said, "each one of you, workers, employers, consumers, to make this freeze work. Working together, we will break the back of inflation."

As part of these emergency measures, the Federal Reserve announced that any non-banking company, such as Wilshire, which owned or operated a bank would have to register with the Fed by December 31, 1971. The Fed's stated objective was to prohibit risky investments "incompatible with the interests of prudent banking."

Regulators initiated a massive reevaluation of America's banking industry. Any non-banking company found operating even one bank would be forced to divest or pay daily fines until the parent company complied. If that failed to convince parent companies to sell their banks, they faced a forced shutdown by the US government. The Fed's intentions were announced and reported in the press.

The Sunday Record

Bergen County, NJ, January 30, 1972

Fed Set to Regularize Holding Companies

The Federal Reserve announced it would be "regularizing" holding companies by registering all significant corporate holders of bank stock. This follows the discovery that companies not usually identified with banks held big blocks of bank shares. . . . Under the new Fed rules, even a one-bank company . . . must declare whether it will divest itself of its bank stocks or of its unpermitted outside operations.

Had the significance of the announcement been clearer to Siggi from the outset—or had the Fed not given holding companies a full ten years in which to comply—he might have taken more immediate action. Perhaps because things were going so well at both Wilshire and TCNJ, objections by the Fed struck him as directed at others, not him.

"I don't think it's intended to apply to us," he told a reporter.

How could anyone object to how he was growing his companies? Look at the results. His tireless efforts to build Wilshire had resulted in renewed leases, new wells, and increased profits. Wilshire's revenues in 1971 were $13 million, up 38 percent from the previous year.

Siggi took no heed of the Fed's announcement and applied to the New Jersey Commissioner of Banking for formal approval to merge TCNJ and Wilshire Oil Company of Texas. The Commissioner approved the merger without hesitation, and all that remained was the Fed's permission to purchase the remaining shares of the bank's stock. Wilshire filed the request and the Fed issued its reply in July 1972.

The Herald-News
July 28, 1972

Federal Reserve Board Orders
Wilshire to Drop Bank Holdings

WASHINGTON—The Federal Reserve Board ruled yesterday that Wilshire Oil . . . must either divest its oil and other activities or to sell its interest in the Trust Co. of New Jersey, a Jersey City bank. In denying Wilshire's application to purchase the remaining shares of the bank, the Reserve Board said the company's non-banking operations are incompatible with the interests of prudent banking. The Board held that Wilshire Oil must divest its oil and other business if it wishes to retain its banking interest, or the firm has to sell its interest in The Trust Company if it were to continue its non-banking activities. Siggi B. Wilzig, Wilshire's president, said the company will appeal the decision. He declared that the Federal Reserve board's reasoning is totally false and totally unacceptable.

The deadline imposed by the Fed for separating TCNJ from Wilshire was December 31, 1980: eight years away and more than enough time, Siggi thought, to find a way out.

Meanwhile, Wilshire now had stakes in more than 700 wells and 80,000 acres of oil fields. As a result, 1973 was the most successful in Wilshire's history. Revenues increased a whopping 75 percent, soaring past $22 million, with a net income increase of 240 percent to nearly $4 million. Not incidental to all this success was the fact that all three of Wilshire's divisions—oil and gas production, banking, and electronics—were part of industries basic to the American economy.

In 1973, the Arab oil embargo cut foreign supplies of oil to the United States and sent tremors through the economy. The demand for domestic energy was a windfall for Wilshire, and the need to activate the cash cow was greater than ever.

To start the flow of money from TCNJ, Wilshire needed to own 80 percent of the bank's stock. At that point, the regulating threshold would be met, the two companies could file a consolidated tax return, and the upstreaming could begin. Tired of waiting for official permission from the Fed, Siggi went ahead and acquired more and more shares of the outstanding stock.

"*I did it!*" he wrote at last on a calendar sheet dated Friday, January 19, 1973. "*87 percent of TCNJ!*"

"Siggi B. Wilzig is probably the best example of the modern-day American dream," reported *Electronic Buyers' News*. "All it takes is guts, tenacity, brains, hard work, and making the right decisions."[54] Had he been offered a chance to edit the story, Siggi might have added "and the *chutzpah*"—Yiddish for nerve—"to stand up to the government."

In January 1974, TCNJ's board elected Siggi the bank's new president.

"People started treating him like royalty," Ivan Wilzig described, "especially once he sat on the thrones of both Wilshire, an American Stock Exchange–listed oil-and-gas-producing company, and TCNJ, a full-service commercial bank listed on NASDAQ.[55] After his tragic Holocaust past, to be president, chairman of the board, and chief executive officer of either one of those companies would have made him a superstar on Wall Street. But to take over both companies? That was unheard of."

Competition for bank customers was fierce in North Jersey, which was so over-banked that there might literally be a different bank at each corner of a four-corner intersection. But Siggi saw to it that TCNJ offered customers a more satisfying experience than any of its competitors, and customers were so appreciative of the personal attention that they called the Trust Company of New Jersey "Siggi's bank." Banking

at TCNJ never degenerated into a clinical exercise of deposits and withdrawals but remained a meeting of neighbors and friends in an inviting atmosphere.

"Other banks pay one hundred cents on the dollar, just like my bank does," Siggi would say, "and their money is just as green. The only difference between the other banks and my bank is superior personal service."

Siggi spent huge sums to change stodgy branches—some of them dating from 1896 when the bank was founded—into modern customer-friendly banking centers. By December 1974, renovations to the Union City branch, which had begun earlier that year, were completed. Gone were the metal bars separating tellers from customers. Gone, too, were the cold institutional benches and desks, replaced by comfortable padded chairs and plush carpets. Tables were crowded with kosher donuts and urns of hot coffee. It was holiday time and colored helium balloons floated through the air with messages wishing customers Merry Christmas and Happy Hanukkah, although Union City was a decidedly non-Jewish outpost of New Jersey, home to a Cuban population second only to that of Havana. The arrangements might have been extravagant for this part of the state—people in Union City counted their pennies—but it was the holiday spirit that mattered, regardless of the size of customer accounts.

Siggi had a parking spot for his car and driver at each TCNJ branch with a sign that read RESERVED FOR BANK PRESIDENT. He arrived at the Union City branch and a guard held open the door. Siggi greeted him by name. The floor was crowded. He surveyed the premises and walked over to listen in as a woman spoke with a young teller. The woman was pointing to her passbook and speaking in emotional tones. The teller was nodding his head while signaling under the table with a hand to get the bank manager's attention. The manager arrived.

"What's wrong?" he asked.

The teller explained that there was a problem with a Christmas Club account. The woman had come to redeem her savings and was expecting more than her actual total.

Krojanke, West Prussia, 1930: Siegbert (second from left, bottom row), his father (center), and other family members. His father earned a living selling pelts from a horse-drawn wagon.

1932: Siegbert, age six, holds a candy-filled cardboard cone, a traditional gift to celebrate a German child's first day of school.

1941: The unloading platform of Auschwitz-Birkenau. Most Jews were sent immediately to their death.

In Auschwitz, prisoners were fed one bowl of rancid soup, less than seven hundred calories per day.

1945: Hans Goebbels, a major general in the SA and brother of Reich Minister of Propaganda Joseph Goebbels, is interrogated by Captain Edward Levy of the US Army Counter Intelligence Corps after Hans Goebbels's arrest by Siggi and his investigative team. Courtesy Anna Rosmus, from *Valhalla Finale*.

1946: Twenty-year-old Siegbert Wilzig, in better health a year after his liberation from concentration camp Mauthausen.

Siggi with fellow Auschwitz survivor Larry Nartel, during their time as traveling salesmen, in 1950.

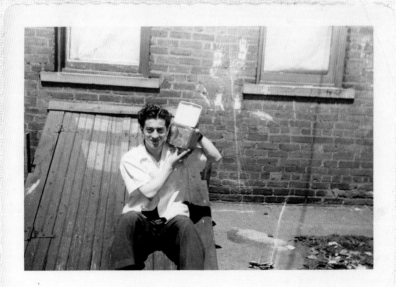

Siggi displays a "love light" from the National Pictures catalog, circa 1950.

1951: Naomi Sisselman, the future Mrs. Wilzig.

1959: Twenty-three-year-old Siggi, dressed for success.

By 1973, the openings of Trust Company of New Jersey branches were feted with theme parties, such as a Wild West celebration in Edison, New Jersey (above), and a fire brigade in Clifton, New Jersey (below).

In 1975, Siggi was the first Holocaust survivor to address cadets at West Point.

Wilshire President Siggi signs papers for the sale of Wilshire Electronics in 1980.

1985: Dean Eric J. Schmertz presents Siggi with an honorary doctorate of law from Hofstra Law School, where the Siggi B. Wilzig Center for Banking Law—at the time the only such center in the nation—had been established.

The woman pointed to the number at the bottom of the page. "I don't have enough money to buy Christmas presents for my family," she explained in broken English. "I read in the paper if I join Christmas Club program and save five dollars each week, then at end of year I have $400. But they say it's only $260 and I don't know what to do," and she buried her head in her hands.

The manager studied the woman's passbook. "You had to start the contributions in January in order to make $400," he said. "You started in June. All your interest was credited. I'm sorry, but the number is accurate."

Siggi stepped in and moved the manager firmly aside while extending his hand. "Madam, how do you do? I'm Mr. Wilzig, the bank president. Here's my card."

Siggi took the passbook and pretended to study the numbers carefully before handing it back to her. "It was our mistake, madam. We miscalculated the interest. The real number is $400. You can buy all your presents. Don't be upset."

The woman embraced him. With a wink and a stern nod to the manager, Siggi signaled that he should give her the money. Then Siggi wished the woman merry Christmas and went to greet another customer. TCNJ was not the only bank in town. Customers had options. It would not do to penalize someone because she had not understood the rules. Why give her a reason to switch to another bank? He wanted his customers to be happy.

"My father treated his employees like family, and he expected his employees to treat the bank's customers like friends of the family," commented son Ivan.

Siggi's generosity was not limited to bank customers. When son Ivan landed the part of Avram the bookseller in his high school's production of *Fiddler on the Roof*, Siggi paid for an elaborate party for the cast and crew. The story of Tevye, a poor Jew attempting to maintain family and

tradition in 1905 Czarist Russia, resonated with Siggi, and his apprecia-tion for the show included dozens of pizzas, followed by a cake with a frosted fiddler perched on a chocolate-covered roof. The party lasted into the morning hours, with the show's chorus singing to the accompaniment of guitar and mandolin and Siggi mesmerizing the teenage cast with his energetic rendition of the show's theme song, "If I Were a Rich Man."

In years to come, the Broadway tune about dreams of wealth became his anthem for celebrating happy occasions. Whenever a new branch of the bank opened, whenever he landed a major new customer, whenever one of his children came home with a "straight-A" report card, out of no-where Siggi transformed into the musical's main character, Tevye, danc-ing joyfully, snapping his fingers, and singing with eyes closed: *If I were a rich man, daidle deedle daidle dum.*

"Picture J. R. Ewing as Tevye," wrote a reporter, referring to the ego-centric oil baron in the hit television series *Dallas*. "That's what Siggi Wilzig became."[56]

"He had a beautiful voice," Ivan said, "and sounded like a professional singer, but he'd sing at the oddest times: in restaurants and public places, dancing in the aisles, oblivious to everyone around him, the whole world his stage."

Siggi loved to sing tunes from Broadway musicals. Every day, he would segue from "If Ever I Would Leave You" from *Camelot*, to "Try to Remember" from *The Fantasticks*, to "What Kind of Fool Am I" from *Stop The World—I Want To Get Off*, to his favorite song, "Impossible Dream" from *Man of La Mancha*. He sang "Maria" from *West Side Story* so often people wondered if that wasn't his wife's name. Often, he seemed more like an entertainer than a banker.

"His outbursts in public made us laugh the first few times we saw it happen," Ivan recalled, "but after a while we got used to it and just started singing along. People would ask us, 'Does your father own the restau-rant?' We'd tell them, 'No, he's just happy to be alive.' People thought he was nuts and laughed at him, but he didn't care. He had thick skin. We

were proud to have a father who could have that much fun and not care about what the people around him thought."

When he was in a particularly good mood, Siggi put on an even odder show by clicking his heels together, raising his right hand, and shouting "*Heil Hitler!*" with the same exuberance as if wishing someone "Have a nice day," to the utter consternation of whoever was in the room. Imitating Nazis was his way of saying, "Screw you, Adolf, you and your master plan. It didn't work out quite the way you expected, did it? Not only are we Jews still alive, but we're happy, we're healthy, and we still have our sense of humor despite everything you did to exterminate us from the planet."

CHAPTER 10

The Bank with Heart

By 1975, it had become difficult to get an appointment with TCNJ's quixotic, show-tune-singing, Nazi-impersonating president, chairman, and CEO. The waiting list of people wanting to talk with Siggi about loans, mortgages, property transactions, investments, and other financial matters was a month long. His popularity had three primary causes. First, Siggi was the only Holocaust survivor to reach such a powerful position in both oil and banking, and many in the Jewish community—particularly Holocaust survivors—were proud of him, had confidence in his business acumen, and came to him for all their financial needs. Second, Siggi made it his business to have a personal relationship with as many of the bank's major customers as possible. And third, he took time out of his busy schedule to give customers, large and small, free investment advice. As a result, while the 1970s may have been an era of high inflation and low returns for other banks, TCNJ was growing.

In the 1970s, the nation was populated by three kinds of banks: a handful of giants such as Chase and Citibank; medium-sized community banks such as Nassau Trust Company, the State Bank of Albany, and TCNJ; and mom-and-pops so small they were exempt from oversight by

the Federal Reserve. To expand TCNJ, Siggi set out to be the best community bank in New Jersey. To start, he created a slogan anyone could admire: The Bank With Heart since 1896. He even designed a logo: two red hearts entwined. Soon, the slogan and logo would make their way into New Jersey magazine and newspaper ads and adorn billboards up and down the Garden State Parkway and the New Jersey Turnpike.

Next, Siggi created two teams charged with expanding TCNJ across New Jersey. While one team worked to replace antiquated fixtures and furniture in the older branches with more contemporary interiors, the other spread out across the northern half of the state to find locations for new branches. Each branch opening was fêted with the good cheer of a national holiday, complete with theme celebrations such as a mermaid festival or Texas barbecue. The Clifton branch ribbon-cutting ceremony featured Siggi waving to crowds from the driver's seat of an antique fire engine. For the opening in Passaic, he commissioned construction of a buccaneer pirate ship. In Edison, he took his place on the running board of a Wild West covered wagon. Food was everywhere at these openings: pyramids of bagels, trays of smoked salmon and white fish, platters piled high with pastrami, corned beef, and turkey sandwiches. One table was always stocked with the finest kosher foods for Orthodox Jewish customers.

"My God," one customer exclaimed. "You never see a spread like this in a bank."

"What, you think I'm going to have an opening like those other banks," Siggi replied, "with cheap pretzels and dip? Here's my card. If you need anything, you can call me directly."

"My father hated the expression 'there's no such thing as a free lunch,'" noted son Ivan, "as if no one is ever nice just to be nice, or as if you always have to get something in return for giving someone a gift. He loved serving a free lavish lunch and giving out gifts by the bagful to every person who walked through the door—no catch, no gimmick. But of course, he hoped that his generosity would be remembered when people needed banking services in the future."

Gift bags awaited everyone who attended a TCNJ branch opening. Even non-customers who happened to be passing by walked away with bags full of pocket diaries, calendars, keychains, pens, and a bright yellow yardstick that stuck out of the top of the gift bag and drew everyone's attention to the name of the bank. In those days, no one ever threw away a yardstick. It was an expensive item to give away for free but worth the cost, as it meant a permanent advertisement for the bank in someone's home.

"TCNJ branch openings were always extravagant," remembered Steve Landau, a former vice president. "Everyone had fun."

All TCNJ customers were treated respectfully regardless of the size of their accounts. Siggi greeted each customer with the warmth of a beneficent uncle, handing out red enamel double-heart pins with gold borders, and speaking to them in language usually reserved for family.

"My dad would pepper almost every conversation with a Yiddish expression, even when talking to gentiles," Ivan recalled. "And then suddenly he'd remember he wasn't talking to a fellow Jew and needed to explain in English what he just said. Pretty funny if you think about it: gentiles learning Yiddish when all they wanted was a low-interest-rate loan or higher-yield certificate of deposit."

Siggi treated his employees with the same personal attention as his customers and, as a result, employees remained loyal to him and to the bank. At one point, the bank had three department heads who had worked for TCNJ for more than fifty years: Ed Davin, Irene Miller, and John Bell.

"He cared deeply about his employees," commented Bob McCarthy, head of human resources at TCNJ and one of Siggi's inner team. "One of the women on the second floor had an eye irritation. Siggi noticed it as he was walking by and immediately sent her with his driver to see a specialist, telling her, 'Don't worry about the cost.' As a result of that kind of care, we probably had the lowest turnover of any commercial bank in the state."

Antonietta Olivo, who worked in TCNJ's customer service office starting at age nineteen, remembered another instance of Siggi's generosity.

"Once when it was my birthday," she described, "I was running to meet my boss who had offered to take me to lunch. I turned a corner and literally ran into Mr. W., who gave me a big smile and said, 'That's what I like to see. Run, run, run! Where are you running today?' I told him it was my birthday. He said, 'I have something for you. But it is not for working hours.' Two hours later, his driver brought me a bottle of champagne and said, 'From Mr. W., for when you get home.'"

Siggi opened his heart to all employees, customers, friends, acquaintances—and as if he didn't have enough to do, he spent hours, days, weeks helping others at the expense of the business and his own family. Even though he had his hands full fighting off the Federal Reserve, nothing kept him from going to someone in need. At any hour of the day or night, even at two o'clock in the morning, he gave whatever time was needed to serve as someone's marriage counselor, business advisor, or family mediator. He'd literally drop everything to help settle someone else's family emergency.

"Customers would go to him whenever they had problems," recalled son Alan. "Fathers and sons would be arguing, and the only person they'd trust to mediate was Siggi Wilzig. It's no coincidence he came up with that double-heart logo for the bank."

"My mother was hurt that he spent so much time with others and less time with his own family," remembered daughter Sherry, "but in his mind taking such personal care of others justified having survived the camps. It gave his life purpose and meaning."

In one job interview a young woman asked Siggi, "What do you look for in a new employee?"

"You don't have to walk or talk or think as fast as me," he replied, "but you have to walk faster, talk faster, and think faster than your average person. Are you prepared to do that? Otherwise, you will not really fit in."

"Well," asked the young woman, "I have degrees in fine arts and religion. What are the chances of getting hired?"

"Fifty percent at best," Siggi said without hesitating. "I would hire anyone from law school or business school right away, but in your case I have to be convinced that you don't talk me into giving you a job and then the first opportunity to become a teacher you take a walk. I want you to honestly tell me, 'Mr. Wilzig, I heard about you, I like what I hear, and I want to work for you. Now, please tell me what courses I have to take to qualify for a job at TCNJ.'"

"It could be seen as a weakness that he felt he had to personally interview every single candidate for an administrative job in the bank," said Phil Kupperman, advisor to TCNJ from the accounting firm Arthur Andersen, "including tellers transitioning from the union into management. On the other hand, people idolized him because of such personal attention. He was loyal to them, and a lot of people saw him as some kind of a god."

"In later years, when he sold Wilshire Electronics, for example," Sherry recalled, "he refused to sign the papers until he was satisfied the new owners were not going to let any of the employees go, that their jobs were protected. It made for a longer negotiation, but he wanted people taken care of."

In addition to conducting interviews with all potential new employees, Siggi delivered the welcoming speech when school groups visited the bank. The big yellow buses pulled up, and he escorted the students and teachers inside, showed them the vault, and explained how a bank operated and the importance of knowing how to spend and save wisely. Before they left, he reached into a teller's box, drew out a handful of singles, and gave out dollar bills to all of the children, each student a potential future depositor.

Interviewing lower-level job candidates, lecturing twelve-year-olds, keeping a hospitality table filled with cake and coffee—the competition laughed at such mom-and-pop tactics. When the chairman of First Jersey Bank, one of the largest commercial banks in the state of New Jersey, heard that TCNJ was extending its drive-through hours, he scoffed. "Bad idea," he said. "All you'll get that late at night is the riffraff."

Siggi's response was characteristically blunt. "They are not riffraff," he declared, pointer finger raised in emphasis. "They are human beings and valuable customers." His respect for others less fortunate than himself was immense.[57]

Just as immense was his love for the State of Israel.

CHAPTER 11

"I'm Still in Auschwitz"

On June 29, 1975, more than eight hundred guests in their best formal attire assembled in the grand ballroom of New York's Waldorf Astoria to attend the State of Israel Tribute Dinner for Siggi B. Wilzig, an event that would prove to be a fundraising milestone for Israel Bonds.[58]

The who's-who of New Jersey society turned out for the gala evening. Limousines glided to a halt before the hotel's Art Deco and gold-leaf entrance. Liveried doormen welcomed guests and directed them to the main ballroom on the third floor, where city and state dignitaries mingled with New Jersey business leaders and society notables. Governor Brendan T. Byrne conversed with Banking Commissioner Richard F. Schaub, while Congressmen Dominick V. Daniels and Robert A. Roe swapped stories about Washington politics. Arthur Eisenstein, educational director of the Jersey City Jewish Community Center, accepted a business card from TCNJ customer Dominic Marino, president of Matco Transport.

Siggi circulated from table to table, greeting guests, checking to see that everyone was comfortable and pausing to shake hands with Fenwick Hill Garvey, executive vice president of John J. Ryan Investment Bankers, and Roy Weledes Jr., vice president of Manufacturers Hanover Trust.

Weledes, a prominent banker and non-Jew, liked Siggi and respected how many hurdles he had overcome to succeed in the restricted world of commercial banking.

Auschwitz survivors were in attendance as well, including Larry Nartel, head of TCNJ's purchasing department, and Joseph Bukiet, a major real estate developer. Executives from Siggi's companies had tables of their own at the front of the room, with TCNJ executives leaning over their chairs to chat with executives from Wilshire Oil Company. A ten-piece orchestra played, and couples danced.

People took their seats, filling nearly one hundred tables in the hotel's grand ballroom. At one end of the room, six American flags and six Israeli flags adorned a raised platform. In front of the flagpoles, two tables for speakers and VIPs extended sixty feet across the platform, each table covered with a white linen cloth and set with Waterford crystal and Limoges china. At a podium positioned between the two long tables, the dinner chairman, Thomas Lynch, stood waiting for the room to quiet. To his right, in a sharply tailored tuxedo, sat the evening's honoree, Siggi B. Wilzig. The room fell silent.

"A young survivor of the horrors of Auschwitz and Mauthausen," began Lynch, "a man who later served in US Army Intelligence, now aged forty-nine and our guest of honor this evening, Siggi Wilzig is the youngest chairman and president of any major bank in New Jersey as well as chairman and president of Wilshire Oil Company of Texas. His Midas touch has grown the oil company's revenues from $1 million to $30 million in ten years and elevated the bank's assets from $180 million to $316 million . . ."

A few more words followed, then Lynch sat down and New Jersey's former governor, Robert Meyner, approached the microphone.

"How he manages to run his multifaceted financial empire and still have time for philanthropic and community activities is phenomenal," Meyner exclaimed.

Siggi sat on the boards of the National Israel Bonds Cabinet, Congregation Adas Israel, the Hillel Academy, the Daughters of Miriam Cen-

ter for the Aged in Clifton, and the Jewish Hospital and Rehabilitation Center of New Jersey, among others. It was no coincidence that two of the boards he chose to join focused on the health and happiness of senior citizens. Siggi lost both his parents at an early age: he was powerless to keep them from being murdered. Now, from a position of power and wealth, he helped as many elderly people as possible.

Meyner sat down and Israel's Deputy Ambassador Mordechai Shalev called Siggi to the podium and presented him with the Prime Minister's Medal. Israel's Prime Minister Yitzhak Rabin had been scheduled to make the presentation personally, but tensions with the Arabs had kept him in Israel. Ambassador Shalev read the inscription into the microphone: "For dedicated service as a humanitarian, champion of brotherhood, and friend of Israel."

Guests rose to their feet and applauded. Some called out his name, others shouted "Bravo!" Siggi paused and looked out at the vast ballroom, casting a solemn calm over the audience, and people sat. He adjusted the microphone and began by thanking his hosts, expressing his love for Israel, and extending his gratitude to family, friends, and coworkers for their loyalty and support. Then he asked the audience to rise for a moment of silence.

"We stand," he explained, "for the millions of Jews who died in the Holocaust and for the many Righteous Gentiles who died alongside them. We stand particularly for more than one million Jewish children who were murdered, nearly all of them under the age of twelve." The room went still. After a moment, he asked them to be seated.

"I'm not liberated," he told the audience. "I'm in Auschwitz every day."

That sent a chill through the ballroom, but those who knew him were not surprised by the admission. Siggi exorcised his demons by revealing them to the world. Nonetheless, the evening was meant to be festive, not depressing, and he kept a careful balance in his speech, adding moments of humor and poetry where appropriate. "How can we understand such horror?" he asked his audience. "Still, I never gave up my belief in the Almighty. He may have created rats and poisonous snakes and Nazis,

but He also created beautiful birds, butterflies—and for Jews the greatest miracle of all: Israel, a homeland for the Jewish people."

When he finished his speech, guests stood and clapped, acknowledging Siggi: oil man, banker, philanthropist, entrepreneur, career maker, civic icon, leader of the Jewish community, but above all, survivor.

He thanked the audience, descended from the stage, took Naomi in his arms, signaled for a spotlight to follow, and like Fred Astaire with Ginger Rogers, spun her around the dance floor to a Viennese waltz, with the houselights dimmed and candles flickering off the mirrored walls and gloriously set tables. He whirled his wife left then right, hands extended, demonstrating for guests that his fancy footwork was not restricted to boardrooms. How far they had come from their early days together, when a vacation with their kids meant sleeping in cheap motels in the same room as their children, Ivan and Sherry. If any part of him missed those early years, it was a small part. Their todays were rewarding, and their tomorrows looked bright.

Things had been moving so fast, his ascension in business so jet-propelled, that no one seemed the least fazed by the irony of seeing Israel's highest civilian honor bestowed on someone who had never set foot in that country.

His children would all visit the Promised Land at some time in their lives, but Siggi's support of the State of Israel came in other ways. For instance, whenever there was a friend or family member who married, celebrated an anniversary or birthday, or sadly passed away, he donated trees to Israel through the Jewish National Fund in multiples of eighteen. In Hebrew, letters have numerical value. *Chai*, the Hebrew word for both life and the number eighteen, have the same numerical value. To honor smaller customers or to mark a moderately important occasion he'd donate eighteen trees; for a dear friend or for a big event, he'd donate 180 trees. For an even more special friend or larger occasion, he'd donate 360 trees, and so on. Over the years he planted many acres of trees, but he always found a reason for not going to Israel himself.

"If we are going to visit Israel," he told his family, "first we should go to Auschwitz and Mauthausen, but that would be too long a trip. So,

either we divide it into two trips, or we wait until I have enough time to do it all." Coordinating his hectic schedule with that of his family proved impossible and, despite his best intentions, a trip to Israel never happened.

There were other reasons that prevented him from visiting the Holy Land, and first among them was lack of faith in anyone other than himself to handle an emergency at work: bank robbery, check kiting, credit card fraud, money laundering, discovery of a corrupt loan officer—banking was fraught with risks, and every risk was a threat to his personal fortune and that of the other TCNJ shareholders. Because he trusted only himself to know how to handle a crisis, proximity to his office was critical. Kutsher's Hotel in the Catskills was acceptable: only two hours from New Jersey by car. Miami Beach was only three hours by plane. Israel, on the other hand, was a twelve-hour flight away, not nearly close enough for him to quickly respond to whatever emergency might arise at the bank.

The other reason he never made it to Israel was that, according to his understanding of Orthodox Jewish law, a Jew who sets foot in the Promised Land should not act like a tourist. He should stay there and make it his home. Despite his infinite love for Israel, Siggi saw himself as too young to retire and move there.

The Waldorf event was a great success. Out came checkbooks from purses and jacket pockets, and by the end of the evening more than $2.5 million had been raised for Israel Bonds, a record-breaking sum for the twenty-five-year-old organization.

West Point

Despite threats from the Federal Reserve, Siggi was a busy man. Notwithstanding the frustration of having to spend time and money fighting the Fed, TCNJ was now among the three hundred largest banks in America based on deposits, and the upstreaming of tax moneys from TCNJ to Wilshire had helped the oil and gas company purchase new properties and expand its drilling operations. The timing for this expansion could not have been better. Thanks to an energy crisis, domestic oil supplies were in high demand, and Wilshire was generating record-high revenues—and that in turn led to another unexpected benefit: in the mid-1970s, Wilshire was invited to list on the New York Stock Exchange, a prestigious move up from its previous listing on the American Stock Exchange.

Siggi's spirits were high when one morning he noticed a young man in the lobby of the Journal Square branch, wearing an Army uniform and yarmulke. Yarmulkes were not a rarity in TCNJ branches, since Siggi was the banker of choice for the northern New Jersey Orthodox Jewish community. Still, a believer in Army uniform was a rarity.

In the mid-1970s, Major William "Billy" Schwartz served as chief of ophthalmology at the United States Military Academy at West Point, the legendary campus that looked out over the Hudson River from a high point fifty miles north of New York City. Admission to the exclusive officers' training school was intensely selective and highly prized. Many of the 1,300 cadets made it in because they had been recommended by members of Congress. Every Friday night, Billy and his wife, Debbie, and the forty other members of West Point's small Jewish community gathered in a chemistry classroom for Sabbath services. Billy played an active role in the congregation and built their first *sukkah*, the temporary tent topped with branches and leaves that celebrates the fall harvest. When Billy's wife became pregnant, he planned to leave the army and open a private practice. That would require more money than his modest income provided. Someone suggested Billy approach Siggi for a loan.

"We ended up talking for so many hours," Billy recalled, "that Siggi sent someone out to bring back a kosher cake. He told me about his Holocaust experiences and how he felt he had survived in order to tell people about them." They came to terms on a loan and Billy returned to West Point.

One of Billy's patients was Major Harold R. Winton, head of the military academy's history department. World War II was a common topic of study for the young officers-in-training, but Winton admitted to Billy that his department's elective courses on the Holocaust lacked the vividness of real-life experience and could use something that would "put the Holocaust in human terms." Billy suggested that Siggi would be the ideal candidate, the first Holocaust survivor to speak at West Point, and Winton agreed.

West Point, or the United States Military Academy, was the training ground for the highest echelon of America's military officers. Since its founding in 1802, alumni had included Douglas MacArthur, George S. Patton, Omar N. Bradley, Alexander Haig, Norman Schwarzkopf, Presi-

dents Grant and Eisenhower, Rhodes Scholars, heads of state, ambassadors, governors, and cabinet members. Americans, possibly including graduates of West Point, had liberated him from the concentration camp Mauthausen, and if ever there was another Holocaust these were the men and women who would again be called upon to respond. More than two hundred cadets and members of the officers' corps filled the West Point auditorium on December 9, 1975, to hear Siggi's talk.

A small riser had been positioned in front of the podium. Siggi stepped up and adjusted the microphone, buying time as he surveyed the uniformed audience. His family watched from the front row.

"When I was a child," Siggi began, "someone in uniform was someone to be afraid of. But I'm honored by your invitation to address you here. Someday, one of you may be president of the United States. You'll need to know what Jews went through in the Holocaust so that you will be vigilant that it never happens again."

Siggi had prepared enlarged photographs to illustrate his talk. Students at West Point were accustomed to images of war. In their courses on warfare, they screened hours of battlefield footage and analyzed the havoc created by different classes of weapons: here is what a human being looks like after getting hit by a hand grenade, and this one by a mortar. Yet few in the room had ever seen images like those Siggi held up that evening: emaciated corpses sloping upward in piles as tall as a house; mountains of human hair, eyeglasses, and shoes; walking skeletons staring at the camera, only minutes from death. Here is what happened to us, he told them. Here is what we looked like. This is what they did to the Jews and other so-called enemies.

"Why did the world stand by and do nothing?" he asked the cadets that evening. "Was there some kind of conspiracy of silence? With all due respect to the non-Jews here today, might it have been a conspiracy among those who believed that the Jews killed Jesus? An American captain, a pilot, spoke about this to the *New York Times* last year. He had been sworn to secrecy, sworn not to reveal that the government knew about the camps. But the government did know. They knew as early as 1943."

He quoted New Jersey Congressman Robert Kean, who declared to Congress on March 19, 1943, that if America and England did not take immediate action, the blood of millions of Jewish men, women, and children would be on their hands. "Two million have already been killed," Kean told the Congress, "and the killing goes on."[59] At the time Kean made his plea, Siggi had been in Auschwitz nearly one month.[60]

Siggi then offered the thought-provoking observation that when Hitler was elected chancellor of Germany in 1932, he had little money and few resources. If at that moment Western nations had been more concerned about the growing threat to Europe's Jewish community, the Holocaust might have been prevented.

"On *Kristallnacht*, in 1938," he said, recalling the night his brother, Joe, had been rounded up, "seventy-seven thousand Jews were arrested and ten to twelve thousand killed—and only one column appeared about it in the *New York Post*. The Western nations did nothing. Let me encourage you to watch the televisions series *The World at War*.[61] In that program, there is an interview from 1973 with the man who had been the imperial marshal of the British armed forces. The reporter asked, 'There were reports of these mass killings. Why didn't you bomb Auschwitz? Planes were within two miles.' 'Oh,' the imperial marshal said, 'you know, we heard those reports about the Jews. But we didn't believe it.' 'Why not?' asked the reporter. 'Well,' the marshal said, 'I must tell you something—and I am not antisemitic, mind you. I know many Jews. But the Jewish people have a habit of gravely exaggerating. First we had to take care of the Nazis.' Those were his words.

"But when the time came to fly home after their bombing runs," Siggi continued, "and they could not fly heavy with the weight of the remaining bombs, instead of dropping their bombs on Auschwitz, they dropped them in the ocean. If only they had bombed the camp, *how many hundreds, thousands of lives could have been saved?*

"To add insult to injury," he said, "after the war the German government never even apologized. Instead, they offered survivors like

me one dollar and twenty-five cents for each day of torture and starvation. One dollar and twenty-five cents for each day I was in Auschwitz, for each day of torment to my mind and body, and not a cent for those they murdered, including fifty-nine members of my family. The Nazis murdered six million Jews, a million children under age fourteen, millions of Christians—and almost fifty years later, this is what they offer? I never spent their blood money. I gave it all to charity."

Siggi's younger son, Alan, remembered that moment at West Point. Even then, as a ten-year-old, he knew there was something unusual about so many soldiers dressed in crisp uniforms, sitting up straight, all in rows, with tears streaming down their faces.

"There's nothing wrong in expressing a bit of feeling," Siggi said in conclusion. "I thank you from the bottom of my heart."

The audience responded with a ten-minute standing ovation. After his talk, a group of Jewish students approached Siggi. "Models are very big here," a cadet told him. "We have models of bridges, models with input and output, but we've never had a model for the Holocaust until you came here. It's hard to admit this," the cadet added through tears, "but this is the first time in my life I feel as much like a Jew as I do an American."

The *New York Times* reported that Siggi's presentation had been "vivid" and "personal."[62]

"I've met four American presidents," Siggi told an interviewer twenty-five years after his West Point speech, "Carter, Reagan, Bush, and Clinton. If someone asked me how it felt, naturally I would say it was an honor. But nothing could ever take the place of what happened at West Point. By scheduling that one talk, the US Military Academy did more than anyone can imagine to preserve the memory of the six million Jews who perished in the Holocaust."

The reception at West Point was still fresh in his mind as he looked out a week later from his office window in TCNJ's Jersey City headquarters.

From that height, eleven stories above Journal Square, Siggi could see most of Manhattan across the Hudson River, including Wall Street and the Twin Towers of the World Trade Center. He held a phone to his ear. On the other end was New Jersey Governor Brendan T. Byrne. In addition to his other achievements, Siggi had become an important influence in many politicians' careers. Had he been a natural-born US citizen, Siggi told his family he would have announced his candidacy for president. Because he hadn't been born in America, the alternative was to help elect those who shared his views, in particular politicians who fought anti-semitism, were pro-Israel, and actively sought restitution for Holocaust victims.

Just as Siggi's customers and friends bought whatever stock he touted, significant portions of the North Jersey Jewish community donated to politicians he endorsed and voted as he recommended. His bank had branches in five counties, a presence which led to relationships with most of the local candidates for public office. To those politicians whom he respected the most, he delivered the North Jersey Jewish vote. People running for mayor, governor, congressman, senator, or president—all had a better chance with Siggi and his followers on their side. Those votes had helped elect Governors Robert Meyner, Thomas Kean, James Florio, a coterie of other pro-Israel politicians such as Congressmen Frank Guarini and Robert Menendez, and today's caller, New Jersey's Governor Brendan T. Byrne.

"If you want to be in politics in New Jersey," Byrne once told associates, "you have to go through Siggi."[63]

Byrne knew how politically powerful Siggi had become. He himself had been reelected with Siggi's help, and he was calling with the customary appreciation by offering Siggi a prestigious appointment of his choice, such as trustee of the New Jersey College of Medicine and Dentistry or as a member of the New Jersey Turnpike Authority, which came with a decent fee just for attending a few meetings throughout the year.

"I'm not interested in an appointment to any of those committees," Siggi said, "and I don't care about the money. I want to be the first Jew on the New Jersey Banking Advisory Board."

Byrne granted him his wish, and the appointment was one more af-
firmation for Siggi that Hitler had lost his campaign to wipe out world
Jewry, and that Jews had not only come back from the edge of extinction
but were breaking down barriers that had been in place for a very long
time.[64]

The Super-Salesman

Norman Bickoff grew up near Siggi's sister, Jenny, in Passaic, New Jersey, and loved Siggi like an uncle. Norman's family regularly had Siggi over for meals and for gatherings of fellow Holocaust survivors.

"I was just a kid then," Norman recalled, "and I remember thinking those gatherings were strange. They were like parties but not parties, everyone talking in hushed tones. Later, I understood they were discussing who had survived, who had died, who made it to America and who didn't."

Norman's father was a real estate broker and taught his son the business. As a child of the sixties, Norman desired to apply his training to help poor people in inner cities. In 1974, he found a building in foreclosure and decided to renovate it as low-cost housing. He went to banks, looking for construction funding. When bankers asked him what kind of people would be living there, he answered candidly, "Blacks, mostly." Bankers shook their heads and showed him the door.

Norman's parents advised their son to speak with Siggi. Norman bought a pinstripe suit, prepared the financial plan for his housing project, and showed up at TCNJ for the meeting. Siggi flew into the room, looked at Norman, and cut to the chase.

"Oh, you got yourself a fancy suit and now you think you're a big shot?" Then, with a chuckle, he said, "Tell me about the deal."

"I showed him the numbers," Norman described. "Siggi looked me in the eyes like he was searching for something. Then he picked up the phone and spoke to someone and said, 'Put fifty thousand in Norman Bickoff's account.' And that was it! I was just starting out in business, but he didn't think twice about it."

The next time Norman had a project that needed financing, he showed up at TCNJ headquarters and waited outside the chairman's office. When Siggi emerged from a meeting, Norman ran after him and explained the new venture.

"It didn't take long," Bickoff recalled. "Siggi looked directly into my eyes, he asked me a couple of questions, I answered them correctly—and in one second he said, 'You got the loan.' Then he picked up the phone, called someone and said, 'Put a hundred thousand into Norman Bickoff's account.' Then he handed me the phone and said, 'Here. The guy on the phone is my mortgage officer. He's the one you have to deal with from now on. Stop chasing me around.' Then he said, '*Zei gezundt,*' a Yiddish phrase meaning 'be healthy and farewell,' and walked out the door."

Abrupt departures, whether from a room or from a phone call, were classic Siggi. He made hundreds of split-second decisions every day involving millions of dollars and had no time for lengthy courtesies and hung up on everybody without saying goodbye, even his wife and children. Very often people would keep talking into a void, and only after hearing the disconnected dial tone did they realize that he had hung up long ago.

"Maybe he helped me with my loans because my parents were good to him when he was just starting out," Norman reflected. "They didn't know he would become a powerful man. Back then, he was just this poor refugee who talked with a strange accent. Helping him was pure *chesed,* Hebrew for 'loving kindness,' on my parents' part. Still, now that he was running a bank, heaven help you if you didn't follow his instructions. He'd think you were being disloyal and dismiss you immediately. Loyalty was a big

deal to him. He even wrote it into the loan documents: I had to have all my accounts with him. He wasn't always warm and fuzzy, but thanks to him I've been able to help poor people with their housing needs."

Siggi reserved his best performances for successful doctors and dentists who had the resources to make substantial investments but knew nothing about business. Son Ivan recalled his father frequently passing him in the hallway on the way to a meeting and remarking, "I've got another dumb doctor coming in for advice."

"He knew they weren't dumb," Ivan explained. "He had the highest respect for medical professionals. But when it came to business, most of them were clueless."

A typical exchange took place with a New Jersey heart surgeon who had already taken out a loan from TCNJ and was seeking guidance on his investments. Siggi received the doctor and his wife in his eleventh-floor conference room. On this occasion, to impress the wealthy doctor, Siggi had the bank's chef, Erik, prepare a lunch of fresh salmon brought in that morning from the Fulton Fish Market. TCNJ was the only bank in New Jersey with a private chef overseeing a kosher kitchen.

After a pleasant lunch, Siggi examined the doctor's portfolio. "You may be a genius when it comes to surgery," he said, "but when it comes to business, you're an idiot. You make a lot of money, so why do you keep these penny stocks? *Schmuck!* What you need is a financial enema. Get rid of this crap and buy stock in quality companies.

"And look at this," he said, pointing to the doctor's bank statements. "You have multiple personal checking and savings accounts in nine different banks. That makes you a little fish in all nine banks. If you put all your accounts in my bank, you'd be a big fish."

"Well, you have my main business account," the doctor said. "The problem is you're five miles from our home. There are no convenient TCNJ branches near us. My wife and daughter have their personal accounts in a bank only two blocks from where we live."

Siggi stared at him and turned up the volume. "Was my bank too inconvenient when you wanted to borrow money? Was it too inconvenient

when that other bank wanted to charge you prime plus 3 percent—*and I gave you a loan at prime plus 1 percent?!*"

By now, the doctor was cowering, head lowered, and feeling like a complete ingrate. "No, you're quite right, Siggi," he said, but the tirade was not over.

"Now show me the interest you're paying on whatever loans you have with other banks," Siggi demanded, "and I'll charge you less on all of them."

"How much less?" the doctor asked.

"*Schmuck!* Less is less!" Siggi bridled. "What difference does it make? You've been with that other bank for twenty years and they didn't appreciate you! *You're banking with me ten minutes and I'm charging you less!*"

"But they pay a higher rate than you on my savings accounts," the doctor said.

"Fine. I'll pay you more," said Siggi.

"How much more?" the doctor asked.

"What are you, an ignoramus? More is more! You're a winner as soon as you give me the money! Here's what you're going to do. You are going to take out every penny you have in those other banks—*immediately if not sooner!* And you are going to deposit that money here.

"Oh, I'm sorry," Siggi said sarcastically. "Are we too far away?" he continued with even heavier sarcasm.

"I'M SENDING AN ARMORED CAR TO PICK UP ALL THE DEPOSITS FROM YOUR OFFICE!"

And he did.

The customer was amazed by Siggi's great rates and couldn't figure out how his bank ever made any money. "Siggi," he asked, "how can you afford to give me such special treatment?"

Siggi smiled and answer candidly, "I know that you're going to play golf this weekend at your country club with all your successful friends. After the game, when you're in the steam room and someone next to you says he doesn't like the rates at his bank, or he tells you his bank turned him down for a loan, do you know what you are going to say? You are

going to say, 'Charlie, you must immediately call my friend, Siggi, the chairman of the board of my bank. He always approves my loans.' And do you know what your friend is going to reply? 'The chairman of the board of your bank *personally approves your loans*? What's his number? I'm calling him right away.'

"That's why I give you such special treatment," Siggi said, "because you will be my goodwill ambassador to all your friends. You will be referring at least one new customer to me each month, and that's how I'm going to make up for the losses I take with you."

Siggi went through this scenario with major customers three or four times a day, almost every day, for years on end, and for the longest time eldest son Ivan also couldn't figure out how the bank ever made money.

"If my father was charging customers less interest on their loans than they had been paying at other banks," he commented, "and if he was paying them more interest on their CDs than other banks, how could TCNJ be making a profit? My father was like the banking equivalent of Crazy Eddie, the pitchman in the electronics business who was always bragging on television, 'Our prices are insane!' and vowing never to be undersold. But once I understood that my father's strategy was spoiling certain customers in order to create a constant stream of customer referrals from them, I understood the method to his madness.

"They don't teach you this stuff at Harvard Business School," said Ivan, who attended hundreds of such meetings in his father's conference room. "My father was thinking outside the box before that phrase was invented."

Siggi wasn't the sole owner of TCNJ—there were thousands of shareholders—but as its largest shareholder and chairman of the board, he had an unassailable sales pitch. To a dentist and his wife who were hesitating to move their investment portfolio and trust accounts to TCNJ, Siggi declared, "So you're telling me you're happy with your present bank because you know the bank president? Well, I've got news for you. That guy who is

the president at your other bank—he's nothing but an employee. He could get fired tomorrow. Or he could quit if another bank offers him more money. Then where would you be? That can't happen to you here because I'm not simply an employee. I own the bank! I'm not going anywhere and every penny I make goes into buying more bank stock. And look at how well the bank is doing. See for yourself."

From the inner pocket of his suit jacket, Siggi pulled out a quarterly earnings report. Siggi's jacket amounted to a walking office. The pockets bulged. He pointed to the report and quoted the bank's most recent profitable numbers.

"Liars can figure," he proclaimed, finger raised for emphasis. "But figures never lie! That gigantic bank you're working with now—they make huge risky loans to foreign countries, in the hundreds of millions. If even two of those loans go bad, they'll be out of business tomorrow. Our bank, on the other hand, doesn't make any foreign loans. Our customer base is mainly in the New York–New Jersey metropolitan area, not foreign countries. That's why there's less risk to you banking with us."

Meanwhile, the dentist's wife was nudging her husband in the ribs. "Sweetie, do whatever Siggi says. He's making a lot of sense." That was the opening Siggi wanted.

"Where does your husband take you on vacation?" he asked casually.

"Every summer we spend two weeks in Saint-Tropez," the wife answered with a nod of satisfaction.

"How would you like to spend *four* weeks there instead of two?" Siggi asked. "Tell your husband to pay attention, or you'll end up with *no* weeks in Saint-Tropez."

"What? No Saint-Tropez? Oh my God!" the wife gasped. "What should we do?"

Siggi studied their portfolio and stroked his chin. "Well, since you asked," he said, tapping his fingers together and feigning deep thought, "I'm not a financial analyst, but I'm taking my time to give you good advice—and do you have any idea what my time is worth? *Ten thousand dollars an hour!* Are any of those other big bank presidents going to sit

down and tell you what to buy and sell? No! They don't even know you were born. They wouldn't know if, God forbid, you should die. They have hundreds of dentists. Why should they care about you? They have General Motors and IBM as customers. To them you're a nobody. But to me, *you're* my General Motors! *You're my IBM—MY MOST IMPORTANT ACCOUNT!*"

"What . . . what do you recommend?" the dentist asked, perspiring, weak-kneed and holding onto the edge of the long mahogany table for support.

"Well," Siggi said, calmly, "legally, I can't *tell* you to buy Trust Company or Wilshire—but I can tell you *I* bought it, *my children* bought it, and *all my friends* bought it. But I'm not telling you what *you* should do. You have to decide on your own," and then he winked obsessively as though nursing a nervous twitch.

"Anything else I should buy?" the dentist asked, furiously writing everything down.

"Well, I see you don't have any stock in energy companies or construction firms. Personally, for technology I like Selas[65] and for construction I like Jacobs Engineering."

If it was good enough for Siggi, it was good enough for the dentist, who would have done anything to stop the browbeating. Investment and trust accounts were successfully transferred. End of meeting.

One effective way to grow the bank's loan portfolio was convincing his business customers to borrow more money than they'd applied for. For example, one customer seeking a loan manufactured and distributed machine parts. Siggi already had an idea from his loan officer's reports how much the customer wanted to borrow and got straight to the point.

"Why do want to borrow only $500,000?" he asked. "I appreciate that you need money to expand your business, but you own the land, you own the inventory, you own the machinery—why not borrow more?"

"Why should I borrow more than I need right now?" the customer asked.

"Because things can change drastically in an instant," Siggi said. "What happens if the price of raw materials goes up? You'll be stuck and have to come back to me for more money. And who's to say the Fed won't raise interest rates? Borrow more now, while the rates are low. Your application says you made $5 million this year and have plans to expand over the next five years. If that's correct, then chances are you will need another loan very soon. That will mean paying additional fees on that second loan, maybe even on a third loan. Save yourself a fortune in fees by borrowing more now. It will cost you much less than coming back later. Don't be foolish!"

As compelling as Siggi's arguments were, the customer hesitated to take on more debt. "My one company doesn't have enough collateral to cover a bigger loan," he argued. "I'm already borrowing the maximum I can."

"You don't have to be concerned about that," Siggi reassured him. "You have two companies, one manufactures, the other distributes. We'll cross-collateralize the loan. That way, your other business will provide the additional collateral you need to get the larger loan approved by my bank's commercial loan department."

In reality, approval from the bank's commercial loan department was irrelevant. If Siggi wanted someone to get a loan, the loan would go through.

"But that puts both my businesses at risk," the customer objected. "I don't want to do that."

"You and I know that both companies are doing well," Siggi replied confidently, "so why are you concerned? I'm giving you the best deal imaginable. You'd be crazy not to take it."

By now the customer was squirming with uncertainty. "No," he said finally. "My father always taught me to keep the two businesses separate."

"That made sense *then*," Siggi said, "when both your businesses were small. But now it's necessary because you're borrowing millions of dollars."

"Okay," the customer said, "now I know where you're coming from and I agree."

"Also," Siggi added, "I'll need a second mortgage on your house as additional collateral."

"*What?*" the customer cried. "*My house?* I don't want to give you my house."

"Why not?" Siggi asked innocently.

"My wife would kill me!"

"*Fine!*" Siggi exploded. "*THEN BORROW THE MONEY FROM YOUR WIFE! OR GO TO ANOTHER BANK!* Is your *wife* giving you the loan," Siggi barked, "or am *I?* Is *she* the one running the business, or do *you* run the business? If you don't have faith that you can pay back the loan, it must be because you lied to me when you said the business is doing well. Did you lie to me?" Siggi asked, rising from his chair, the temperature in the room rising with him. "*Did you lie to my loan committee? Why should I be comfortable lending you anything?*"

"Siggi," the customer gasped, the air in the room suddenly thinner, "I appreciate what you're saying, but be reasonable."

Now the customer was forced to imagine what it would be like having to move all his accounts to another bank. No doubt the new bank would also require collateral. In addition, the new bank's loan officer would want to know why TCNJ had refused to lend him the money. If the loan had not been approved where the customer had been banking for years, why should anyone else lend him money?

Siggi read his customer's mind like an open book and offered reassurances. "I've looked at your statements," he said, nodding in appreciation. "You will have no problem paying back the loan. I know your businesses are solid. But what happens when the examiners tell me *they* think the loan is too risky? What happens if they argue with me that your business is seasonal and unpredictable? If you give me a second mortgage on your house, I'll have an answer for them. Here's what I will tell them: 'I know the man! He's good for the loan. Who cares if his profits are slightly higher or lower in any given quarter? This is a brilliant businessman. He's successful and growing—and on top of that, I have the second mortgage on his house! The loan is completely secure.'"

Siggi draped an arm around the customer's shoulder. "That is how I will convince the examiners that I didn't make a mistake giving you the loan," he said, "and that is why it makes sense for you to take the bigger loan, cross-collateralize it, give me a second mortgage on your home, and sign a personal guarantee, in case the examiners want to make trouble and start questioning me."

Just when he thought the pressure couldn't possibly get greater, the customer blinked in disbelief. "Personal guarantee? Siggi, you didn't say anything about a personal guarantee. I thought we already agreed on the terms."

Siggi shrugged and lifted his hands in the air, palms up. "What's the problem? *Of course* you have to give a personal guarantee. For a loan this size, my customers always sign a personal guarantee."

Every shred of common sense told the customer he should run away before things got worse. But where would he go? When all was said and done, Siggi was his best bet for growing his business. It was just that, logically, the deal was getting crazier by the minute.

"Siggi," the customer pleaded, "you're asking me to put everything I own on the line. If the loan goes bad, you could sue me and take away my house."

Siggi tilted his head back, as though insulted. "Do you really think I would ever do that? What good would that do anybody? Sue you? Foreclose on your house? That's not how we do business here. Remember, *we're THE BANK WITH HEART!* That's our motto and we live by it. Don't worry. The personal guarantee is just a formality. My biggest customers all give me personal guarantees. If the Wilfs and the Halperns, two of the wealthiest families in New Jersey, have to sign personal guarantees on certain deals, don't you think you should, too?"

At last, seeing himself elevated to the ranks of such successful business moguls, the customer nodded his head in agreement, and the deal was sealed with a handshake. Papers were drawn up with the various new conditions: a loan increase from $500,000 to $1,500,000; additional collateral from his other company; a second mortgage on his home; and

a personal guarantee. Once the borrower had given Siggi everything he wanted, Siggi made sure the customer walked away feeling like a winner. He picked up the phone and called his son.

"Ivan, I'm sending my most important customer down to your office. I want you to get him the best seats to any sports event he wants. The sky's the limit." He hung up and turned to the customer and said, "I'm going to take the best care of you. And by the way, you should be getting your Certificates of Deposit from me as well. Just show me on paper whatever your last bank was paying you on your CDs and I will pay you more. Now, am I the best banker you ever met in your life or not? Now you know what it's like to bank with a genius. And now that you're on our VIP list, go see my son downstairs and pick out your tickets."

The Jewish community benefited most from Siggi's willingness to approve risky loans.

"When I moved to Passaic, the Orthodox community was very small," recalled Rabbi Heshie Hirth of Yeshiva K'Tana. "Mr. Wilzig was instrumental in helping us grow. I would go to him, he would listen and do whatever he could to help us. He'd turn to somebody in his office and say, 'The Nazis tried to kill us. They didn't succeed. We are going to rebuild, and this is the man who is going to do it. Give him whatever he wants.' It meant taking a risk, since we had no money. One time, we needed several hundred thousand dollars to build a *mikveh*, a bathhouse used for ritual immersion. He invited me to his home and talked about the Holocaust, not about the loan. It was clear he was still angry about having been subjected to those horrors in the camps. He boiled over when he spoke about it. But he put the emphasis on rebuilding the Jewish people. The next week, we had our money. No questions asked."

The *mikveh*, along with other facilities, transformed Passaic into a premiere location for Orthodox Jewish families. In Siggi's mind, the risk in approving loans for such projects was easily outweighed by the

reward of helping the Jewish people with their financial and religious needs.

Siggi's rapport with customers resided as much in his ability to sell himself as in the quality of his advice. It was the utter spectacle of his public persona that made a lasting impression. He dominated conversations with colorful stories, riveting reminiscences, and unassailable arguments, all delivered at breakneck speed. If Siggi and Naomi invited another couple out to dinner, no one else got in a word. Meals with Siggi were one long monologue. The fact that Siggi monopolized conversations left little room for Naomi to show how dynamic a person she was in her own right.

"One of his bank directors came to see me after I had surgery," Naomi remembered. "At the end of his visit, he said to me, 'You're a fascinating person, but I never heard you speak before.' And we'd been to dinner with him and his wife many times. It was just Siggi's way."

To the Holocaust survivor community of New Jersey, Siggi was a hero who had made it big and proved that the Jews were alive, strong, and smart. He took care of their money as though it was his own, and TCNJ was their bank of choice. Builders and real estate developers—including the Halperns, Wilfs, Pantirers, Zuckermans, Bukiets, Kushners, Kaplans, Pomerances, Osters, Fisches, Sarnas, and many more—all banked with Siggi. The New Jersey survivor community took pride in having one of their own as head of the bank where they did business.

"He felt a different kind of loyalty to survivors than to the general public," said Phil Kupperman, one of Siggi's closest business advisors. "As time went on and those people became bigger successes, they borrowed more and more from Siggi, and that added to his own success."

American-born Jewish billionaires including the Simons and LeFraks also did business with him and leased him space to open branches of

TCNJ in their shopping centers. In addition, smaller businesspeople of all religions and ethnicities fell into his embrace, and as long as they remained loyal and did all their banking with him, Siggi took care of them, too, like family. If TCNJ opened a new branch and needed eight desks and twenty chairs, a customer who ran a furniture company got the business. When customers had fender-benders, Siggi sent them to a body shop owned by someone who banked with TCNJ. If a business owner needed office supplies, Siggi recommended a supplier who banked with TCNJ. He revamped his customers' finances, made introductions that expanded their business network, brought them new business, and did everything possible to be of service—provided they did every stitch of their banking with him. That was the one criterion for receiving his blessings: unwavering, unqualified, total loyalty. If he suspected that a customer was keeping an account, even a small one, at another bank, he had a memorable way of addressing the offense.

"Let me see your wallet," Siggi said to a customer seated in his boardroom, who had come to discuss a loan.

"Why do you want my wallet?" the customer asked.

"Never mind why. Just give it to me."

The customer handed over his wallet. Siggi opened the wallet and pulled out the credit and ATM cards. He took the cards from other banks, grabbed a pair of scissors from a nearby desk, cut the cards in half, and drop the pieces on the table.

"*Are you crazy?*" the customer yelled. "I can't believe you just did that."

"No," Siggi said, "*you're* crazy for banking anywhere else," and he launched into such compelling arguments that there be could no doubt who was in the right. The customer hemmed and hawed and offered feeble excuses for why the cards were in his wallet in the first place.

"I . . . I forgot those," he said. "My wife and I had an old account there when we first got married. I don't do any meaningful business with them. It's just for convenience since we pass by their ATM on the way to work . . ."

"*I don't care!*" Siggi yelled. "In twenty-four hours, I will get you the same credit card and an ATM card from our bank. You lied to me! You said all your money was in my bank! Why do you have these cards? *Get your money out of there! Now!*"

"Okay, okay," the customer stammered, "but I have a question. Two days ago, on the phone, you offered me a lower interest rate on my loans than my current bank. Doesn't that have to be approved by your loan committee?"

"I *am* the loan committee!" Siggi exploded. "If the deal you get is one penny different from the deal I offered you, you can tell me to go to hell and keep your accounts where they are. Now, do we have a deal or not?"

"Yes," the customer nodded, "I believe you."

"Good!" Siggi said with a nod and a smile. "Now get out of here quick, before I change my mind."

"Okay, but don't forget," the customer added, "when it comes to my mortgage you promised to waive the filing fees and processing fees, right?"

Siggi seethed. "Yes, I said that. Read my lips. I'm—waiving—the—fees."

"But how will my loan officer know you said to waive the fees?"

By now, Siggi's foot was tapping. "I'm going to write it down on a piece of paper," he said, his temperature rising.

"And do you remember," the customer asked cautiously, "that we also agreed that my brother-in-law could get the same deal?"

Siggi looked at the man without blinking. "You know," he said softly, rising slowly from his chair, "there are some people who are jealous of my success. There are others who do not like me because of my religion. But you will never find one person in the entire world who says, 'Siggi doesn't keep his word.' My word is my bond."

By now the carotid artery in Siggi's neck had begun pulsing feverishly and his face had turned dangerously red. He took a step closer and spoke in a soft, muted voice.

"When you ask me for something and I shake your hand—it's a deal," he said. "You will never hear me say, 'Oh, I misunderstood you,' or 'Oh, I didn't understand what you were saying.'

"You see," he said, sidling up to the customer's face, "I may *speak* with an accent"—and then, leaning in, words exploded from his throat with the force of a cannon—

"BUT I DON'T HEAR WITH ONE!"

What an Athlete!

Apart from being a world-class screamer, Siggi was also a world-class storyteller, comedian, and charmer. For example, from the vest pocket of his pinstripe three-piece suit hung a gold pocket watch. On the watch hung an elaborate key-shaped gold fob, which he kept in full view by leaving his jacket open. The shiny fob attracted innocent inquiries, like the sequined lure of a hook dancing before the eyes of a curious fish.

"What's that?" a customer asked.

"Oh, that?" he said casually. "That's my Phi Beta Kappa key. I got that at Oxford."

"You went to college at *Oxford*?" the customer exclaimed.

"No, first I graduated from Cambridge. Oxford is where I did graduate studies. One year at Princeton, two years at Harvard, then I transferred to Cambridge—*then* I did graduate studies at Oxford."

"Can you write my son a letter of recommendation to Harvard when he applies?"

"*Schmuck*, I was pulling your leg. I was in Auschwitz and never even finished junior high school."

In his passion to impress upon potential customers that they were dealing with a banker unlike any other in the country, each of Siggi's stories was wilder and more breathtaking than the last, and his sense of humor knew no limits. At one party, Siggi attracted attention by running his fingers through his luxurious mane of hair while singing the jingle for Brylcream, a popular hair cream famous for slicking hair back and keeping it perfectly in place. *"Brylcream—a little dab'll do ya,"* he sang, loud enough for those around him to hear. A woman guest took the bait and complimented him on his beautiful head of hair. Siggi responded by furrowing his eyebrows and studying her coiffure as though appraising a work of art.

"You know," he said with matter-of-fact insouciance, "I own a chain of exclusive beauty salons. Let me see. Turn around, please. Hmm. Madam, you are very beautiful. But I can make you twice as beautiful," he said, running his fingers through her hair, fussing now à la Vidal Sassoon, primping and fluffing as though liberating her head from a lifetime of hairspray and blow dryers.

"Yes," Siggi surmised, "I'd take off a little here, a little there. My dear, I can make you look ten years younger."

"Really!" she gasped at this stroke of good luck. "Can I get an appointment?"

"Appointment!" Siggi exclaimed, eyes bulging at this offense to his artistry. "Goodness, no! We're booked for the next two years!" Then he stormed off as if grossly offended. So polished were these stories that unsuspecting listeners swallowed them in one gulp. How could claims delivered with such conviction be anything but true?

Siggi's charm was irresistible. If he saw an elderly woman in the lobby of his bank, he felt an instinctive desire to extend his largesse and initiated a conversation by running up to her and, with excitement in his voice, proclaiming, "Madam! You look so elegant! You look gorgeous! Your hat matches your dress, your dress matches your shoes—*you look like a movie star!*"

Turning to her escort, an elderly well-dressed man, he added, "And you, my friend, are a gentleman and a scholar for having such wonderful taste in women."

The elderly woman might not have heard such praise in a long time, and in short order, after hearing all that Siggi was prepared to do for her, expressed her desire that Siggi's bank serve as executor of her will, trustee of her various bank accounts, and top advisor on her investment portfolio.

It only took minutes for Siggi to work his magic.

If Siggi learned that sports were important to a customer—noticing for instance an autographed photo of a famous quarterback on a customer's office wall—his creative powers kicked in.

"Ah, I see you're a football fan," he commented one time while visiting a customer at his real estate office. "The Giants are doing great this year!" Siggi had no interest in sports and no idea how the Giants were doing.

"Oh," the customer said, surprised. "You follow football?"

"Are you kidding?" Siggi said, as though insulted. "I never miss a game. I used to be quarterback on my college team. No one completed more passes than me. I had the best arm in the league. Then I got this bum knee," he said, rubbing a fictitious wound and shaking his head back and forth at the loss of such an illustrious career.

"I'm sorry to hear that," the customer sympathized.

"Don't feel sorry for me. I was joking," Siggi admitted. "There was no football team in Auschwitz."

"Oh my God, you were in Auschwitz?" the customer said.

"*Was* I?" Siggi said and rolled up his sleeve. "How many other bank presidents do you know with a tattoo like that on their arm?"

In another customer's office, Siggi noted the photo of a teenager in a bathing suit. "I see your son is a swimmer," he said.

"Yeah, state champion in the hundred meters," the customer replied proudly.

"Fantastic! I wasn't much of a swimmer myself—but when it came to *diving*, nobody was better than me. In college, I specialized in the triple backward somersault. But I can't do that anymore after my injury," Siggi lamented, massaging a spot on his lower back with such conviction that the customer nodded in sympathy.

"Are you in pain now?" the customer worried.

"Not at all, I was only pulling your leg," Siggi confessed. "I don't even know how to swim—and there were no diving teams in Auschwitz."

"You were in Auschwitz?" the customer gasped.

"*Was* I?" Siggi exclaimed, and once again rolled up his sleeve to reveal the number tattooed on his arm. Then he recounted story after story of his life in the camps. Most other salesmen would warm up a potential customer by discussing possible family connections—"Oh, your parents came from Italy, too?" Siggi had practically no family left from his life before coming to America, so he broke the ice with crazy sports stories—anything to establish a lighthearted, friendly rapport before exposing them to the horrors he had known in the camps.

When Ivan was a young child, he noticed the tattoo on his father's arm. "What's that?" the boy asked.

"It's my phone number," Siggi replied. "I have a very bad memory, so I had that done so I would remember it," shielding his son from the horrible truth. Ivan believed him. After all, what reason would his father have to lie to him?

That same desire on Siggi's part to protect young children from the brutal reality of the Holocaust was illustrated on another occasion. Ivan recalled a time in elementary school when classmates bragged about their fathers' military service in World War II.

"My dad was a private first class in the Army," one kid said.

"My dad was an airman first class in the Air Force," said another.

"Oh yeah?" said a third, "My father was a corporal in the Marines."

"Ivan," one of the kids asked, "what did your dad do in the war? What branch did he serve in?"

"I don't know," Ivan confessed. "I'll have to ask him."

On hearing his son's dilemma, Siggi thought for a moment. Clearly, he could not have his son telling innocent classmates the truth about his father's years in the concentration camps. So he said to Ivan, "When you go to school tomorrow, tell them your father was a lieutenant in the French Navy," an invention as big as any he had ever created. The fabrication earned Ivan the envy of his classmates: lieutenant was a higher rank that those of all the other fathers.

Siggi's tall tales were matched by a self-confidence that he could do whatever he applied himself to, an assumption tested one day when Ivan wanted to play golf with his father. Neither of them knew anything about golf. Most other bankers in America played golf and belonged to at least one country club, since that was where most deals with customers were solidified, but Siggi declined. Why spend a day closing one deal on a golf course when he could spend the same amount of time in his office and close a dozen deals? Besides, New Jersey country clubs didn't serve kosher food and he didn't drive on the Sabbath, so it made no sense to join one. On the other hand, Kutsher's Hotel and Country Club in upstate New York was kosher and happened to have a golf course.

"One time when we were on vacation there," Ivan recalled, "I asked my father if he would try playing golf with me, and he agreed. He said, 'How hard could it be? You hit a ball with a stick.'"

Father and son donned shorts and sneakers, rented clubs, and walked over to the nearest tee. There they found two sets of balls: two large red cement balls about eight feet apart with a tee in the middle, and about twenty feet farther back two large blue cement balls set up the same way. There were no signs explaining what anything meant, but Siggi and Ivan assumed the red balls were markers for amateurs, since those balls were

twenty feet closer to the hole, and that the blue balls were for professional golfers. Since they were amateurs, they decided to tee off from the red markers. The reality was that the red-ball tee area was for women and the blue-ball tee area was for men, so from the start they had it all wrong.

Down the green, off in the distance, they spotted a flag flying above the hole, and they could vaguely see other golfers around the hole, finishing up their turn. Siggi and Ivan were convinced that as beginners they could never hit a ball hard enough to go that far and took turns warming up, hitting balls one after another in quick succession, as they had done a few times at a driving range.

Whack! Siggi sent a ball sailing down the green. *Whack!* Ivan did the same. Father and son sent a hail of golf balls sailing toward the flag.

At first, golfers putting by the hole couldn't quite believe their eyes. Then they started waving their arms and jumping up and down. Siggi and Ivan waved back, acknowledging what they assumed was an expression of camaraderie from fellow golfers, and carried on whacking balls in their direction. The screaming grew louder. Siggi and Ivan strained to hear what was being said and finally made out the words: *"Idiots! Are you crazy? Stop it! Get the hell off the course!"*

Who knew you had to wait for the other players to finish the hole before you took your turn? After causing so much drama, father and son had had enough and broke for lunch. And so ended the Wilzig experiment with golfing.

Siggi often pretended to be expert in things about which he knew nothing. "If he saw someone riding a horse," Ivan recalled, "he'd yell out, *'Sit straight! Pull in the reins! Loosen the horse up before you gallop!'* My father never rode a horse in his life, but he sounded so sure of what he was saying, the rider would say, 'Thank you!' and my father would reply, 'No problem. I'll make a rider out of you one day—*no matter how long it takes!'*

"Why did he have such an extreme sense of humor? Because he went through the most extremely evil time in history," Ivan explained, "and he followed in the line of great Jewish comedians who countered tragedy with humor to help heal the wounds."

Cookin' with Gas

He may have known nothing about sports, but Siggi's knowledge of business was encyclopedic and new TCNJ customers benefited from his guidance. He visited their places of business, analyzed their work habits, found ways they could be improved, and delivered his opinion.

"I see all your employees run out at noon for lunch," he told the owner of a printing and binding plant. "Do you know what happens then? Half your people are going to wait in line for a table, then eat, then spend more time paying the check and maybe make a call to a girlfriend or boyfriend—all excuses for coming back to work late. Now, look at this empty room you have over here. If you made it into a lunchroom, you'd have your employees under your eye. You could sell them a cheaper and better lunch, and they'd be back to work on time.

"Now here's the next thing you should do," Siggi said. "I saw you have one person folding, a second person stapling, and a third person gluing. One guy can do all three of those tasks. You just have to reorganize the production line."

Six months later, the customer called. "I did everything you told me

to do, Siggi, and now I'm producing 20 percent more than before. You're a genius!"

Siggi could advise on a wide range of subjects because he had job experiences that other bankers lacked. He had worked in both leather goods and bowtie sweatshops, sold neckties and loose-leaf binders door to door, manufactured change purses, revamped a furniture business, managed a cemetery headstone company, bought and sold a tire company and an electronics distribution company, revitalized an oil- and gas-producing company—he'd done it all and retained every detail in the database of his extraordinary memory.

For someone whose formal education ended with grade school, Siggi had an uncanny ability to understand complex financial formulas and translate them into action. He was a self-made man with a laser focus who could study obstacles from unusual angles and find innovative, unexpected ways around them. Then he reached out to the people he trusted most—those who had the formal training he lacked—to get his plan implemented.

"I'm dumbfounded just thinking about how he ever learned, on the job, every type of investment vehicle the bank had," commented daughter Sherry. "Someone who hasn't attempted to earn a business degree might not grasp how extraordinary that is, to be self-taught in so many complex areas and become—not just reliable as a fiduciary for other people's money and investments, but brilliant at it. Think about all the courses you have to take in business school: finance, accounting, real estate investments, risk management, information technology, operations—this is a man who never took high school math. How did he manage to run three major companies: an oil-producing company, a commercial bank, and an electronics distribution company? It's like someone becoming a surgeon without attending medical school, or going to the moon without ever studying physics."

Siggi understood the commodities market, the currency market, the stock market, the bond market, and global economics, as well as corpo-

rate law, corporate taxes, corporate accounting—a vast range of specialized fields of knowledge.

"Siggi had a saying," recalled Dan Kaplan, audit partner at Arthur Andersen, at that time one of the country's top accounting firms and the firm that serviced both Wilshire and TCNJ for more than twenty years. "He used to say that for him CPA (Certified Public Accountant) meant Cleaning, Pressing, and Alterations. It was his way of underlining that he had about as much training in finance as a tailor—none. Yet he could discuss accounting and tax matters with me and my partners for hours, and 90 percent of what he said was completely accurate."

To impress his biggest customers, Siggi took them to the prestigious Marco Polo Club, a private restaurant located inside the Waldorf-Astoria, New York's crown jewel of Art Deco hotels. Membership to the exclusive club involved an elaborate series of applications, recommendations, and interviews. Clientele included Hollywood celebrities, heads of state, barons of industry, and the upper echelon of New York society, who used the club's private entrance on Lexington Avenue to avoid photographers. These VIPs counted on management's discretion to not publicize their presence. Siggi's clients were naturally impressed by the recognizable faces and how responsive the restaurant staff was when Siggi walked in.

"Louie," he said to the maître d', "you know I keep kosher. Are you sure there is no meat broth or shellfish in this soup?" If he was going to question the creations of New York's finest chefs, what better way than surrounded by celebrity non-Jews and before one of TCNJ's important customers? It was an irony he relished, having survived the Holocaust with nothing more to eat than putrid soup and rotten scraps of food.

Every day over breakfast, and every day in his car while being chauffeured to his office, Siggi perused the *Wall Street Journal*, the *New York Times*,

and two magazines: *Newsweek* and *Time*. Based on what he learned from these four publications—plus what he gleaned from TV news shows and from credit ratings listed in *Moody's* and *Standard & Poor's*—he instructed his brokers what stocks and bonds to buy or sell. Constantly throughout the day, he had his assistant bring him a piece of paper listing the bid, ask, and closing prices of his top twenty stocks.[66] He was on the phone all day giving instructions to his brokers about what to buy and what to sell, right up until 4 p.m. when the market closed. A single good transaction before the clock ran out could turn a day of losses into a day of profit for shareholders, and heaven help anyone who interrupted him before 4 p.m.

"Not now! The market isn't closed yet! *Leave me alone! Come back later!*" he barked at officers who entered the boardroom unannounced, occasionally throwing papers at them from behind his mahogany desk if they didn't leave immediately.

"In his boardroom, Siggi had a little wooden phone booth that he used for highly confidential private calls," remembered lawyer Bob Margulies, who negotiated leases for the bank branches. "The whole reason for the privacy booth was so no one could hear him buying and selling millions of dollars of stocks and bonds. But he yelled so loud, everyone heard everything through the shut door. It was comical."

"He certainly was a dramatic figure," said Bruce Shoulson, an attorney with Lowenstein Sandler from the years when his firm handled the bank's legal affairs. "He was unrestrained in some respects. I remember a dinner our firm put together for clients and management. Siggi was always on the lookout for new customers and there was a gentleman there, a Jewish man who owned a successful business but who banked with an institution run by non-Jews. Well, people are standing around talking when all of a sudden we hear this scream that shook the room: *'YOU BANK WITH THE GOYIM?! WITH GENTILES?! STOP IT! YOU'RE GONNA GIVE ME A HEART ATTACK!'* Everyone's jaws dropped."

That was the kind of outburst—and classic Jewish guilt trip—Siggi was known for.

Shoulson remembered being in Siggi's office when one of the bank directors mentioned to Siggi that he was going to do something on his own initiative. "Siggi started screaming like a banshee," Shoulson recalled. "He ran to the window—this was on the eleventh floor—and yelled, '*What are you trying to do, kill me?! YOU WANT ME TO JUMP AND KILL MYSELF?!*' screaming at the top of his lungs with the window wide open and the wind blowing through the boardroom. I thought the poor director was going to faint."

John Mendyk, who worked in the TCNJ mortgage department in the 1980s, remembered Siggi's explanation for his high-volume tirades. Working late one night and knowing that the boss's chauffeur had already left for the day, Mendyk offered to drive Siggi home. Lately, Siggi had been yelling at Mendyk a lot and making him feel like he was going to get fired. He glanced at his boss in the passenger seat and weighed the consequences of asking something that Siggi might interpret as impertinent. Mendyk took the risk and said, "Boss, why are you always yelling at people—and at me in particular?"

Siggi took no offense and replied, "Because I care about you. When I stop yelling at one of my employees, it means I've given up on him and he won't be with the bank much longer. But I see something in you. I yell because you have a future here at the bank and I want to motivate you."

Other bank presidents may have yelled when they were angry and ready to fire someone. Siggi's thunderous outbursts meant he cared. Mendyk's job was secure—at least for now.

Moments like these defined life with Siggi B. Wilzig, in the office and at home. In public, he could be complimentary, even obsequious toward someone who might be important to the growth of Wilshire Oil Company or TCNJ, but in private the extreme behavior emerged. However educated someone might be, Siggi was capable of verbally dismembering

him if he seemed unwilling to accept Siggi's point of view. His summary judgment of more or less every man he met was "What a *schmuck!*"—a Yiddish term meaning idiot or contemptible person. In Siggi's lexicon, the word was not an insult but an instruction, meant to startle people into seeing how inferior their judgment was compared with his. The problem was that he declared "*Schmuck!*" with such conviction that not everyone understood the explicative was meant for their benefit.

"I got so accustomed to hearing Siggi say, '*Schmuck! You really went to Harvard?*'" said Harvard Law School graduate Joe Steinberg, "that I began thinking it was my first name: *Schmuck* Steinberg."

Steinberg was a highly respected partner at the law firm of Lowenstein Sandler, and when Siggi cast aspersions on him, it was in jest—the two had an affectionate and productive working relationship—but in Siggi's eyes, more or less everyone really was a *schmuck* for not following his advice and not recognizing how lucky they were to have him advising them at all.

"The thing is," Steinberg said, "his advice was almost always right. If you followed it, you made money. What could customers do except take the yelling and the insults and admit they were wrong for not listening sooner?"

Schmuck was not the only label Siggi applied to people. When evaluating the job performance of his employees, for instance, he differentiated between "workhorses" and "racehorses." A workhorse was someone who did the minimum, followed the same routine day in and day out, and rarely came up with a great idea. A racehorse was someone with potential, an individual who showed initiative, ambition, and the ability to go beyond the call of duty. Racehorses could look forward to a prosperous future with the bank since they merited regular raises and steady promotions. "Of course, you need workhorses in any business," he explained to his children. "All businesses need people to do the basics. But there's no point spending precious time trying to turn a workhorse into a racehorse."

Bank personnel knew they were subject to Siggi's evaluations, and it kept them on their toes. Still, it was occasionally hard to know if he wanted someone to exercise more initiative or less. On one occasion, a loan officer walked into his office and said, "Siggi, one of our customers is opening an import-export business in Aruba in the Caribbean and needs financing for the expansion. I think we should lend him the money."

"*NOT IN A MILLION YEARS!*" Siggi yelled. "Not only is the weather harsh and unpredictable in those islands, but they have corrupt governments that can arbitrarily make things very difficult for local businesses."

"But Siggi," the loan officer foolishly persisted, "the customer knows this is out of our market area, that TCNJ doesn't normally make this kind of a loan, so the bank can charge him a high interest rate and huge fees for such an accommodation . . ."

"*NOT FOR ALL THE TEA IN CHINA!*" Siggi yelled. "I'll never lend money to anyone on a Caribbean island. One hurricane and the whole place is underwater—and no electricity."

The loan officer made the mistake of pushing his point. "But Siggi," he said with utter sincerity, "you know this customer. He keeps a lot of money in our bank . . ."

"*I DON'T GIVE A DAMN!*" Siggi roared. "*IT'S NOT NEGOTIABLE! NOW GET THE HELL OUTTA HERE BEFORE I CALL THE POLICE AND HAVE YOU ARRESTED!*"

The loan officer hurried out of the room, scared half out of his wits.

At another loan committee meeting, an officer spoke up in favor of a potential borrower based on an evaluation provided by the borrower's son.

"The son?!" Siggi exclaimed. "The son is *dangerously dumb. Schmuck. Use your brain.* He's only been working with his father for two years. Why are you quoting him?"

"Well," the loan officer said, "his companies' assets are cross-collateralized, so I believe we're protected and it's safe to make the loan . . ."

"*Believe?! Who cares what you believe! Don't play lawyer!*" Siggi snapped. "Give it to one of our attorneys to review."

"Siggi, I've been doing this for years," the loan officer dared reply. "I thought I could save the bank a few thousand dollars in legal fees."

"Sure—and cost me millions in lawsuits!" Siggi bellowed. "Give it to the damn lawyer!"

"I understand your concern," the officer replied, "but there's something else you should consider. The son has given us promising figures for the company's growth next year . . .'"

"*Promising??* What kind of *meshugas* is that?" Siggi said, using the Yiddish term for nonsense. "Who cares what one year's projected figures are? Go back and study the numbers for the last *three* years. Unless you study the financial figures for at least that long, you can't make an intelligent decision. You don't have to be a genius to figure that one out."

"Okay," the loan officer finally conceded, "you're probably right. I'll get the necessary papers from his accountant."

"Now you're cookin' with gas," Siggi said with a smile, nodding his head in agreement. "It's a good thing I like you so much, otherwise I'd fire you."

Just as he could unleash on his employees, he had choice words as well for any customer who failed to heed his advice. "*Bist du meshugah?!*" he yelled in Yiddish at Jewish customers. For non-Jewish customers he used the English: "*Are you crazy?!*" Sometimes the put-downs were amusing. "I don't know how so-and-so could have made that ridiculous investment," Siggi might say. "If he's such a great businessman, how could he let himself be suckered into buying something so worthless? Goes to show you. *Even smart chickens shit on their own feathers!*" he would conclude, quoting an old Yiddish saying.

Siggi's witticisms were well known to his family and senior staff, but those who knew him best understood that the humor did little to erase the nightmares of his past. The person who knew him best of all was Leon Katz, his rabbi. Rabbi Katz was cast in the old-school, Eastern European mold of holy men who assiduously studied the Old Testament

and could quote verses for any occasion. Everyone in Congregation Adas Israel agreed that Rabbi Katz was a *mensch*, a Yiddish word that meant more than its literal translation of "a man." A *mensch* in Jewish culture was a righteous person, an unselfish upstanding individual who could be trusted and whose behavior was worth emulating.

"Siggi would call on the phone to see if the rabbi was home," described Rabbi Katz's wife, Rivkah, "and if so, he always wanted to come over. They'd dismiss me from the room so they could have private conversations, and they would talk about anything and everything."

Rabbi Katz served as Siggi's therapist and confidant, the one person with whom Siggi could discuss his nightmares and flashbacks. Siggi and Rabbi Katz spoke for hours about the meaning of life, the role of evil, and whatever business issues were on Siggi's mind.

Both men had witnessed children die. One of the rabbi's sons had died in a fire at age thirteen, and his oldest child, a daughter, had died from a heart attack. Siggi and Rabbi Katz also shared an existential dilemma, namely how to reconcile a beneficent God with the murder of more than a million children in the Holocaust.

"How come you never go to synagogue on the Sabbath?" Siggi's young son Alan once asked.

"I have a mixed relationship with God," Siggi replied. "I go to synagogue on all the Jewish holidays to give thanks to the Almighty. Without the will of the Almighty, there's no way a shorty like me should have survived the Holocaust. But I don't go to synagogue every week. I have a hard time being thankful for the murder of a million and a half Jewish children, or the murder of my innocent seven-year-old nephew and two-year-old niece.

"Besides," he said, "I take the Almighty's commandment to rest on the seventh day literally. I need that time off to recharge my battery for the week to come."

To escape the ugly memories of Auschwitz, Siggi sought out moments of beauty such as a Jewish wedding, a vacation in the mountains or at the beach, and an occasional visit to the elegant Biltmore Hotel in Phoenix, Arizona.

Setting aside its status as one of the nation's premiere hotels—the place where Marilyn Monroe had been photographed bathing in the hotel swimming pool and Irving Berlin had written many of his memorable songs, including "White Christmas"—the Biltmore featured unique and exquisitely manicured flower gardens. Siggi was occasionally obliged to attend business meetings in the area concerning loans or other TCNJ matters, and on those occasions, he chose the Biltmore specifically for its gardens. The hotel's thirty-nine acres of topiaries and seasonal plantings soothed his heart and soul, and the tranquility created by these moments briefly overshadowed the nightmares.

"They had fifty-four gardeners on staff, just to take care of the flowers," he once recalled. "I live in Auschwitz every day, but when someone walks with me through those gardens, they see a different side of me. Why am I looking at flowers? The answer is, to forget Auschwitz. An occasion has to be really beautiful, really moving, whether it is a Jewish child being born or a lovely garden—the opposite of Auschwitz. So when I go to the Biltmore for three or four days, it's like anyone else going on vacation for three or four weeks. It stays with me for a long time."

To combat nightmares of Auschwitz, Siggi became the worst kind of workaholic: the kind for whom the only cure was more work. Reporters saw his achievements, but few understood the demons that plagued him or their impact on his family life. "His unflagging idealism has propelled him to live a full life. . . . He displays very few mental or physical scars," wrote one naive journalist, oblivious of the horrors fueling his obsession with long hours and frenetic multitasking. Siggi suffered from severe headaches, for which there was little he could do. Over-the-counter

medications did nothing to alleviate the pain. The only thing that helped was the barbiturate Fiorinal, which he took so that he could continue immersing himself in the pressure of work.

"Do you want to know why I work so hard?" he asked his assistant in the 1990s. "It started when I was a teenager in Berlin and Jews were forced into slave labor. We worked harder than the non-Jews because we were more scared than the non-Jews. When the SS came to take us away, German army officers in charge of our factory said, 'Let them stay. They do better work than the others. They work harder, they're more intelligent—let's keep 'em.' And if we didn't work harder, then they threatened to send us to 'the east.' They never said to concentration camps, but we knew what they meant."

"Work so hard" meant working at maximum speed and maximum volume. For instance, he never just talked on a phone. He walked and paced and yelled while secretaries followed, holding the cord above their heads before it swept papers off his massive conference table. He communicated with his whole body the way circus barkers do, in a choreography of mouth, hands, and feet that expanded speaking from vocal to physical expression. His voice boomed like a cannon, but the outbursts weren't always amusing. Ehab Zied, an Egyptian chauffeur who worked for Siggi for nearly twenty years, recalled one such incident.

"Mr. Wilzig was fanatical about only eating bananas without the smallest blemish," he said. "One time he called me around midnight and yelled into the phone, '*Come here! Get here immediately!*' I lived about a mile away, so I got in the limousine and raced to his place. I thought maybe he was very sick. I got there, and he was pointing to a banana that the family's other chauffeur had bought. '*Look what this guy bought me!*' he screamed. I looked, and the banana had some black spots on the skin due to being overripe. '*Take it out of here!*' Any spots or splits in his bananas and he would go crazy."

A banana with brown spots looked rotten and reminded Siggi of rotten food in Auschwitz, but only those close to him understood that. Oth-

ers witnessing one of his tirades might have thought him deranged. The condition known as post-traumatic stress disorder would not be added to the American Psychiatric Association's *Diagnostic and Statistical Manual of Mental Disorders* until 1980, yet even then the behavior of Holocaust survivors would elude effective diagnosis.

Telling Siggi he might have a psychological condition would have meant nothing to him. In his eyes, psychiatrists were all fakes. By his reckoning, people were either mentally ill or sane based on his own diagnostic guidelines. For instance, if a visitor to his office twitched, stuttered, or exhibited an odd shuffling of the feet, such behavior was sufficient for Siggi to conclude the person was mentally ill.

"Der mensch ist leider nicht normal," he would whisper in German to Ivan or Sherry—meaning, "Unfortunately, this person is not normal"—and he would stand and look at his watch and tell his visitor, "We have to leave now. The tire just blew out on my car and we have to get it replaced. I wish you the best of luck in all your endeavors. Thanks for coming in." Then he would run out the door.

Siggi didn't need a psychiatrist to tell him who was crazy. He, on the other hand, was the sane one, the strong one, the one who resisted grabbing the electric fence to commit suicide. Erratic behavior from him was the privilege of a man whom the SS had failed to destroy. "Every day I'm alive," he would frequently say, "is another day Hitler didn't kill me."

And if Hitler had failed to kill him, what chance did the Federal Reserve have?

Government *Schmucks*

As described by *New Jersey Business* magazine, "Wilzig is the only Nazi concentration camp survivor in the world to head both a major New Jersey bank and a New York Stock Exchange–listed oil company."[67] By any reasonable assessment, he was contributing to the growth of the American economy—but not by the Fed's. By their assessment, he was a renegade who had to be reeled in.

Conversely, by Siggi's assessment, regulators were government *schmucks* who didn't know what they were talking about. They could insist all they wanted that he must divest himself of one of the companies that he'd made successful, but he simply wasn't going to do it, not without putting up a fight.

"Siggi had a deep-rooted hatred of authority," noted former bank director Don Brenner, "which no doubt came from his experiences in the camps. He could not tolerate anyone telling him what to do. The animosity was very deep-seated and very obvious."

———

The thought that the US government would threaten to dismantle his success in business was on Siggi's mind during one of his weekly visits to bank branches in December 1974. Traveling in cold weather brought out the arthritis in his hands, no doubt exacerbated by the bone-crushing labor and freezing temperatures in the camps. He nonetheless looked forward to these weekly rounds of bank branches and to seeing the surprise on customers' faces when he introduced himself—"How do you do? I'm the bank president"—and then he would hand out heart-shaped gifts, echoing TCNJ's motto as The Bank with Heart: crystal candy dishes, wooden jewelry boxes, ceramic cookie plates, and—for the kids—heart-shaped lollipops and chocolates.

Trust Company became one of the largest banks in the State of New Jersey the old-fashioned way, purely through internal growth: one customer at a time, one branch at a time. Siggi didn't approve of what he saw elsewhere in the industry—banks expanding through mergers and acquisitions, as though buying someone else's hard work equated to having done the work yourself. Where were the personal relationships with customers in such impersonal expansions? And without a personal relationship with a bank officer, what would stop major customers from withdrawing their money? If depositors knew no one of authority in their own bank and had no one to call or turn to in a crisis, why should they remain loyal? The slightest excuse would mean losing them to another bank, and the loss of even one prominent account for Siggi spelled disaster.

He had an expression: "The best piece of new business is to keep the old business." Attracting new customers was essential to the bank's growth, but it was far more important to not lose any existing customers. "If you lose your old loyal customers," he told bank employees, "you'll never make it up. It'll take you thirty new one-million-dollar customers to compensate for the loss of one thirty-million-dollar customer."

So he poured himself into building a loyal following by showing up, shaking hands, handing out gifts, listening to customers' woes, and offering remedies. The Federal Reserve, however, would not be placated by such courtesies, and small gestures would not convince them to let Siggi

keep his companies together. He would have to turn up the voltage of his prodigious brain to figure this one out—and that's when he came up with an idea more outrageous than any he'd ever conceived before.

He would sue the Federal Reserve.

Did he pause to consider what had just occurred to him? Perhaps it required no reflection at all. Where others walked, he ran, and sometimes the ideas came so fast it was hard to know which hemisphere of his brain was operating or how or why. The impulse to sue the Federal Reserve—the central banking system of the United States, whose board members were appointed by the president and authorized by Congress to oversee the finances of the most powerful nation on earth—was irrational, mad, and a classic Siggi move. Agents of the Fed had the audacity to tell him to his face that the interests of the American people would be best served if he divested one of his two companies, that his simultaneous control over both an oil company and a commercial bank constituted a conflict of interest and posed a risk to the public. Siggi could not disagree more, but by suing the Fed he was taking on a formidable opponent.

The incoming chairman of the Federal Reserve Board of Governors, "Tall Paul" Volcker (six foot seven) was born in 1927, the son of German immigrants. He grew up in New Jersey, graduated *summa cum laude* from Princeton University at age twenty-two, earned a master's degree in political economics from Harvard two years later, and by age twenty-five was a full-time economist at the Federal Reserve Bank of New York. Chase Manhattan Bank wooed him away in 1957. Five years later, the Treasury Department hired him as director of financial analysis. From 1969 to 1974, Volcker served as undersecretary of the Treasury for International Monetary Affairs, then from 1975 to 1979 as president of the Federal Reserve Bank of New York.

Volcker's appointment as the new chairman of the Federal Reserve got great press—"Finally, a tough chair for the Fed!"—and he quickly announced his intentions to put an end to runaway inflation. As he would

do thirty years later in response to the financial crash of 2008, he blamed the debacle of the 1970s on insufficient regulation of the financial sector. Memories of the Great Depression loomed over the pairing of commercial companies and banking subsidiaries, and Wilshire's ownership of TCNJ embodied everything Volcker pledged to suppress.

"The Fed threatened Siggi," recalled Phil Kupperman, "and Siggi's response was that it would be settled before a judge. He was ready to fight this all the way to the Supreme Court. It's fair to say the Fed had other means of regulating him and that, in his mind, the central bank was trying to put out a fire with too big a hose. He was ready to challenge the legitimacy of their demands."

Like other federal agencies with civil enforcement power, the Federal Reserve preferred quick settlements. If Siggi would simply agree to divest, the whole matter could be settled and everyone could go home. He would no longer run both companies, having had to choose one or the other, but he would still be rich, respected, and a credit to his people—but there was no way Siggi would let Tall Paul or anyone else separate him from either of his two corporate entities. He had to win, yet this would be a war even his extraordinary brain could not handle alone. He needed a powerful ally, so he picked up the phone and called Sullivan and Cromwell's renowned banking lawyer, Rodgin Cohen, Esq.

In 1972, two years after joining the firm of Sullivan and Cromwell, Rodgin Cohen became Siggi's chief legal expert in his battle with the Federal Reserve. In the near future, the *Financial Times* would describe Cohen as "one of the biggest players on Wall Street," and the *Wall Street Journal* would call him "the country's leading banking lawyer." A call from the renowned lawyer was the only acceptable reason for interrupting Siggi in a business meeting. Seeing the two short men walking side by side turned heads. At five foot six, Cohen was just slightly taller than Siggi. Cohen was also the smartest man Siggi had ever met.

"He only weighs a hundred pounds," Siggi would say, "but ninety of them are brains."

Cohen possessed an unparalleled ability to explain complex principles of law and banking in laymen's terms, and Siggi was not alone in his appreciation for the grand master of banking law. "When I worked in Washington," said Robert K. Steel, a board member of Wells Fargo bank and a former top official at the Treasury Department, "Rodge would always give a balanced read of the pros and cons of a situation with a knowledge so expansive you'd have to go to five other places just to get his level of sophistication."

In December 1974, Cohen received notice that the Federal Reserve was going to make good on its threat to divest Siggi B. Wilzig of control over his two companies. "The notice came in a telephone call from the deputy general counsel of the Fed," Cohen remembered. "A senior associate in our firm took the call. He came and told me right after, and we called Mr. Wilzig."

Siggi, Cohen, and their legal team traveled to Washington, DC, to meet with agents of the Federal Reserve. Officers of the Fed sat on one side of a long conference room table; Siggi, Cohen, and the legal team sat across from them. The Fed officers cited the Bank Holding Company Act (BHC Act), which stipulated that a non-banking company could not own or operate a commercial bank. The assumption behind the BHC Act, they said, was that an oil man like Mr. Wilzig knew nothing about banking and that his risky oil drilling jeopardized bank customers' money.

"Mr. Wilzig," the Fed officers said, "we have notified nearly four hundred parent companies across the US that they must get rid of their banking subsidiaries. Your company, Wilshire, is the only holdout. The time has come for you to comply as well—or there will be consequences." They laid the compliance papers on the desk and awaited his reply.

As he had done many times before, Siggi rolled up the sleeve of his white shirt and pointed to the Auschwitz prisoner number tattooed on his arm.

"The last person to threaten me was Hitler," he said. *"And no one is going to do it again!"*

He rolled down his shirtsleeve, put on his jacket, picked up the papers, and left.

Like a war room, Siggi's office on the eleventh floor of TCNJ headquarters buzzed with senior staff arguing how to press their case against the Fed, proposing tactics and discussing the enemy's strengths and weaknesses. If Siggi was commander-in-chief in this battlefield scenario, renowned banking lawyer Rodgin Cohen was his secretary of defense.

"We cautioned him," Cohen recalled, "not in terms of legal results so much as in terms of the Federal Reserve not taking kindly to being sued. He listened and said, 'I've lived through worse, much worse than this. We're gonna take them on.' It was a bold move. Nobody sues the US government. As far as I know, no one had ever done it before. But that wouldn't have deterred him. Siggi was someone who would look at the Himalayan Mountains and say, 'I can climb that.'"

The Wilshire team's first responsibility, Cohen told them, was to familiarize themselves with the Fed's main weapon, the Bank Holding Company Act of 1956 and the amendment of 1970.

Bank Holding Companies (BHCs) were of two kinds: banking organizations looking to expand their businesses across state lines, and nonbanks—such as Wilshire or retail giant Sears, Roebuck, and Company—that owned or controlled banks. Through the 1940s, federal law placed no limits on such expansions and BHCs proliferated.

Things changed in the 1950s, when Transamerica Corporation became the archetype of what was perceived as a dangerous concentration of economic power. Transamerica controlled, among others, Bank of America in Arizona, California, Nevada, Oregon, and Washington, as well as several non-banking enterprises: insurance firms, real estate and oil operations, a fish packer, a metal fabricator, cargo shipping operations, and

a taxicab company. Concerns over Transamerica's control of nationwide financial resources triggered a move for restrictions. The result was passage of the 1956 Bank Holding Company Act (BHC Act) designed to separate banking and non-banking interests by forcing parent companies to make a choice: get rid of their banks or get rid of their non-banking business.

At first, the BHC Act only applied to parent companies with two or more banks, since a single bank didn't amount to much in the scheme of things. When the BHC Act was first passed in 1956, there were only 117 one-bank holding companies, with assets of $11 billion. By 1969, however, the number had grown to more than 890, with total assets exceeding $181 billion—more than 40 percent of all US bank deposits. So lucrative were these one-bank operations that more than thirty additional large commercial banks had announced plans to create their own one-bank holding companies.

"The Act was created because companies were evolving into bigger operations," explained Alex Paul, who handled applications for mergers and acquisitions for the Federal Reserve until 1972. "For instance, customers traveled. Why not create a travel agency for them? Customers leased cars. How about opening a leasing company? And why stop at cars? Customers ship products. Why not lease boxcars? Why not own and lease airplanes? How about providing banking services while we're at it?"

The Fed sprang into action and met with President Nixon, intent on keeping BHCs from getting out of control.

"Banking must not dominate commerce or be dominated by it," Nixon told the press in March 1969. "To protect competition and the separation of economic powers, I strongly endorse the extension of Federal regulation to one-bank holding companies and urge the Congress to take prompt and appropriate action."

"Appropriate action" emerged as the 1970 Amendment to the BHC Act, which changed the definition of a holding company from two banks

or more to one bank or more. Wilshire's ownership of its one bank was now at risk. The real question was whether Siggi "controlled" TCNJ prior to the 1970 Amendment. If so, then Wilshire was grandfathered by law[68] into the Wilshire-TCNJ relationship and Wilshire could continue to own the bank.

"We're going to argue," Rodgin Cohen told the group, "that Wilshire acquired its controlling position in Trust Company of New Jersey prior to the amendment in the BHC Act and that the Fed's insistence on Wilshire divesting is consequently wrong. Wilshire bought into TCNJ and has run it for years based on the original statute." Siggi and everyone hearing Cohen's game plan agreed it was a strong position to take.

Everyone except the Federal Reserve.

Sullivan and Cromwell presented their arguments to Federal Reserve officials in the fall of 1975 but failed to convince them that Wilshire had gained control of the bank prior to the 1970 amendment. Siggi and his team may have acquired a *position* in TCNJ prior to the amendment, government officials replied, but not *control*.[69]

Cohen interpreted the situation differently. Regardless of how much stock Wilshire owned or when, Cohen argued, Siggi effectively controlled the company by his actions. The BHC Act stipulated that if someone held the power to determine operational decisions and if his orders were followed unconditionally, then even if he did not own a controlling percent of the stock he was nonetheless deemed to "control" the company. That definition could have been written for Siggi at TCNJ.

"I visited the bank in the late 1960s," recalled Alex Paul, "and saw that whatever actions were taken by Siggi, others followed. A big loan application usually goes to the board. But Siggi would tell the board, 'I know Charlie. I like him and I'm not worried about the loan,' and the board would approve the loan based on his assessment. That's control."

Cohen's arguments to officers of the Federal Reserve, however, fell on deaf ears, and their decision remained unchanged. Despite Siggi's undeniable control over the affairs of his bank, and despite arguments offered

by the nation's preeminent banking lawyer, Rodgin Cohen, the Fed was adamant that Siggi did not control his own bank.

A war with the Federal Reserve was inevitable, and in Siggi's opinion the cause of the war was not President Nixon's desire to "break the back of inflation." The real cause was antisemitism. In Siggi's mind, the Fed's aim was to stop him, a Jew, from taking over a commercial bank. To support his claim, Siggi described for his son Ivan that in 1969 a thirty-year-old entrepreneur named Saul Steinberg attempted a takeover of Chemical Bank, the sixth-largest commercial bank in America. Like Siggi's attempt to take over TCNJ, it was a daring move for a young Jew with no banking experience. Steinberg had earned a fortune in his early twenties as founder of Leasco Data Processing Equipment Corporation, a company that leased IBM computers at prices lower than IBM's. Leasco went public in 1965 and in 1968 acquired Reliance Insurance Company, a 150-year-old company with a lot of capital: just what Steinberg needed to wage a takeover of Chemical. The attempt failed, and in Siggi's estimation the reason was as obvious as it was familiar: Steinberg was a Jew, and just as the antisemitic banking industry would not allow Steinberg to take over America's sixth largest bank, neither would it allow Siggi, another Jew, to maintain his power in both banking and oil. When Siggi was asked whether the Federal Reserve intentionally tried to block Jews, Siggi had a ready answer: "You bet your ass."

"He was more certain of that than anything else he ever told me," son Ivan described. "All you had to do was look at how few Jews were in the banking and oil industries. This wasn't paranoia on his part. It was a certainty that infuriated him."

Whether Siggi's suspicions of antisemitism were justified or not, he was now obliged to either comply with the Fed's order to divest or face the consequences.

"You have a deadline," regulators warned Siggi. "Divest yourself of either your bank or your oil company. And do it by December 31, 1980—or we'll do it for you."

Threats from the Federal Reserve did not intimidate Siggi. The January 31, 1983, issue of *Forbes* magazine published a profile that said it all.

"What's the Fed," the article concluded, "when you have survived the Gestapo?"[70]

A Reckoning at Midnight

Siggi had lost the first round with the Federal Reserve when the courts determined that Wilshire did not have control of TCNJ prior to the BHC Act amendment of 1970. Still, for several years Siggi managed to keep his two companies together by having his legal team stall divestiture as long as possible. The math was simple: the longer his lawyers could postpone separating Wilshire and TCNJ, the longer Siggi could continue to upstream tax moneys from TCNJ to Wilshire. The lawyers consequently conveyed to the Fed a variety of suggestions for how Wilshire might comply with the Fed's demands, but they never made a firm proposal.

Now, however, the clock was ticking: Wilshire had until December 31, 1980, to divest or face severe consequences. Siggi's attorney, Rodgin Cohen, suggested there might still be a way for Wilshire Oil to qualify for exemption and thus continue upstreaming TCNJ's tax money: show that TCNJ was not a "bank" as defined by the Fed.

A bank under the BHC Act was an entity that did two things: it serviced depositors by allowing them to withdraw funds on demand, and it made commercial loans. If Siggi could find a way, Cohen said, to either divest the bank of its "demand deposits" or else discontinue making

commercial loans, then TCNJ would no longer be a bank as defined by the Act, and TCNJ tax money could continue flowing to Wilshire unimpaired.

Siggi approved the idea, and on November 5, 1980, the TCNJ board sent out a letter informing depositors that beginning November 19, TCNJ would reserve the right to require two weeks' notice prior to a withdrawal from its accounts. In theory, this meant that customers could not withdraw their funds "on demand," thus negating one of the two activities that defined a bank according to the BHC Act.

To reassure customers that the notice would not really affect their ability to access money on demand, the letter went on to say that "the Trust Company has never exercised its right to require notice and has no intention of exercising a notice provision on any type of account."

When Federal Reserve officers got wind of the letter in early December, they condemned it as a transparent attempt at an end run around their demands. Compliance with the Fed's order to divest meant that Wilshire was to immediately get rid of its bank, not send letters to customers pretending the bank was something other than what it was.

On April 1, 1981, the Fed issued a Final Decision and Order, declaring that Wilshire had failed to divest itself of TCNJ as ordered. The oil and gas company now stood in violation of the BHC Act and must immediately place its shares of the bank in a trust overseen by the Honorable Richard J. Hughes, former governor of New Jersey. Per the order, Siggi was to immediately resign as president and chairman of Wilshire, and the company was to pay a fine of $1,000 a day until complying. Siggi was delighted and did a little dance around his mahogany conference table. "I'll gladly agree to those terms for as long as they want," he told his executive vice president, Ed Davin. "Why wouldn't we pay a thousand dollars a day when Wilshire is making so much more than that by upstreaming from TCNJ?"

The victory was short-lived. A follow-up letter arrived from the Fed, saying Wilshire's ability to upstream moneys from TCNJ had come to an end.

As a way of reassuring Wilshire's 27,000 shareholders that despite the ruling all was well, that year's letter to shareholders highlighted good news. The new president, Jacob Schmidt, and the new chairman of the board, Nathan White, announced the sale of Wilshire Electronics for a whopping $13 million to Marshall Industries. Marshall, a West Coast electronics distributor, had paid a premium price to acquire Wilshire Electronics' East Coast territory, which enabled Marshall to distribute nationwide. Consequently, Schmidt and White's letter went on to announce a 36 percent increase in the oil company's revenues.

Almost as an afterthought, with regard to the well-publicized loss of their suit against the Federal Reserve, the letter mentioned that an appeal had begun. Should they lose the appeal, the letter explained, "the two companies will have separate management. Mr. Wilzig will remain as chairman and president of the Trust Company of New Jersey, and Mr. Nathan White, a Wilshire director for thirteen years, will serve as chairman of the board and chief executive officer of Wilshire."

The appeal was argued on October 26, 1981. On December 31, 1981, the Third Circuit of Appeals ruled against the appeal—but Siggi's lawyers were ready with a backup plan for delaying a final decision.

"The Fed had in mind that Siggi would have to either shut down the bank or else sell it," described Jeff Parker, who was second-in-command after Rodgin Cohen in Siggi's case against the Federal Reserve. "Our strategy was to tie the case up as long as possible without him having to do either." The lawyers filed for a restraining order, which would stop the Fed from taking any further action against Wilshire. The US Supreme Court granted the order based on the assumption that, given additional time, TCNJ could find someone to take over its commercial loans. In addition, Parker and his team moved for a writ of certiorari, a legal mechanism by which the Supreme Court would order the lower court to deliver its records for review. It was a delay tactic—the Supreme Court rarely

overturned another court's ruling—but it did show that Siggi was serious about taking his case all the way to the Supreme Court.[71]

Although the court agreed to the restraining order, it imposed a deadline of midnight on February 3, 1982, to comply. The clock was now ticking: Wilshire had only a few weeks in which to separate TCNJ from its commercial loans.

Siggi dreaded the loss of TCNJ's commercial loans. He'd worked relentlessly for fifteen years to build up the bank's loan portfolio, which now exceeded $100 million. But what choice did he have? If he was going to keep his companies together, TCNJ had to stop being a commercial bank, and that meant finding another bank that would agree to take TCNJ's commercial loans.

The obvious choice was Manufacturers Hanover Trust. Manny Hanny, as it was known, had been TCNJ's correspondent bank[72] for years and Rodgin Cohen, TCNJ's legal advisor, was also Manny Hanny's longtime legal advisor. In addition, Charlie French, TCNJ's executive vice president and senior lending officer, had worked at Manny Hanny prior to joining TCNJ and maintained close friendships inside Manny Hanny's senior management. The synergy between TCNJ and Manny Hanny was strong, and everyone working on this last-ditch effort to keep Wilshire and TCNJ together was convinced the deal with Manny Hanny was the right solution. Phone calls went quickly back and forth between the two banks, and a tentative deal was struck, subject to official confirmation by Manny Hanny's higher-ups.

To complete the deal, hundreds of thousands of pages of collateral documentation in support of the commercial loans had to be transported from TCNJ to Manny Hanny's Manhattan offices before midnight of February 3. TCNJ hired a fleet of trucks, and the bank's executives arranged themselves into an assembly line, stacking boxes and filing cabinets into the rented vans. By early evening, February 3, the vans were full, locked, and on their way. All that was needed now was a call before

midnight from Manny Hanny to the Wilshire-TCNJ management confirming that the deal was done.

In Siggi's office, the mood was ebullient. "Everyone was jovial," daughter Sherry recalled. "We had succeeded in keeping together what my father had worked so hard to achieve. After years of fighting, after so many attempts to conform to the Fed's demands—it was dramatic, a feeling of victory, that we had won and were going to keep the companies intact."

Siggi lived for moments such as this, when going out on a limb paid off. Beating the Fed at its own game was more than solving a bank problem; it was a victory for the underdog and a validation that the Almighty could work miracles.

"We had been there all day organizing the transfer," said Sherry, "but by ten thirty, with an hour and a half to go, the call had not yet come. Then there was an hour to go, then forty-five minutes. Things got quiet and the mood started to change, like waiting for a stay of execution. The clock was ticking."

Ten minutes to midnight, nine minutes to midnight—four minutes to midnight, three minutes to midnight—then midnight came and went. No call. The deal was dead. "We went from nervous to panic to shock," Sherry described, "from total victory to total loss."

If traffic was passing at that late hour in the streets below, no one in the TCNJ boardroom heard it. Everyone was slumped in their chairs, too numb to hear or feel anything other than exhaustion and defeat.

"My God, I can't believe this!" Sherry said. "What the hell happened?!"

Indeed, what had happened? According to B. J. Douek, an associate at Sullivan and Cromwell, the logical explanation was that Manny Hanny officers had been pressured into changing their mind, maybe via a call from the Fed ordering them to kill the deal. Whatever the cause, Siggi's one hope for keeping his companies together crashed at midnight.

"It wasn't Manufacturers Hanover's fault," Douek said. "They would have preferred to let the deal go through. They were a correspondent bank for TCNJ and would have wanted to provide any additional service they could. But no doubt the Fed made it clear, 'We don't want you to do this.' And the Manny Hanny officers weren't going to take on loans if the Fed threatened to put the loans on their watch list. Can anybody prove it happened like that? That the pressure came from above? The Fed certainly won't admit it.

"Imagine what this was like," Douek explained. "Here we were in this card game, and Siggi's team had put together the winning hand by getting Manny Hanny to take over the commercial loans. Just at that moment, the Federal Reserve descends, like God from on high, and stops the game cold. 'We did everything you asked,' we told them. What was their answer? 'You would have won this—had it been someone else you were fighting. But it's us, the Federal Reserve, and we say you are flouting the law. We don't like the way Mr. Wilzig runs his business. He had ten years to make the necessary changes, and he failed to do so.' It was infuriating, completely unfair. We had won! Then the government stepped in and stole our victory."

The ruling to divest was now irreversible, and by the end of February 1982, the spin-off of Wilshire's subsidiary business, TCNJ, took place.

"My father's reaction to bad news was always the same," noted son Ivan, "namely, 'This isn't over.' Some powerful force, whether it was the Nazis or the Federal Reserve, might knock him down, but like a boxing champion he would find a way to get back up and win. No one could ever take from him that survivor's power to fight back."

"More than anything else," noted Rodgin Cohen, "Siggi was an incurable optimist. It was one of his best features. Siggi said, 'All right, we're not able to keep the two companies together. We have options. We have the possibility of changing this somehow in the future and getting Wilshire back into banking again. Also, there might be a change in Congress.' For Siggi, no setback was permanent. The challenge was to keep going and look towards the future."

In the spin-off, Siggi received the same deal as other shareholders, namely for every thousand shares of Wilshire he received one hundred and eleven shares of TCNJ. Overnight, as Wilshire's largest shareholder, he became TCNJ's largest shareholder. Everything he achieved had, in a sense, always been for his children, who for a long time had enjoyed civilian life. Now the moment had come for his sons, Ivan and Alan, and his daughter, Sherry, to get more deeply involved in preserving and perpetuating his achievements. He had built two stagnant businesses into an empire, and it would have been the greatest tragedy if there were no heirs to follow in his footsteps.

Siggi's eldest child, Ivan, now twenty-seven, had earned a college degree from the University of Pennsylvania and a law degree from the Benjamin N. Cardozo School of Law, an excellent background in Siggi's opinion for running a company. But when he proposed that Ivan replace him as head of Wilshire Oil Company, Ivan refused.

"Why not?" Siggi demanded. "Who in their right mind wouldn't want to be president, chairman, and CEO of an oil company listed on the New York Stock Exchange? Who wouldn't want that glamour and power? The perks are great, the money is great, the hours are great, you'll get to travel . . ."

"Not for any amount of money," Ivan said. "Hanging out with map-makers and geologists? No thanks."

If his son Ivan had no interest in the job, Siggi wondered, who else could do it? His youngest child, Alan, would eventually graduate from the Wharton School of Business and join the bank in 1987, but in 1981, at age sixteen, he wasn't ready. Siggi's middle child, Sherry, on the other hand, was twenty-three and had already begun learning her father's business. In some ways, Sherry was the child most like Siggi—for example, in analytical skills and business savvy—and with her at the helm, Siggi saw a way to maintain control over the affairs of Wilshire.

His mind whirled around the possibilities. There would be questions and no doubt more heat from the Federal Reserve for putting his own young, inexperienced daughter in charge. Still, it was a good solution since Siggi could protect his daughter and advise her from the sidelines.

"Putting Sherry in charge of Wilshire was the only possibility left," explained Rodgin Cohen. "We had lost on the argument that Siggi had control of the bank prior to the BHC Act. We had lost on looking to divest TCNJ of its demand deposits or its commercial loans. Sherry was the final Plan B."

With that final Plan B, Siggi succeeded in retaining de facto control of his two companies. Resuming control of Wilshire through his daughter began by training her during the tenure of the company's new president, Nathan White, a cousin of Siggi's wife, Naomi. When White passed away a year later, Siggi continued to train Sherry during the term of White's successor, Sam Halpern, a wealthy and prominent refugee real estate developer. After two years of preparation, Sherry was ready to become the youngest head of any oil and gas company traded on the New York Stock Exchange. Siggi could no longer be president, chairman, and CEO of Wilshire, but by having negotiated a favorable divestiture agreement he was able to assume the title of senior consultant.

"I can still do everything I was doing before except sign checks," he bragged to his son Ivan.

"I was good at the legal and stockholder side of Wilshire's affairs," Sherry later described, "but in reality, my father still ran the company. He was the expert when it came to Wilshire's oil and gas deals and everybody knew who was really still in charge."

A typical business consultant would normally only advise a company and help carry out its agenda and plans. In Siggi's case, because he had negotiated so successfully with the Fed, he could make all strategic, investment, and financial decisions, and nothing significant at Wilshire was going to be done without his blessings. The company was still his to direct, run by his own former management team, board friends, and rela-

tives—the same team that would now loyally continue listening to him as though he were still chairman, president, and CEO.

If Siggi had earned such loyalty, it was in large measure because he never stopped caring for his employees. He took particular pride in knowing that TCNJ was perhaps the only bank in the country to give stock options not only to senior management but to entry-level administrative employees as well, such as secretaries. In simplest terms, a stock option was the right to buy a certain number of shares within a specified time and at a locked-in price. When the stock rose above that fixed price, the employee could exercise the option of buying at the lower fixed price, thus showing a profit, at least on paper.

"Congratulations," he told them. "You own a piece of the bank. The harder you work, the bigger the bank's profits. The bigger the profits, the higher the price of our stock. The higher the stock price, the richer you become."

Siggi loved being a hero to his employees and they loved him for the personal care and attention he bestowed on young and old alike. When Siggi appointed his middle-aged comrade, Larry Nartel, to head TCNJ's purchasing department, no one said anything: the story of how Larry had saved Siggi's life in Auschwitz was well known. Larry was not a go-getter and the job could have been handled more efficiently by a younger man, but nonetheless Siggi would not deny Larry his position due to age. Purchasing agents were notorious for getting paid off by suppliers, and Larry was the only person Siggi trusted, regardless of how few hours Larry was able to put into the job. In later years, when Larry's energy waned even more, some executives questioned why Siggi kept him on. "Are you crazy?" Siggi said. "Who do you think I am, Mengele, that sadistic Nazi doctor who decided who shall live and who shall die? I don't care if Larry only comes in one hour a day. *I'll keep him till he's a hundred!*"

Larry was not the only older employee protected by Siggi. "We never laid off anyone because of age," he once described for an interviewer. "If someone is so sick that they can no longer work, then you can't help it, and that's gonna happen to all of us eventually. But to fire someone just because he walks a little slower or takes more time to get something done? Never!"

Caring for employees also included end-of-year bonuses, which Siggi prepared with his daughter Sherry, even though she wasn't part of the bank. Siggi trusted her judgment about such matters and was confident that she would keep his personal feelings and comments about employees confidential.

"That one lives alone and has a sick child," he told her, "so give her an extra $100. And that office manager? He only owns one brown suit. Give him an extra $100. And that secretary over there needs to see the dentist. Give her an extra $100."

"Caring so much about each of his employees was a very human, decent, and un-businesslike thing to do," Sherry said. "I'd taken business courses at Wharton, and his way of handing out bonuses couldn't have been more different from what I learned about the 'businesslike' way to handle job performance evaluations. His level of concern for employees was not a quality taught in business school."

Which made the day TCNJ's unionized employees went on strike all the more painful.

Strike

In 1984, there were nearly 13,000 independent banks in the United States.[73] TCNJ was one of only a dozen that were unionized, a tiny percentage compared with other industries. At the time, 20 percent of working Americans were union members. Banks had less need for unions since banking carried few of the risks of more manual-labor-intensive industries such as mining and transportation that involved heavy equipment and dangerous conditions. Nonetheless, employees everywhere wanted maximum vacation time, overtime pay, protection against layoffs and wage cuts, and other benefits. The range of issues between union employees and management at TCNJ was more or less the same, and some degree of conflict between them was predictable.

Union organizers had gained a foothold in TCNJ in the 1940s when the bank had only twelve branches. In those days, whenever the bank president approved increases for department heads and staff, managers first took their share and then gave something to their assistants. The money disappeared before getting down the ladder to the hourly employees. People were rightly outraged and called in a union representative to set things right.

Being a unionized bank had its pluses and minuses. It was good for keeping a larger bank from taking over TCNJ since no larger bank would want a union influencing the minds of their nonunion employees. The downside was that, if and when the time came to sell TCNJ, Siggi didn't want a union scaring away potential buyers. As far back as anyone could remember, TCNJ had maintained a reasonable rapport with Local 142. Then in 1983, a bigger shop, the Office and Professional Employees International Union, took over from Local 142 and troubles began.

"The problem was the new union delegation," explained Ed Davin, executive vice president of the TCNJ's operations department and union liaison. Davin had worked with the union for years and was friendly with union employees. He had effectively defused an earlier strike in 1978 that ended up lasting only three hours, but the ambitious new leadership was a problem.

"They were nice enough people," recalled Bob McCarthy, the bank's human resources director, "but when it came to economics, they were asking for the moon and the stars: unreasonably high salary increases, double the vacation time, and extended sick leave. They called it 'union proposals.' A more accurate word would be 'demands.'"

"Don't worry," Davin and McCarthy reassured Siggi. "We've made them a generous offer they can't refuse."

But the offer never reached union members. The new delegates sat on it, pretending that the members had voted it down, and continued to press the bank for unreasonable wage increases and other contract changes.

In some measure, Siggi himself was responsible for the strike. He insisted on issuing quarterly earnings reports that offered glowing accounts of the bank's financial condition: profits are up, stock value is up, and TCNJ is the fastest-growing bank in New Jersey. Naturally, union officials read these reports and wondered why their members weren't getting a bigger piece of the pie. In addition, Siggi's annual letter to shareholders projected the image of a corporation making millions, which further goaded union officials to demand their share of the bounty. "Our members are contributing to your success, too," they argued. "Where's the payback?"

To handle his side of the negotiations, Siggi brought in Eric J. Schmertz, one of the nation's most renowned labor lawyers. Schmertz, dean of Hofstra University's Law School, had resolved numerous high-profile labor disputes, including strikes by both the Radio City Music Hall Rockettes and New York City cab drivers in the 1960s. When union leaders learned that Schmertz was handling the negotiations, they knew a strike was likely since Schmertz had never bowed to pressure from a union before and he wasn't likely to start now.

A strike by TCNJ's union employees meant that management would have to run all of TCNJ branches, including all back-office operations, without the usual staff, a daunting prospect that had bank officers looking for replacements anywhere they could find them. Davin and McCarthy petitioned department heads for referrals. They headhunted among the friends and relatives of administrative employees and brought in temps from a local employment agency, Commerce and Helpmates. McCarthy called a meeting of his human resources team. "We're hiring," he said and sent them out to join in the personnel search.

This was the middle of June 1984. Many potential hires had already made summer plans and needed an incentive to cancel vacations and rearrange time with their families. "Let's pay them double," Davin suggested, and Siggi agreed. This was an emergency and extraordinary measures were called for.

By the first day of the strike, Siggi and his senior staff had managed to find sixty people, including his wife Naomi and the children, to replace the three hundred slots vacated by striking employees. The tactic sent a message to the union: You're not only in for a fight, but you're going to lose.

It had never mattered to Siggi whether employees were union or not; they were all his extended family, and he made sure they were looked after. Even his well-known penchant for yelling never focused on lower-level employees: he reserved that privilege for executives. Yet despite all the goodwill he could muster for his people, here they were marching up and down, chanting over and over, "One! Two! Three! Four! Throw Siggi

out the door!" He could understand working-class people wanting more. Everybody wanted more. It was their lack of loyalty that galled him. He knew these people by name. He gave them car loans, mortgage loans, and student loans, all at preferential rates whenever possible, and here they were spitting in his face. When they needed anything, he was there for them in an instant. He bent over backwards for them—and this is how they repaid him?

Union officials met with Siggi and his team and debated terms. "When it came down to negotiating," recalled McCarthy, "Mr. Wilzig got excited. He had the fastest mind I'd ever seen. If the union was demanding twenty dollars more per week for each union employee, Mr. Wilzig was way ahead of everyone. He had already calculated how much each additional dollar was going to cost the bank in terms of salaries and benefits, down to the penny. I'm sure it was the challenge of adversity that inspired him. He lived for it."

The strike lasted three weeks. Eventually, strikers realized management was not going to budge and a settlement was reached. Siggi could forgive workers for wanting more money, but contending with treason had worn him down. It was time for one of his rare, much-needed breaks.

"Millions At Stake!"

In the lean years when he was still a salesman, Siggi took his family on vacation to Asbury Park or Atlantic City. For the price of a handful of quarters he could indulge his children in games of Skee-Ball and pinball and buy as many hot pretzels and saltwater taffies as their adolescent stomachs could hold. Once his personal fortunes grew, he drove Naomi and their children to Kutsher's Country Club and Resort Hotel in the town of Monticello, in the Catskill Mountains.

"At Kutsher's, we had a card game every Sunday," described Arnie Young, who owned a large industrial tools company and had known Siggi since the 1960s. "It started right after breakfast and went on for hours. Whether the game was seven-card poker or ten-card gin rummy, he played like his life depended on it. He got so excited over cards you'd see this big vein bulging across his forehead. It worried me. I talked with him about it, but he would just yell, 'You don't understand! *Four dollars is not the point!*' It wasn't about the money. It was about winning. After having lost everything in the camps, winning meant everything to him."

Siggi loved Kutsher's. He loved sitting by the pool. He loved being with other Jewish vacationers in a place where he could not only relax but also network and find new customers for his bank. He was wealthy and could have taken his family to any of the resorts in the area, but Kutsher's was his preference. Grossinger's, fifteen miles north, catered to a more religious crowd. The Concord, a 1,200-acre behemoth with its own landing strip and post office, was the resort of choice for a more assimilated Jewish crowd. Kutsher's was Siggi's preference for several reasons. For one, Kutsher's was family-oriented and offered a wide range of sports and other activities for kids. Then, too, he enjoyed the entertainers, many of whom had gotten their start in show business at Kutsher's. A typical weekend might feature the likes of Woody Allen or Jerry Seinfeld, or old-time greats such as Duke Ellington, Louis Armstrong, or Dean Martin. Another incentive for choosing Kutsher's was that the hotel's owner, Milton Kutsher, treated Siggi like royalty, providing him with reserved VIP tables in the dining hall and nightclub and arranging for him to have two private phones: one in the card room and one by the pool, a privilege extended to no other guest.

"Put my calls through immediately," Siggi instructed the front desk.

"But Mr. Wilzig," an unsuspecting employee argued, "we have a policy of no calls . . ."

"Milton Kutsher approved it," Siggi corrected him. "*Put my calls through immediately! THERE ARE MILLIONS OF DOLLARS AT STAKE!*" The calls were put through.

"Sell fifty million short-term treasury bills!" he yelled into the phone. "Buy a hundred million long-term treasury bills!" all the while playing cards and drawing a crowd of vacationers around his pool chair, mesmerized by the show.

"Who is that guy with his own phone by the pool?" they wondered.

Once the crowd began to grow, Siggi hung up the phone, turned his attention to the assembled audience, and the stories began to flow. He regaled vacationers with anecdotes of life in prewar Germany and re-

membrances of the Holocaust. A crowd of five grew to ten, then twenty or more in bathing suits and flip-flops, hypnotized by the dapper business mogul with the explosive voice. Kutsher's was less his vacation spot than a satellite office and one-man theater in the Catskills.

"My kids called Siggi the Worm Man," said Lenny Boxer, a prominent Manhattan real estate attorney and fellow Kutsher's vacationer. "He would go down to the lake and bait a hook. Then he'd catch a fish, put the fish back in the water—still on the hook—and wait for a little kid and his father to walk by. Then he'd say, 'Hello, young man, have you ever gone fishing?' and hand the kid the rod. He'd point into the lake and say, 'Watch that red and white plastic float. When the ball moves around, it means the fish is nibbling. When the ball goes all the way down, there's a fish there for sure. Then there's a good chance you might catch him.' After a minute, the fish would swim off, the float would disappear under the water, and Siggi would yell, 'Look! You got something! Pull back! Pull back!' And up from the water jumps a two-pound bass—and the kid goes crazy. 'Look, Daddy! I did it! I did it! I caught a fish!' It made the kid's summer something special."

The gimmick made Siggi's summer special as well. A child's happiness meant everything to him, knowing what nightmarish experiments had been done to children in Auschwitz by Nazi monsters calling themselves doctors. Siggi's fondness for fishing included turning his hotel-room bathtub into a fish tank so all the kids in the hotel could stop by and have a look at the tub full of sunfish, bass, catfish, carp, and pickerel. The children were in awe but finding a bathtub full of flopping fish drove the maids at Kutsher's crazy. Siggi smoothed things over by letting the maids take home their pick of the catch.

"See this man?" comedian Freddy Roman would say from the stage of Kutsher's nightclub, spotting Siggi seated in the front row. "This man is the best banker in the world. You need a mortgage loan? A car loan? He's the guy to see. He's a banking genius."

During winter holidays, Siggi brought his family to the Saxony Hotel in Miami Beach, Florida. Completed in 1948, the Saxony was one of Miami's first luxury hotels and featured air-conditioned suites and an Olympic-sized swimming pool. By the 1970s, the Saxony was also the hotel of choice for religious Jews looking for kosher food. It had "Shabbos elevators" (elevators that automatically stopped at every floor on the Sabbath when any kind of work, including making electrical contact by pushing an elevator button, was forbidden). From the pool deck, guests enjoyed a view of the hotel's six-hundred-foot-long private beach—an ideal place for card games among regulars.

Dr. Jerry Quint, a New York heart surgeon, was not one of the regulars. His young daughter, Kelly, had made it into a figure skating competition at the Fontainebleau Hotel down the block, and Quint was passing time at the Saxony while waiting for his daughter's rehearsal to end. He stood on the hotel deck, watching six guys in shorts and polo shirts play poker. One of the players left the table and Jerry asked if he could join the game. The others waved him in, and Quint sat down next to Siggi.

"Siggi was the world's worst poker player," he recalled, "and the other guys read him perfectly. None of them spoke English very well, but it didn't matter. Whenever he had a really good hand, Siggi pretended it was the worst hand imaginable—totally transparent. '*Oh! What a terrible hand!*' And if he had a terrible hand, he yelled out, '*Ah! What a hand! Nobody can beat this hand!*' He lost a lot of money. It drove him crazy."

The game came to an end and players prepared to leave. Dr. Quint looked at Siggi's arm and saw his concentration camp number. He knew what it meant. Quint's stepfather had also been in Auschwitz, where his wife and five children had died in the gas chambers. Quint gently took hold of Siggi's arm and kissed the number. Siggi affectionately put his hand over Quint's. Quint gave Siggi his card and said, "If there's anything I can do for you, please call me."

One day, Siggi invited Dr. Quint to join his family for dinner in the hotel dining room. Also having dinner that evening at the Saxony was another couple, seated at a table next to the Wilzigs, Elie Wiesel and his wife, Marion. Siggi leaned over his chair, struck up a conversation with the renowned author, and discovered they had much in common. Wiesel was also sixteen when he was deported to Auschwitz, and like Siggi he had also lied to guards that he was eighteen and by doing so escaped the gas chamber. Both men had been separated from their families on arrival at the Birkenau selection ramp. Both had mothers who were sent straight to the gas chambers, and both had fathers who died in the camp.

During dinner, the two Auschwitz survivors commiserated over reports of antisemitism on the rise again. Thirty years after war's end, antisemitism had grown into a network of terror that threatened ordinary citizens in their homes and schools and on buses and planes. The 1970s were a particularly violent decade for Israelis, who faced constant tragedy and armed attacks. In 1970, operatives of the Popular Front for the Liberation of Palestine (PFLP) fired two bazooka shells into a school bus, killing twenty-five people, including nine children. In May 1972, three men entered the waiting area of Tel Aviv's Lod Airport, pulled vz. 58 assault rifles from violin cases, opened fire, and killed twenty-six civilians.

Four months later, eight terrorists from the Black September faction of the Palestine Liberation Organization (PLO) scaled a six-foot chain-link fence and entered Olympic Village in Munich. Aided by neo-Nazi insiders who provided details of the village layout, the attackers broke into rooms where Israeli athletes slept. Within twenty-four hours, eleven of the Israelis were dead. On Yom Kippur, October 6, 1973—the holiest day of the Jewish calendar—a coalition of Arab states led by Egypt and Syria launched a surprise attack on Israeli-occupied territories. In April 1974, three members of the PFLP crossed the Israeli border from Leba-

non, entered a residential building in the town of Kiryat Shmona, opened fire, and executed eighteen residents.

More attacks followed in hotels and marketplaces, on buses and public roads. In March 1978, a PLO faction known as Fatah hijacked a bus on Israel's Coastal Highway and opened fire on passengers, killing thirty-eight people, including thirteen children. Israelis chose less crowded routes to their destinations and looked in all directions when circulating in public. Parents instructed their children to walk away from loaves of bread, packs of cigarettes, or anything else lying on the ground that might be booby-trapped. No one knew when or how the next attack would come.

The US government was warning that if you were Jewish, or if you were the president of a bank or oil company, you were a number-one terrorist target—and Siggi was all three, which explained why he would only hire chauffeurs during those years who were licensed to carry a gun.

The continued murder of innocent Jewish men, women, and children thirty years after war's end was a deep concern that bound the two survivors together. That evening's conversation was the first of many, and in the months to come, Siggi would find that Wiesel had already envisioned a role for him in one of the most significant Holocaust memorials in the world.

The Holocaust Museum

On March 16, 1977, President Jimmy Carter addressed a town meeting in Clinton, Massachusetts. If ever there were to be a resolution to the Middle East crisis, he said, there would need to be a homeland provided for the Palestinian refugees. The statement caused dismay in Israel. Speaking to students in Tel Aviv, Israel's Premier Yitzhak Rabin suggested that Carter's words could lead to serious difficulties between Israel and the US. The American president needed to make some gesture of reconciliation. A museum dedicated to the Holocaust in a prominent Washington location might go a long way to healing the rift that threatened the friendship between their two nations.

On November 1, 1978, Carter established the President's Commission on the Holocaust and gave its chair, Elie Wiesel, the duty of submitting a report "with respect to the establishment and maintenance of an appropriate memorial to those who perished in the Holocaust." Michael Berenbaum, deputy director of the President's Commission, wrote in his 1979 *Report to the President* that Americans had a "distinct responsibility" to remember the Holocaust. American soldiers had liberated some of the concentration camps, survivors now lived in America, and the nation suf-

fered from a "disastrous" legacy of indifference to the Jews of Europe. By constructing a museum, the US government would not only memorialize those who perished but would "instill caution, fortify restraint, and protect against future evil or indifference."

The President's Commission included four community leaders, five rabbis, and a number of other distinguished men and women. Members were sworn in on February 1, 1979, in the White House's Roosevelt Room, charged with the mandate of creating America's most important edifice to Holocaust memory. By this time, Wiesel and his family had become friends with the Wilzigs. Elie admitted to Siggi he knew nothing about business and needed his help to raise funds and keep the Commission on track. When Wiesel was appointed to head the US Holocaust Memorial Council by President Jimmy Carter, he asked that "Wilzig be the first person to serve with him."[74]

"Wiesel had done immense good positioning the museum in the public light," Berenbaum recalled, "but not much in terms of funding or development. Wiesel enlisted Siggi to join a board of trustees, called the US Holocaust Memorial Museum (USHMM) Council, and go through the financial plans. Siggi was smart as a whip and could take that on."

The appointment to the council came with an invitation to dine with President and Mrs. Carter at the White House. Thirty years after his arrival in America as an impoverished refugee, Siggi was a dinner guest of the president of the United States.

Passions ran high over the creation of the USHMM. How much of the horror should be depicted? Should revolts and armed resistance such as the Warsaw Ghetto Uprising play a central role in the narrative, as they did in Israel's Yad Vashem Holocaust museum? Should Hitler's words be displayed on museum walls? What historical sequence should be followed in telling the story of the Holocaust? Should human hair be included among the artifacts on display or would that be too upsetting for visitors?

And what of America's role? Should the permanent exhibit be limited to America as liberator or should it include evidence of US indifference to the slaughter of Europe's Jewish population?

"To the American military," said historian David Wyman, "Europe's Jews represented an extraneous problem and an unwarranted burden." The Air Force, he stated, as Siggi had in his many talks on the subject, "could have eliminated the Auschwitz killing installations." Did that tragic fact deserve a place in the permanent exhibits?

Of all issues relating to museum content, the most contentious was determining who should be commemorated: just Jews, or should other victims also be represented? If so, who else and to what extent?

"That was Wiesel's biggest fear, that the museum would betray the Jewishness of victims' memories," said Berenbaum, who presided during the early years of planning. "You have to remember, at that time survivors were worried not only about who would be remembered but whether the Holocaust itself would be remembered at all. It was less about their personal immortality than about the event. These were people who had lost everything imaginable, and the possibility that there would be no remembrance of what had occurred to the Jewish people was overwhelming. If Siggi was aggressive about anything, he was aggressive about the museum maintaining a focus on the Jewish specificity of the Holocaust."

On this central issue of whose story was to be told, Siggi made his position clear to council members. "The worst thing that can happen is to compare the Holocaust to anything else," he said. "The Holocaust is a distinct, unique experience. Of course Jews were not the only ones murdered. And yes, we must remember the millions of Christians who also died in the war. But it is as Elie says, 'While not all victims were Jews, all Jews were victims.' So you have a distinction here. I'm a founding member of this council, and this is one of our functions. We don't say we were the only ones who suffered. But there was a vast difference. Never did Hitler or his henchmen say of *any other people*, 'Take everyone from grandfather to grandchild and kill them all.'"

Many on the council agreed. Other ethnic groups had been murdered, but only Jews had been singled out by the Nazis for total extermination. For some members such as Irving Greenberg, comparing destruction of the Jews with any other genocide was "blasphemous." Others disagreed. Gypsies—more accurately, Roma—argued that they, too, were murdered not because of anything they had done but because of who they were. The one Roma representative on the council accused fellow members of "overt racism" and "willfully downplaying" Roma suffering.

Historian Raoul Hilberg reminded members that the Holocaust, although unique, was not "without its precedents and not without its implications" and argued in favor of including the Armenian victims of Turkish genocide in 1915 along with other non-Jewish victims of the Nazis. Another council member, historian Lucy Dawidowicz, disagreed, arguing that "never before had one people denied another people the fundamental right to live" and that maintaining the Jewish core of the Holocaust was crucial to the purpose of the museum. Council Chairman Miles Lerman concurred, adding that "if you are introducing the Armenian tragedy to the Holocaust, why not the tragedy of the Cambodians? Why not the tragedy of the American Indians?"

Survivors were growing old. They saw their ranks thinning by the day and worried about the future of Holocaust memory, particularly given the threat of "deniers": those who claimed the Holocaust never happened. Losing the Jewish center of the Holocaust struck many on the council as fuel for Holocaust denial.

It was common knowledge among council members that Holocaust denial had been on the rise since the end of World War II, when French journalist Maurice Bardèche, a self-proclaimed fascist, published articles claiming that gas chambers had only been used inside concentration camps to disinfect clothing, that photos and documents used as evidence of the mass murder of Jews had been falsified, and that in any case Jews had deserved harsh treatment since they were Germany's enemies.

Momentum was fueled by other deniers, or "revisionists" as they were sometimes called, including Pat Buchanan, an arch-conservative journalist; David Duke, a far-right politician and former Grand Wizard of the Ku Klux Klan; and David Irving, an English author who declared there never were gas chambers in Auschwitz, only mockups built after the war, and that Adolf Hitler had never known about the extermination of Jews or, if he had, he opposed it.

What good, council members asked, was building the museum at the physical center of American commemorative space—adjacent to the National Mall, the geographic core of Washington, DC monuments—if it did not serve as an insurance policy against such blatant distortions of history? In the words of conservative rabbi Seymour Siegel, the museum needed to establish "on a scientific and unshakable basis the truth of our story and the accuracy of the event."

Yet council members acknowledged that every museum had a particular editorial perspective on history and its own interpretation of events. Which story would the Washington museum tell? Was this to be a Jewish museum and close its doors on Yom Kippur, or an American museum and remain open? Should the emphasis be on the Allies as victors or on Jewish resistance, such as the Warsaw Ghetto Uprising and the creation of the State of Israel? Should inscriptions on the walls of the museum's Hall of Remembrance be biblical ("May their memory serve as a blessing"), or testimonial (such as the last line of Anne Frank's diary, "Despite everything, I still believe people are good at heart")? Should the architectural design be benign and fit seamlessly with other structures on the Mall, or should it evoke something unsettling and different in the architectural landscape? Every issue generated debate.

One person who remembered Siggi's participation during these turbulent months was Eli Pfefferkorn, who worked closely with Wiesel. Pfefferkorn had survived months in Majdanek and other concentration camps, then a death march to Theresienstadt, where he was liberated by the Red Army

on May 8, 1945. Pfefferkorn first went to England as an orphan, then came to the United States, earned his PhD in history at Brown University, and served as the USHMM's director of research.

"Observing Siggi was a fascinating exercise," Pfefferkorn wrote in his memoir, highlighting "his compact physical build brimming with energy, head boasting a shock of curly hair, and overall meticulously dressed." Pfefferkorn continued, "Wiesel had invited Siggi to look into the fiscal operation of the council. Recognizing the urgency of the situation, he took time out from stewarding everyday business of his bank and came to Washington. The quality of steely resolve that undoubtedly navigated him to the ownership and the presidency of the bank also guided him in probing the council's structure. Undaunted by the entrenched bureaucracy, he laid open the council's operation, resulting in recommendations on how to streamline its management."[75]

Once he was appointed by Wiesel as chief advisor to the chairman, Siggi conducted a review of the museum's hiring policies and was appalled. "In my thirty years in business," he wrote to board members, "I have never seen such a lack of hiring controls." He cited in particular the failure to check references, the failure to consider applicants' salary histories—noting that "in some cases, persons hired have been given salary increases of 25 to 90 percent"—and the failure to conduct adequate background checks. "*The PLO could have been working for us!*" he chided sarcastically.

Siggi instituted measures which he described as "the minimum requirements used by any responsible business or organization." These included job descriptions, detailed employment histories of anyone looking to work for the museum, two business references, two personal references, and credit reports. "If someone is broke," he told board members, "or has judgments against him, we obviously would not hire him to handle cash or checks for the council."

Still, responsible oversight of its staff did nothing to reduce accusations by White House officials that the council was advocating an "overly Jewish" view of the Holocaust. The board itself, officials warned, did not

reflect sufficient ethnic diversity. The council had "too many Jews," White House officials were rumored to have said, before politely but firmly asking Wiesel to add another non-Jew, perhaps a Polish American or someone with no connection to the Holocaust.

Wiesel called an emergency meeting of his closest advisers and asked what they thought should be done. How should these outrageous demands from the White House be answered? Jewish industrialist Frank Lautenberg, a future senator from New Jersey, argued that compromise was unavoidable. "Sometimes," he said, "if it is for a just cause, one may sell one's soul to the devil."

According to Wiesel's recollection of that moment, Siggi "flies into a rage and—fortunately—puts [Lautenberg] in his place."[76] Where will it end, Siggi argued, if we give in to such pressure? How many non-Jews will be invited to vote on Jewish memory? Quarrels mounted and emotions flared. The various committees Wiesel had organized were, he wrote, "in a mess."[77]

Then came a dramatic new setback. Technical studies determined that the historic buildings allocated by Congress for the museum were unusable: too small, rotted to the point of collapsing, and beyond repair. Better to demolish them, the studies recommended, and build something new. The council now faced the daunting prospect of starting from scratch, with a new and vastly more expensive design.

Time was running out on the "sunset clause" of the museum's enabling legislation: permission to build would be withdrawn if by sunset of October 7, 1985, evidence was not presented to Congress showing progress on content and funding. Yet the council was divided over even the most basic of issues, and Micah Naftalin, a senior policy analyst with the National Academy of Sciences and later acting director of the council, warned Wiesel that they were "fairly close to zero" in their planning.

Of all moments for planners to be deadlocked on the future of the Holocaust museum, late 1985 was the worst possible. In recent months, neo-Nazis had burned synagogues and desecrated cemeteries across Europe. Deniers had grown more vociferous in promoting their "evidence" that the

Holocaust had never happened. And, as if intended to exaggerate offenses to Holocaust memory, President Reagan chose this moment to commit what White House officials later called "the most serious blunder of his presidency" and one that nearly drove council members to resign *en masse.*

The president announced that on an upcoming tour of Germany he would visit the Bitburg military cemetery. Bitburg contained the graves of forty-nine Nazi SS officers.

CHAPTER 21

Unbecoming Conduct

In November 1984, West German Chancellor Helmut Kohl had visited the White House and proposed to President Reagan that they promote friendship between their two nations by jointly observing the fortieth anniversary of V-E Day on May 8, 1985. Kohl had been informed that Reagan was scheduled to attend a meeting in Bonn that same week and suggested that together they visit Kolmeshöhe military cemetery on the outskirts of Bitburg, a town less than an hour's drive from Bonn. The president agreed.

In February 1985, White House Deputy Chief of Staff Michael Deaver inspected the cemetery. The official explanation of what happened during the inspection was that snow covered the rows of headstones, and that Deaver and his team consequently failed to notice that of the two thousand graves of German soldiers, forty-nine belonged to members of the Waffen SS, Hitler's elite police force. The cemetery housing their graves was the most inappropriate of places for a visit by an American president, yet Deaver approved the site and the White House announced Reagan's travel plans.

Reporters quickly learned about the presence of the SS graves, and the resulting articles triggered international outrage. Survivors were livid, government officials protested, and a wave of objections descended on Washington. In 1946, the Nuremberg tribunal had declared the SS collectively guilty of extreme war crimes, yet here was the president preparing to officially bestow American honors on them by placing a wreath at their tombs.

Secretary of State George Shultz—in Wiesel's words "the humanist on Ronald Reagan's team"—called his ambassador in Bonn, hoping the ambassador could convince Chancellor Kohl to cancel the visit to Bitburg. Kohl was unmoved. German elections were coming up, and a photo of Kohl with the US president bowing before the graves of German soldiers would reinforce Kohl's popularity. Neo-Nazi groups were on the rise in 1980s Germany, and conservative politicians such as Kohl looked for just such opportunities to win influential right-wing votes.[78]

The USHMM council convened an emergency meeting. Some members proposed that they should all resign in protest, while others advocated patience. Senator Lautenberg of New Jersey again urged the council to not rock the boat. Better to remain in the president's good graces, he argued. Besides, there were three weeks before the scheduled trip. Something still might happen to change the president's mind.

Elie Wiesel met with Reagan at the White House and pleaded with him to cancel the visit. "People everywhere, Jews and non-Jews, young and old, Republicans and Democrats alike, will applaud your decision," Wiesel said.

With a sad smile, Reagan replied, "Too late." He had just spoken with Kohl on the phone. The chancellor insisted that if the visit to Bitburg were canceled, it would be a "national catastrophe" for Germany. "I will not give up the idea," Kohl told the *New York Times*. "If we don't go to Bitburg, if we don't do what we jointly planned, we will deeply offend the feelings of [the German] people."

On April 19, 1985, Wiesel arrived at the White House to receive the Congressional Gold Medal. Fifteen minutes into his acceptance speech,

he surprised the audience by addressing the planned visit to Bitburg. "That place, Mr. President, is not your place," Wiesel said. "Your place is with the victims of the SS. I implore you to do something else, to find another way, another site."

In the weeks that followed, fifty-three senators signed a letter asking the president to cancel his visit. Nearly three hundred other government representatives signed a letter urging Chancellor Kohl to withdraw the invitation. Former Army Staff Sergeant Jim Hively sent back his World War II decorations in protest. Reagan's proposed visit prompted a spate of pop songs. The Ramones recorded "My Brain Is Hanging Upside Down: Bonzo Goes to Bitburg," referencing *Bedtime for Bonzo*, a movie from Reagan's film career that costarred a chimpanzee. Frank Zappa recorded "Reagan at Bitburg" with satirical instrumentation using slide trombones and xylophones.

The president exacerbated his predicament by saying in defense of his decision, "These [SS troops] were the villains, as we know, who conducted the persecutions and all. But there are two thousand graves there, and for most of those, the average age is about eighteen. I think that there's nothing wrong with visiting that cemetery where those young men are victims of Nazism also, even though they were fighting in the German uniform, drafted into service to carry out the hateful wishes of the Nazis. They were victims, just as surely as the victims in the concentration camps."

Reagan could not have made a more inflammatory claim. Equating Nazi soldiers with Holocaust victims was, declared Rabbi Alexander M. Schindler, president of the Union of American Hebrew Congregations, "a callous offense to the Jewish people." Council member Hadassah Rosensaft, a survivor of Auschwitz and Bergen-Belsen, telephoned Wiesel in despair.

"How could he? How dare he say what he said?" she asked.

Two days before the scheduled visit, Reagan told his deputy chief of staff, "I know you and my wife, Nancy, don't want me to go through with this, but . . . history will prove I'm right. If we can't reconcile after forty years, we are never going to be able to do it." There was one announced

change to Reagan's itinerary: a concessional visit to the Bergen-Belsen concentration camp, a gesture which some felt would merely make matters worse. Menachem Rosensaft, Hadassah's son and an advisor to the USHMM council, called the president's plan "an obscene package deal."

Pressure had to be brought on Reagan to change his plans. Siggi took to the airwaves.

Starting with his first show in the 1960s, radio commentator Barry Farber's easily recognized Southern drawl, intense delivery, and quick wit made him a favorite with listeners. His on-air interviews for WMCA, a New York–based radio station, garnered a wider audience than any other show on American radio.

"We had Siggi on my show for a variety of topics," Farber recalled, "and when we wanted to find a concentration camp survivor we lucked out again with Siggi."

The interview took place on May 1, 1985, less than a week before Reagan's scheduled visit to Bitburg.

"Siggi," Farber began, "you may remember when you came on my late-night broadcasts in the mid-seventies. You were telling us about being the first survivor to address the cadets at West Point."

"The cadets couldn't understand," Siggi said, "when I told them that, to the best of my knowledge, I was the only one to survive from a school of fifteen hundred children. They couldn't grasp that I was one of only 10 percent of all German Jews to survive the Holocaust, or that the SS had killed fifty-nine members of my family, including three of my brothers, one of my sisters, my seven-year-old nephew, and my two-year-old niece."

Then his focus shifted. "These are the same SS that President Reagan is going to honor next week. Barry, you have known me for quite some time, and you understand why I'd be hesitant to talk about myself just now, when what I experienced is overshadowed by what President Reagan is planning to do."

"Siggi, forgive me," Farber said. "I didn't realize you'd be going through this kind of emotion."

"Barry, this for me is the darkest hour since the liberation. What the Nazis did was blatant brutal murder, and the leader of the free world is giving it a total whitewash. The president isn't even listening to the members of his own party. Everyone with any decency has come out and said that on this one the president is wrong. What happened in the Holocaust was a legalized system of murder that only existed with the help and active participation of the SS, who are buried in Bitburg.

"Over the years," Siggi said, "with the love and affection of my family and friends, sometimes I can escape those memories. What it took my family and friends thirty, forty years to do, the president is about to undo in one day. I'm not the same person I was when you and I were together a few years ago. Every day, I relive in my memory experiences from Auschwitz. I was liberated in Mauthausen concentration camp on May 5, 1945—the same date the president is going to Bitburg to honor the murderers."

Farber, who was not easily jolted out of his usually sanguine disposition, sat stunned. "Siggi, please go on," he said.

"I've tried to see Chancellor Kohl," Siggi said, "to convince him to switch his plans. I would recommend that he go with Reagan to the Tomb of the Unknown Soldier in Munich or to the grave of the late Chancellor Adenauer.[79] Then I had another idea. Let them go and pay tribute to Field Marshal Rommel, a soldier's soldier. At least Rommel didn't kill any children in gas chambers. The future will remember this visit by an American president as one of the worst days in the history of the free world. Reagan has started something that he does not comprehend. I just pray that this is not the beginning of something unspeakable. For me, this is right now more fearful than the possibilities of nuclear war. I voted for this man but truthfully, I hope the president is going mad because that might explain what he is doing.

"The people who made the preparations claimed they didn't know that the cemetery had the graves of forty-nine SS murderers," Siggi said. "They said snow covered the grave markers. That's an outright lie. Ac-

cording to German sources, not my own, the mayor of Bitburg and the man in charge of the cemetery handed Deaver a list showing that the SS murderers were buried there. But the president himself said, and I quote, 'The men buried in that cemetery are victims just as surely as the victims of the concentration camps.' Who can understand this?"

Farber took a call from a listener.

"I think this controversy over Bitburg will die down someday," the caller said, "but what will remain is the fact the Holocaust story is a hoax and your guest is a scurrilous liar. And the evidence for that is very clear. It consists of such things as the aerial photographs of Auschwitz which were taken by American reconnaissance aircraft from May of 1944 through January of 1945. Detailed views of the so-called gas chambers and crematorium totally failed to show any of the type of evidence that should have been visible in the photographs, if the descriptions of Elie Wiesel or people like your guest were at all accurate."

Farber jumped in. "Hold your fire right there. Folks, this is a magic moment in radio. Here we have on the phone one of the people who denies that there ever was a Holocaust, and he's facing a survivor of Auschwitz, Siggi Wilzig."

"Did I understand right?" Siggi asked. "Did this gentleman just say it didn't happen?"

"Yes," Farber said. "He's saying that American reconnaissance photos proved that there was no extermination camp and that the Holocaust was a hoax."

The caller came back on the line. "No, I didn't say there was no camp at Auschwitz. Certainly, there was a concentration camp at Auschwitz. That was clearly shown in the photographs. But what was missing in the photographs are flaming pits, for example, where thousands of bodies were supposedly burned every day as claimed by people like Elie Wiesel—who is another scurrilous liar—or smoke and flames supposedly pouring forth continually from a crematorium chimney—"

Siggi interrupted, telling Farber, "The first time he said it, I thought I misunderstood what he said. But he just said it again."

The caller said, "Well, I'll tell you again if you—"

"No," Siggi said. "I feel sick enough after listening to it the first two times."

Siggi shook with anger. Was this faceless caller deranged? His voice offered no evidence of madness. Whoever it was, he had likely grown up accustomed to the privileges of free speech and the opportunity to be heard, yet for reasons known only to himself he chose to exercise those privileges to publicly deny history's darkest hour. Was there an authentic human being behind such babble? If the caller had posed a question— "Did it really happen the way people say it did?"—that would have been worthy of discussion. But in the caller's voice there was no sign of such uncertainty. He spoke with righteous conviction and it was more than Siggi could bear.

"*You deny that this took place?*" Siggi raged. "*That my parents didn't die there?! That my father wasn't beaten and lay dying in my arms on April 8, 1943?! That the flames weren't there the day I got off the trains?!*"

"What day was that?" the caller demanded.

"The twenty-seventh of February, 1943," Siggi said.

"Well, that's not so because the crematoriums weren't in operation until after February of 1943—"

"*You are an outright ignoramus!*" Siggi yelled. "*YOU'RE A DANGEROUS IDIOT!*" He signaled to Farber to disconnect the caller.

"Next caller," Farber announced quickly. "Your turn."

"My question to Mr. Wilzig is this," the caller said. "Why doesn't the president just change his mind and not go to Bitburg?"

"The first point I want to make," Siggi said, trying to calm himself, "is that I was chosen as one of six survivors to light a memorial candle during Holocaust Remembrance Day in the White House.[80] I stood less than ten feet from the president, and the man had tears in his eyes. I don't believe he was acting. He meant it. So why does he insist on going to Bitburg? I'll tell you. The economy has gone as far as it can go, the national debts are high, those things he can't change, and I think the president wants to find a way to go down in history. He is looking for something revo-

lutionary to be remembered for. To that you should add that Chancellor Kohl lost votes in the last municipal elections, which are a forerunner to the presidential elections in Germany, and Bitburg is in an area that will decide that next election. Nine out of ten times, the Bitburg votes have shown which party will get the presidency. Mr. Kohl also sees that the president lacks a sense of history and Kohl is taking advantage. He sees that the president not only doesn't know European history, but he doesn't even know his own people."

Farber took another call. "Siggi," the listener said, "I think you're overdoing it, I think you're overstating the case. Reagan is a good man. He made a mistake. That's all it is. There's no conspiracy. Don't put those evil motives on Reagan. What you are doing is counterproductive for Jewish concerns."

Siggi shook his head. These callers didn't understand. They were not making the connection between Reagan's "mistake" and its consequences for humanity's future.

"I sincerely hope that you are right and that I am wrong," he told the caller, "but there aren't many people who share your opinion. I believe that President Reagan is a very fine man. If he weren't such a fine man this terrible tragedy wouldn't upset me. I wouldn't expect anything better from a lesser man. But this is not the behavior of a leader of a great nation. When the president said that the SS men buried in that cemetery are as much victims of Hitler as the victims of the concentration camps—when you hear that, sir, then it isn't a question of what I believe. What the president is saying is evil. Let us hope that the Almighty will push aside this dark cloud and that sunshine will come after. I hope so."

This had been the most emotionally charged broadcast of Farber's twenty-five-year radio career. "Siggi," he said, "any last words?"

What could he say to conclude such an inflammatory interview? After a pause, Siggi replied, "When you survived the concentration camps and others didn't, you can't figure out the wisdom of the Creator. But I believe

wholeheartedly that there is a Creator. If I was the only one to survive the Holocaust, I would still believe in the Almighty. When a nobody like me can come on national radio and tell the president of the United States he's wrong, well, then, there has to be a God in heaven."

On May 8, 1985, security was heavy for Reagan's visit to Bitburg. Two thousand police lined the three-mile route from the NATO airbase to the cemetery. When the president arrived, documentary filmmaker Michael Moore and a friend whose parents died in Auschwitz were there holding a banner which read THEY KILLED MY FAMILY. Television cameras caught the confrontation and broadcast the moment live. Reagan spent only eight minutes at the cemetery but managed nonetheless to make matters worse by telling reporters, "We can mourn the German war dead today as human beings crushed by a vicious ideology." With those words, Reagan became the first person in postwar history to absolve the SS of the very crimes for which the international Nuremberg court had convicted them in 1946. One Auschwitz survivor said the president's comments had triggered her worst nightmares since liberation. "It was proof the world had not learned," she lamented. "To equate the SS with us as victims. Mindboggling! To have made that sacrifice and then to think it was all in vain—it was unforgivable."

"With these few steps taken by the president," Elie Wiesel told the press, "forty years of history have been wiped out."[81]

For years, Siggi had been a sought-after speaker, flooded with invitations to speak at public and private gatherings, and until Bitburg he accepted them all. He always found time to speak about the Holocaust for a high school commencement, a college honors program, a continuing education graduation ceremony, a Jewish community center lecture series. Most any occasion was an opportunity for Siggi to convey his message: Speak up

when you see injustice. And when you hear Holocaust deniers spreading their propaganda, be prepared to fight the lies.

His talks always elicited an emotional response from his audience, and their acknowledgement reinforced his sense of being a torchbearer of Holocaust memory. "Maybe I have an ounce of brain, but I'm no genius," he would begin. "I am a very simple individual. The only thing that's special about me is that I survived. I'm a free man, an American Jew, a Sabbath observer. I have an excellent memory, and I remember it all—all of it, much to my pain"—and the memories came pouring out. In addition to West Point, Siggi had lectured about the Holocaust at numerous prestigious colleges such as Brown University, the University of Pennsylvania, and Boston University.

But after the Bitburg fiasco he gave up public speaking. What was the point? When the president of the United States, the most powerful man on the planet, became an apologist for Nazi mass murderers, the world tipped too far off course for Siggi to continue bearing witness.

"It would have been horrible even if he wasn't the president," he told a newspaper interviewer, "but he is the president and he is giving official sanction from the world's greatest democracy to history's worst murderers. I'm not a vicious person, I don't wish him any harm—if I don't hate today's Germans, why would I hate Reagan? But why trouble myself any longer with more nightmares? When I speak in public, I have nightmares. You don't die in a nightmare, but you can come close. In my case, I dream about the gas chambers. I dream I see my own children dying in the flames. Why put myself through that?"

Among other offers to speak, he turned down invitations from the University of California Berkeley, the US Air Force Academy in Colorado Springs, and the Taft School in Western Connecticut. The silence lasted twelve years.

By the 1990s, the spread of Holocaust denial brought Siggi out of his retirement from lecturing, and he once again accepted an invitation to

speak, this time in honor of the Day of Holocaust Remembrance at Kean University in Union, New Jersey.

Yom HaShoah Ve-Hagevurah, "Holocaust and Heroism Remembrance Day," had been inaugurated in Israel in 1953 and signed into law by then–Prime Minister David Ben-Gurion and President Yitzhak Ben-Zvi. The commemoration was scheduled to coincide with the April anniversary of the 1943 Warsaw Ghetto Uprising, the Jews' longest-lasting revolt against their Nazi oppressors. In Israel, every year at 10 a.m. on Yom HaShoah sirens sound across the country in memory of those who perished. Pedestrians come to a halt, drivers stop their cars, public venues shut their doors and flags fly at half-mast. The entire country stands at attention, in silent tribute to the dead. Since 1988, as part of the commemoration, students from around the world assemble at Auschwitz to participate in the "March of the Living," so named to contrast with the death marches and to demonstrate the rebirth of world Jewry. In the US, Yom HaShoah commemorations include services, vigils, and talks by Holocaust survivors. Now, for its commemoration during Holocaust Remembrance Week in April 1992, the Holocaust Resource Center at Kean University invited Siggi to be their speaker.

"We were up all night preparing his talk," said Lisa Goldstein, Siggi's longtime personal assistant. "I helped him write notes on index cards, cutting them up and positioning them with Scotch tape. It had been a long time since his last talk, and he was anxious."

More than a thousand students and faculty filled the Kean University auditorium. Siggi was introduced by Kean University's president, Dr. Nathan Weiss, and then Siggi approached the podium.

"I would feel much more comfortable," he began, "if we were to talk about banking and business. That I understand quite well. But I have to put my comfort aside to speak once again about a subject that is painful yet holy to me."

At sixty-six years of age, Siggi's voice was as strong as it had been a

dozen years before at West Point, but there would be different content in today's talk. At West Point, he had evoked with dramatic oratory the details of his time in Auschwitz, but Holocaust denial had not yet become such a pressing issue. Incorporating this troubling development into the Kean presentation would be a first.

"I have an excellent memory," he began, falling back on familiar phrases and topics. "I remember the Holocaust, much to my pain. Added to that pain is a new, brutal disease that has entered American life: denial of the Holocaust. Deniers ask, 'Was there really a Holocaust?' We might as well ask, 'Was there really slavery in America?' What would your reaction be to someone who says, 'Slavery never existed in America. Slavery is the invention of Black people looking for sympathy'? What would your reaction be to someone who says, 'There never were any lynchings by the Ku Klux Klan'? I expect you students here would object if such lies were spoken.

"Holocaust denial is the worst thing that can happen to a survivor," Siggi told the audience. "For someone who still hears the screaming of children, who still has nightmares of babies torn from the arms of their parents to be thrown into the flames of the crematoria, the cruelty of having to read such statements by deniers in newspapers . . ." He stammered and grabbed the sides of the podium.

"*Damn them all!* It is obscene to deny the murder of innocent people. Never did I think that I would have to raise my arm and swear to you that whatever you hear from me today is the truth . . ." and for the next hour he kept his audience enthralled with memories of what he had seen and lived through in Auschwitz, stories of wholesale slaughter and cruelty beyond imagining, of liberation and of the work being done in Washington and elsewhere to protect the memory of the Holocaust from the propaganda of deniers.

"My good friend Elie Wiesel once said, 'Those who do nothing stand not with the victims but with the murderers.' So, march along with us now," he urged the students and faculty. "Fight this disease and its perpetrators, the David Dukes, the Pat Buchanans, the Robert Faurissons, the

neo-Nazis and the racists. In England, Dr. David Irving says in his book that Hitler did not know until October 1, 1943, that Jews were gassed by the millions.[82] In other words, there never was a Final Solution. There never were any gas chambers—which means what? That I killed my own family? That this number on my arm doesn't exist? And if this is happening now, what will happen when we survivors are gone? That's when you, young people, will share the burden and privilege of keeping the memory alive."

He pulled back, pursed his lips, and raised a finger. "I have a task for you," he said. "I want you to be my deputies. You are the future of America." The finger wagged back and forth. "Don't say to yourself, 'I'm Catholic. I'm Protestant. I'm Black. I'm Hispanic. It doesn't concern me.' We survivors remember the righteous gentiles, and I for one will never forget to mention them: the Danes who saved 95 percent of their Jewish citizens in the still of the night, the Dutch, the Yugoslavians, the Italians who saved 87 percent of all Italian Jews—but where was the Pope?"

While many Italians did their share in helping to save Jews, the complicity of Pope Pius in Nazi policies infuriated Siggi and was a part of almost all his lectures about the Holocaust.

"As a child," he told his audience, "I smuggled myself into a movie house to see the newsreel. And I swear by the Almighty God that I saw the Pope blessing the German weapons and the divisions of Nazi soldiers leaving to fight the Bolsheviks. Many righteous priests and nuns died in Auschwitz, but when the Pope was asked after the war what he'd done to save the Jews, he said, 'I prayed for them.'"

Contrary to his criticism of Pope Pius, Siggi heaped praise on his future successor, Pope John XXIII, who went out of his way during the 1930s as a papal ambassador to save Jews from the Nazis by various means, including the issue of certificates of "baptism of convenience" and personal intervention to secure the release of Jews held in concentration camps. In Siggi's eyes, Pope John was the greatest of heroes.

Among the VIPs invited to sit on the raised front stage were several Holocaust survivors. Siggi pointed to Sam Halpern, by some accounts the most prolific builder in New Jersey history and a survivor of the Kamionka labor camp.

"This man," Siggi said, "was saved by a Polish Catholic family. We remember them and other righteous non-Jews. I appeal to the non-Jewish students here to remember these words of Martin Niemöller, a prominent Protestant pastor who spent the last seven years of his life in concentration camps. Pastor Niemöller said, 'First they came for the Socialists, and I did not speak out because I was not a Socialist. Then they came for the Trade Unionists, and I did not speak out because I was not a Trade Unionist. Then they came for the Jews, and I did not speak out because I was not a Jew. Then they came for me—and there was no one left to speak for me.'[83] That's why it is up to you, Black and white, Christian and Jew alike. You help us fight this denial now because no one is immune. Today, they pick on Jews. Tomorrow, on everyone else.

"Look outside," he concluded. "The sun is shining. In Auschwitz, the sun never shined. I wish for you all, young people, God's blessings that the sun should shine on you forever. And even though I get nightmares, I will continue to speak out. Thank you."

A student raised her hand. "Mr. Wilzig, can the feeling of liberation be put into words?"

"Not really," he said. "Two weeks before the liberation, I was down to eighty-eight pounds. I always told myself I would survive, but I admit that during those last few days I felt that I would not live long. Even after liberation, we were surrounded by the dead and dying. It did not penetrate. When you are almost in the other world, and the two people next to you are dead, how do you rejoice? We were numb. We were not alive. It came slowly, when you were in the hospital and you saw the kindness of

an American Army nurse, or when a soldier offered you some chocolate even though it was too rich and you couldn't eat it. The feeling of liberation developed slowly. You got warmer, inside and outside."

Another hand went up. "Mr. Wilzig, could you have become the business success you are now anywhere else in the world?"

"No," Siggi replied emphatically. "Only in America is such a miracle possible. Only America is the land of freedom and opportunity."

Another student raised his hand. "Can something be done to prevent the Holocaust from happening again?"

"I will tell you what can be done," Siggi said. "Speak out against this foul Holocaust denial that's spreading around college campuses. This denier, Mr. Buchanan, for instance, claims he has it on good authority that in Treblinka, one of the worst camps, so many Jews could not have been gassed at the same time. Why? Because he claims science has proven otherwise. What science? He says that there was a coal mine explosion many years ago in West Virginia and documents showed it took forty-five minutes for a small number of people in the tunnels to die. When pressed, 'Where are these documents, and what do they have to do with 800,000 Jews killed at Treblinka?' he finally admitted reading about them in a neo-Nazi German paper. Challenge them. Call them to task for their words. That is the best prevention."

Another student asked, "If you could show anything you wanted to Adolf Hitler if he were alive today, what would you show him? What would you say to him?"

Siggi smiled and said, "Nothing would pain him more than to see the rebirth of the nation of Israel. We survived him, just as we survived the Crusades and the Spanish Inquisition and Stalin and the murderous PLO. I would show him beautiful little Jewish children," perhaps thinking of his two grandsons, Sherry's sons Jonathan and Jesse, "and I wouldn't have to say a thing."

The applause was sustained and heartfelt. Martha Lester, TCNJ's in-house counsel, was present and remembered the crowd as "eerily quiet while he spoke, but the applause afterwards was deafening."

Rich Fracaro, head of facilities at TCNJ, attended the talk. "What I remember about the Kean College speech," Fracaro recalled, "was the way Siggi gave of himself when he told his stories. You could feel the emotion coming out of him. The message was, 'Never forget, and never let anyone else forget.' He told unforgettable stories to drive the point home and had a way of keeping you on the edge of your seat."

"Perpetuating the memory of the Holocaust is a major concern for Wilzig," stated a profile in *Commerce* magazine. "He is dedicated, he says, to informing Americans that such a horror should not be forgotten lest it be repeated."

Over the fireplace in Siggi's office hung a four-foot-by-three-foot engraved marble plaque—a gift from his wife and children, inscribed with his defining creed: FREE MEN WHO FORGET THEIR BITTER PAST DO NOT DESERVE A BRIGHT FUTURE.

"My father had little respect for Jews who failed to speak about the Holocaust, regardless of whether they were survivors," commented son Alan. "I remember once an Israeli diamond dealer came to see him. This man was looking to get into real estate and needed bank financing. While waiting to see my father, he looked at the plaque over the fireplace and said to me, '*Pshah!* There's no great accomplishment in remembering terrible things. The challenge is to overcome and forget.'

"I got up, walked into the next room where my dad was finishing another meeting, and told him what the guy had said. My father walked into the waiting room and told the man, 'Good luck with your project,' and walked out. That was the end of it."

The Never-Ending War

"Siggi B. Wilzig . . . in the past two decades single-handedly has propelled the bank from $180 million in assets to more than $2.2 billion," declared *New Jersey Business* magazine, "all from internal growth. [TCNJ] is the state's most liquid bank.[84] It has just turned in record earnings for the ninth consecutive year, unmatched by any major bank in the state. It has recorded extremely high capital ratios and has been called the 'healthiest bank' in the state."[85]

On Siggi's watch, the value of the bank's stock rose from $10 a share in 1983 to the equivalent, after accounting for stock splits, of $150 a share in 1992. By the fall of 1992, Siggi had opened forty branches in eight counties. "The plan," he told *Commerce* magazine in October, "is that all branches will be no more than one hour's drive from the Trust Company's headquarters in Jersey City, a distance that permits senior bank officers to respond to a customer promptly. We can stop at their place of business and analyze their needs on the spot."

Siggi had relocated Wilshire's offices to the bank's headquarters on Journal Square, allowing him—now officially Wilshire's "senior consultant"—to call his daughter Sherry into his office on a moment's notice.

Sherry's business relationship with Siggi was strongest among his three children but at times also the hardest. When in a good mood, Siggi showed her the respect of a full-fledged colleague. At other times he was not above criticizing her for failing to get a manicure. Still, Siggi and Sherry made a good team, and Siggi orchestrated Wilshire's purchases and sales through his daughter as though nothing had changed—nothing other than his daughter's hopes for a life of her own.

Ten years before, in 1981, when Siggi had brought in his twenty-three-year-old daughter to be trained as the future head of Wilshire, Sherry proved herself more than qualified to handle the job to Siggi's satisfaction. She excelled as an administrator and was content as her father's surrogate at Wilshire. Still, there were times when she bridled at how completely Siggi dominated her choices in life, going back to college days. In her teens, she had looked forward with excitement to entering the University of Pennsylvania (U of P) in West Philadelphia, where she had been accepted into the honors program. Siggi shook his head and told her Penn was located in a high-crime district where rapes were frequently reported in the press and that she would attend Brown University in the safer city of Providence, Rhode Island.

"But both my brothers went to U of P," she argued. "Why not me?"

"Because *they're* not the ones who are going to get gang-raped," Siggi said. "End of story."

The topic of where Sherry would attend college came up one evening at a "family discussion," which everyone knew was a euphemism for Siggi tearing one of them apart in front of the others. The argument simmered for more than an hour until it risked boiling over.

"But this is important to me," Sherry insisted. "You're not listening to me. Why can't I—" Siggi's face went hard.

"*I don't listen to you?!*" he yelled. "How dare you say such a thing! Take that back. I always listen to you. *YOU'RE QUESTIONING ME LIKE THE GESTAPO!*"

He picked up a vase as if ready to smash it on the floor, terrifying everyone in the room. No one had ever witnessed him carry out an act of violence toward anyone, and it was precisely because Siggi was not a violent person that the gesture was so frightening. Seeing his effect on them, Siggi put down the vase.

"No one who hasn't grown up in [a survivor] household can conceive it," wrote Melvin Bukiet, son of Siggi's survivor friend Joe Bukiet. "Other kids' parents loved them but never gazed at their offspring as miracles in the flesh. . . . So, what do you do with this cosmic responsibility? . . . How could you rebel against these people who endured such loss? Compared to them, what did you have to complain about?"[86]

Sherry had read books that analyzed what Holocaust survivors did to their children, and intellectually she understood where such behavior originated. In 1979, second-generation author Helen Epstein had published her seminal work *Children of the Holocaust*,[87] which included interviews with survivor parents who admitted to expecting only the worst from life and who were consequently overprotective of their children. Siggi did not expect the worst from life, indeed he was an optimist; but he was no exception to being overprotective of his children, and, being Siggi, he was superbly overprotective. Sherry recalled a time during her college years when she left TCNJ's Journal Square headquarters to do some clothes shopping, promising her father she would be back by a certain time. When the hour came and went, Siggi panicked. He ended a board meeting early and sent the directors out to find her. Bank guards along with city and county police with walkie-talkies combed nearby clothing stores, knocking on dressing room doors and asking, "Are you Sherry Wilzig?"

Sherry knew her father jumped to worst-case scenarios as a consequence of what he had seen in Auschwitz, but an intellectual grasp of her father's obsessions did little to resolve her emotional ambivalence over them. She loved him without reservation, yet his extremes were damag-

ing. *You're questioning me like the Gestapo*—how does an utterly devoted daughter live with that?

Still, she was entitled to a life of her own, she was smart and independent and, like her father, possessed sharp analytical skills. From the start, she argued with him strenuously that she would not agree to merely function as his mouthpiece, and Siggi's legal team, led by some of the finest lawyers in the country, would often tell him to listen to her advice. That wasn't easy for a man raised with an old-world notion of where women belonged and how they should behave, but he knew how to listen to people he respected, and after arguing with her he frequently agreed with her recommendations.

Even more important for someone who distrusted almost everyone, Siggi knew he could count on Sherry's loyalty. She represented something new to him: a woman no less aggressive than a man, but one who loved her father and would do anything for him. Still, he was not above manipulating her into doing his bidding.

"There came a time," Sherry described, "when Wilshire was developing a real estate portfolio. As a result, TCNJ sold many of its properties to Wilshire. It was a good move for Wilshire but, as a responsible CEO, I wanted to perform due diligence, send in inspectors and do other basic stuff anyone does before buying property. Who buys a building without knowing if it's structurally sound? My father had no tolerance for that. I was to do what he told me to do because he told me to do it. I'm the chair and CEO of a publicly traded company, and he's forcing me to take risks for which I could have faced serious consequences. I had to stand my ground, which is why we ended up fighting so often."

Ivan reflected on how his father singled Sherry out for his most biting criticism. "Here was this super-intelligent woman confronting our father's European prejudices and telling him to his face that she found his double standards hypocritical and condescending. And they were."

If yelling didn't get Sherry to sign whatever papers he wanted signed, Siggi would put one hand on his heart, hold out the papers with the other, and say, "I'm having chest pains. Sign these," and his

daughter would oblige. How could she do otherwise, knowing all he had gone through?

"I loved the man and still miss him every day," Sherry said, "but I carry some painful memories."

Siggi B. Wilzig's business success reached a new height when he recommended to the Wilshire board that they begin acquiring shares of Jacobs Engineering Group, a giant West Coast engineering and construction company with major government contracts for power plants, bridges, tunnels, dams, and buildings.

"If you look back at Wilshire," said Sullivan and Cromwell attorney B. J. Douek, "its primary asset was its huge stake in Jacobs Engineering. The company was doing extremely well, and Siggi saw the sense in purchasing more and more stock in Jacobs and holding onto it."

"My father nicknamed himself 'eagle-eye,'" Alan Wilzig described, "because he never missed a thing, particularly details in financial reports. He looked at the Jacobs reports and said to himself, 'How is it that last year this company showed revenues of only $1.5 billion when they are sitting on contracts worth $5.4 billion? Hydroelectric dams and other giant projects—they seem to be writing more business than they can handle. They're housed in facilities worth $100 million, their operations are more sophisticated than those of most engineering companies in the world—and yet look at all these backlogged projects. Something's going on. They're never quite catching up with their pipeline.' My father realized that the company was suppressing the value of its stock. But why? Then he saw what was going on. Having gone public in the 1970s, Joseph Jacobs was positioning himself to take the company private. So, my father decided to give old man Jacobs a run for his money."

Joseph J. Jacobs (1916–2004) was the son of a Lebanese immigrant and rose to become a legend in his industry. After earning a doctorate in

chemical engineering, he moved to California and in 1947 founded a one-man consulting company. By 1983, the year Siggi became aware of who he was, Jacobs was heading up Jacobs Engineering, a multibillion-dollar Fortune 500 company trading on the New York Stock Exchange. That was also the year President Reagan presented Joseph Jacobs with the Hoover Medal for civic and humanitarian achievement. In the distinguished founder of Jacobs Engineering, Siggi perceived a man of honor and accomplishment—in other words, a man like himself. He also recognized that Jacobs was sharp and shrewd and on further investigation discovered that he had tendered an offer to buy any available stock in his own company for its original public offering price of $7 per share.

"My father questioned why stock in a company showing so much activity would sell so cheaply, so he read every financial report," Alan Wilzig recalled. "Not only the reports but every footnote in every report. Nothing got past him, and he figured out what this fox Jacobs was up to."

"He's doing exactly what I would do if I was him," Siggi told his son. "He's managing things so that the stock appears worthless. Look at this opinion letter he got from a lousy investment bank. He's trying to fool people into believing the company stock isn't worth owning. But I know that stock is worth $17 a share if it's worth a penny. Jacobs is trying to pull a fast one on investors. Well, it's going to be our plum to share. I see the money sitting on the table as clearly as Jacobs does."

Siggi started buying every share that came on the market, outbidding the company's founder by a few pennies. Jacobs's directors monitored fluctuations in their company's market position and discovered that someone named Siggi B. Wilzig had been buying aggressively. They also found out that Wilzig had a reputation for taking over vulnerable companies. The Jacobs directors decided the time had come to meet this Wilzig and assess how big a threat he represented.

The flight to Pasadena, like all flights for Siggi, was excruciating. Six hours in the air felt like an eternity. Siggi arrived in Pasadena, took a

taxi to Jacobs' headquarters, and the meeting went more or less as he had anticipated.

"I'm trying to buy my company," Joseph Jacobs explained, "and you're buying every share that comes on the market."

"And we both know why," Siggi said. "Your stock is selling at seven dollars a share when it's worth a lot more than that. I'll buy every share I can get, even if I have to pay a premium." Then, as though thinking of it just then for the first time, he added, "Maybe I'll make my own tender offer."

In March 1987, the Jacobs directors attempted to pacify him with a seat on the board. Siggi settled for two seats and gave the second one to TCNJ director Larry Codey. While it may have been prestigious to have two seats on the board of one of the world's biggest engineering companies, it nonetheless restricted Siggi's ability to buy or sell Jacobs stock. Eventually, Siggi resigned as a director of Jacobs Engineering, and since he was no longer an insider privy to confidential information about the company's activities, he could legally pursue what appeared to be a hostile takeover.

"Dr. Jacobs is an extraordinary man who built a first-rate engineering company," Siggi told a reporter, "but there is a time when action should be taken. . . . The man is seventy-six years old. He should get his house in order." Joseph Jacobs did not take the slight well.

"The company is doing damn well," he said. "[Wilzig's] view is to make money on his stock, and our view is to make the company bigger."

"For the right price," Siggi countered, "Dr. Jacobs would be happy to sell his shares just like we would."[88]

In reality Siggi had no interest in a California-based company, so far from his East Coast office, and even less interest in the politics of government contracts. What he wanted, and succeeded in doing, was to give the impression that he was interested in taking over the company, sufficient to intimidate the Jacobs board into making him an above-market or premium offer for his shares—an action known as greenmailing: the purchasing of enough shares in a company to challenge leadership with

the threat of a hostile takeover, thus forcing the target company to buy the purchased shares back at a premium in order to prevent the takeover. The ruse was a classic Siggi maneuver, making one thing seem like another, controlling events with bravado and grand-scale illusions.

"The Jacobs directors saw themselves under attack by this powerful Jewish businessman," Ivan Wilzig explained, "and asked themselves what would stop him from taking them over, just as he had Wilshire and TCNJ. In the end they were glad to buy back privately whatever shares he hadn't sold on the open market, just to get rid of him."

When Siggi finally sold Wilshire's shares of Jacobs Engineering in the mid-1990s, it turned out he'd been more prescient about their potential value than even he had imagined. In the intervening years, shares in Jacobs skyrocketed from $7 to $17, then to $24, and the sale of Wilshire's two million shares netted Wilshire a hefty $48 million profit.

If students of business were to study Siggi B. Wilzig's business methods, they might conclude that success was commensurate with gall and stress. His gall was legendary, but it came at the price of constant stress. Stress prevented him from ever getting a good night's sleep, and the stress spiked radically whenever he discovered that a close friend with Wilshire or TCNJ stock had been selling their shares without conferring with him first. There weren't many shares traded in either company, and even a small number of shares sold at a low price could depress either company's stock value. A number of friends and customers who owned stock didn't understand that, or why selling their shares would consequently cause Siggi such stress. All they saw was a chance to cash out.

"Why should we wait to make a profit?" they asked.

"Because," Siggi told them, "it was thanks to my hard work that your shares became valuable. If you sell at a cheap price, then the value of everybody's shares goes down. I work my ass off so the stock will go up—*and this is how you repay me?! By selling behind my back?!* Why didn't

you come to me first? Why didn't you tell me you wanted to sell? I would gladly have bought your shares from you myself."

When Siggi purchased stocks, he paid for them using a combination of his own funds and money borrowed from brokers. As long as Wilshire and TCNJ were doing well, his brokers had no problem fronting the money for these purchases. But if too many shareholders of either company sold their shares at a low price, the fluctuation drove the value of the stocks down. The drop in stock value signaled to brokers that the stock they held as collateral was worth less now than when they had originally offered Siggi the line of credit—and that automatically triggered a margin call, a warning that he had to pay down his loans or come up with additional collateral.

"Mr. Wilzig," the conversation went, "we see your stock is only worth 70 percent of what it was worth earlier this week. You know, we're always here for you and we always do whatever we can. But we're getting pressure from upstairs to cover our behinds. Can you pay down your loan by tomorrow?"

"I can't raise cash that fast," Siggi replied. "You have to give me till Thursday."

Most of the time, his brokers agreed to give him the extra time. What choice did they have? If they didn't cooperate, he'd fire them and find another firm, and that meant losing the lucrative commissions they'd been making from him over the years. If anyone could turn a situation around, they knew it was Siggi, so usually they gave him the time he needed to get cash by borrowing from another bank. But the stress of having to come up with money and pay down his loans was overwhelming. As a further consequence of the constant buying of Wilshire and TCNJ stock, Siggi was forever cash poor. Whatever wages, bonuses, or cash dividends he earned, he used to pay down his margin loans or else buy more stock in his two companies.

"Here was this high and mighty CEO of a bank," son Ivan explained, "collecting a huge salary and huge bonuses every year, and no one suspected he was often desperate for cash. That was where some of his migraine

headaches came from, not only from nightmares of Auschwitz but from trying to maintain the stock prices of both of his companies. His fortune was tied up in those stocks. Whenever he learned someone had sold their shares without conferring with him first, sending the price of the stock down, it was like a bull seeing red. You were finished in his eyes."

"A few years before, he had had heart problems and was about to undergo a quintuple bypass operation," Sherry recalled. "On the gurney, he called me close to him, and I was expecting him to say something like, 'Sherry, I love you, thank you for staying with me.' Instead, he motioned for me to bend down so he could whisper in my ear and said, 'Sherry! I want you to buy three hundred shares of Trust Company stock. But you have to do it today! Quick! Before four o'clock when the market closes!'"

"I watched firsthand how neurotic a life my father led," Alan Wilzig described. "If TCNJ stock went down even slightly, it was a calamity for him. I watched him live like that for two decades."

Pressure was something Siggi passed along to everyone around him. "He was always going two hundred miles per hour," remembered his driver, Ehab Zied, "the way he talked, walked, and went from meeting to meeting—and he wanted me to drive that way, too. One time, we were at Kutsher's Hotel and Country Club in upstate New York. It was maybe 2:30 p.m. He got a call. The governor of New Jersey wanted to see him in his office in Trenton. But Siggi had to be there by 5:00 p.m., not later. So, he looked at me and said, 'We can make it. Don't worry about getting stopped. I have my credentials. *Just fly!*' We were doing at least 120 miles per hour the whole way. When we got close to the meeting place, he looked at his watch and said, 'Now you can relax. But don't go less than one hundred.' That was a comfortable speed for him, one hundred miles per hour."

Amid all the pressures in Siggi's life, there was one wonderful piece of news. After years of struggle, the US Holocaust Memorial Museum was

finally ready to open its doors. The issues that divided the council had finally been resolved, members had agreed on the specifics of exhibits, construction had been successfully completed, and on April 22, 1993, a crowd of more than a thousand people filled the wide Eisenhower Plaza in front of the museum for its official opening. It was a rainy day, "Auschwitz weather," Siggi commented to a colleague. "My tears are in that rain coming down."

Siggi sat in the front row of the plaza with other museum council members and savored the moment. His efforts at helping see the museum to completion had included fundraising among New York's prominent Jewish real estate developers, a function facilitated by his own prominence as president of a large bank specializing in real estate finance and development. Now the fruits of that labor were on public display.

Flags of the liberating armed forces waved in a brisk wind as VIP speakers took to the stage, including President Bill Clinton; Chaim Herzog, president of Israel; Harvey Meyerhoff, chairman of the memorial council; and Nobel Peace Prize–winner Elie Wiesel. When the museum opened its doors to the public four days later, the first visitor would be His Holiness the Dalai Lama. By the year 2000, annual attendance would surpass two million.

After opening remarks, people made their way into the museum. The discussions were animated: survivors reconnecting with one another, dignitaries responding to questions from reporters. Siggi turned to the people around him and asked rhetorically, "Do you know which car is the best car in the world?" The crowd went quiet.

"A Mercedes," he said emphatically.

Many of the attendees knew Siggi but had no idea where he was going with this. A survivor, glorifying a German car?

"Yes," Siggi said, nodding. "A Mercedes. *Not once* did a Mercedes vehicle break down delivering Jewish children to the ovens of Auschwitz."

Now he had their attention. The discussion continued as they walked past exhibits. He pointed to a reconstructed barracks.

"I see here a bunk from Auschwitz," he said. "My bunk was half this size. There must have been eight of us in it. To collect the dead people's bread, we kept the dead bodies with us in the bunk—one head here, another head there. There was a law among prisoners. If someone stole an ounce of food from someone else, the prisoners would kill him. It didn't happen often, but if someone went crazy from hunger and began to steal, he couldn't be allowed to live."

The crowd around him grew.

"I live with these memories," he told his audience, "and anything can bring them back. When I look at food today, it reminds me of Auschwitz where there was so little food. When I see a woman with short hair today, it reminds me of Auschwitz where they shaved the women's heads and did so much worse to them. What was done to the women cannot be believed. I saw a woman with her breasts cut off staggering out of Block 10.

"I will tell you something that for some reason never gets discussed," he said. "It was not just the SS who did these cruel and inhuman things. I swear on everything that's holy to me, I saw regular German Army doctors also go into Block 10 where they did these sadistic experiments. I recognized their uniforms. The perpetrators were not just SS but also regular soldiers of the German military. So many were involved. And now consider how the world did nothing. America, England, France— *they knew what was happening!*

"*The Holocaust could have been prevented!*" he said and pointed down the hallway to glass display cases housing original documents from the Nazi era. "Go and see the evidence. See what it says about the Evian Conference."

In the summer of 1938, delegates from thirty-two countries met at Evian, a resort town in southeastern France, to decide what to do about the tens of thousands of Jews seeking places to live outside Nazi Germany. During the nine-day meeting, delegate after delegate rose to express sympathy for the Jews and offer excuse after excuse why they could not allow them into their country.

"When the Evian Conference was going on," Siggi told the crowd that had gathered around him on opening day of the museum, "there were six Gestapo agents in the back of the room in civilian clothes. They gave themselves away because in the middle of the conference they started laughing at all these excuses from the French and other nations for why they could not take in the Jews. The French delegates said, 'We have unemployment. If we take in Jews, they will work for less money and take jobs away from the Christians in our country. Then the Christians will hate the Jews even more, so we are doing the Jews a favor by not taking them in.' That was the logic of the French. The British gave nineteen excuses for why they could only take in a few Jewish children. As for the United States, State Department documents show that Roosevelt told his delegate, Myron C. Taylor, to show sympathy for the Jews but the last word Roosevelt gave him was, 'Don't commit yourself to anything that will change the quota.'"

Siggi argued that, had the refugees in question been anyone else, things would have been different. But because they were Jews, they were condemned to death—something worse than death. The nations of the world condemned Jews to a horror that made death desirable. Siggi described seeing so-called doctors in Auschwitz resection a prisoner's stomach without anesthesia. He gave a graphic description of how an SS officer forced an elderly Jewish man to hold a heavy oak chair over his head. When he could no longer hold the heavy chair and dropped it to the ground, the SS officer beat him to death for disobeying orders. He described prisoners as emaciated as walking skeletons, and lice so thick on their chests it seemed like they were wearing undulating white shirts. He was plagued by memories from which he would never escape, and so much of the horror could have been avoided by a small gesture of compassion from the international community, by the stroke of a pen.

"You have to look at the whole history," he told the museum audience, "but tragically, history in this country is not taught in depth. I'm a proud, flag-waving American with an accent, but I must say this, that our children are not being taught well. They learn a profession but not history.

They can build skyscrapers and bridges, but ask an engineer, 'What can you tell me about Napoleon?' he'll say, 'I ate one for dessert last night.' Young people can learn accounting or law, but first they should get a real education. They should learn from the past."

Ceremonies came to a conclusion, and guests made their way home, moved by the speeches and by the historic achievement that the US Holocaust Memorial Museum represented. For Siggi, the satisfaction in attending the museum's opening was short-lived, as the government's objection to his business empire was taking a new and threatening turn.

Defying Orders

Ever since Wilshire waged its case against the Federal Reserve, examiners from the Federal Deposit Insurance Corporation (FDIC) had been keeping close tabs on TCNJ's banking practices. The FDIC was charged with maintaining the public's trust in American banking, and while TCNJ's practices were not criminal, they skirted the edge of what the FDIC considered normal.

One of the FDIC's main objections was to Siggi's habit of buying AAA-rated government security bonds—billions of dollars' worth—and selling them before their full term. His intuition for when to buy and sell treasury bonds had always earned huge profits for TCNJ. Siggi's son Alan recalled a day in the 1990s when his father arrived late for a bank board meeting and plunked himself down at the head of his mahogany table and announced, "Sorry I'm late. I just made four million dollars on the sale of a hundred million dollars in treasuries."

Examiners deemed buying and selling government treasury bonds before maturity to be "trading," which in their eyes was as grievous as high-stakes gambling. "Trading must also go," they insisted. "You are a commercial bank, not an investment bank. You are not authorized to

trade. Focus instead on core earnings and traditional methods for a commercial bank to earn money, such as commercial loans and commercial mortgages."

FDIC regulators also strongly recommended that TCNJ write off or write down loans that had not been performing. It's not that they were wrong. Banking law required that loans that were not being paid off by the borrower be written off as a loss on the books. Siggi knew those rules. He simply didn't care to follow them. If, in his estimation, a loan would earn out eventually, he held onto it no matter how long it took, and orders by bank examiners to the contrary meant nothing to him.

"The examiners got it wrong," Siggi told his board. "They want me to write off debts. But look at this one, for instance. This isn't a bad loan, it's a good customer who hit a bad season. We're going to get a new appraisal—and besides, I have this customer's personal guarantee. The FDIC doesn't know what they're talking about."

To rein in the bank, FDIC examiners spelled out recommended changes in a Memorandum of Understanding (MOU) and warned that failure to comply would trigger a Cease and Desist Order (C&D). While an MOU was a series of strong recommendations, ignoring a C&D carried serious consequences. These included imposing stringent controls over loan practices and restricting the bank's ability to open new branches. If TCNJ stockholders learned that a C&D had been issued, it could shake their confidence and prompt them to dump their shares; and if customers found out about a C&D, it could trigger a run on the bank, meaning they would withdraw all their money—and that could be life-threatening to TCNJ. In the worst-case scenario, the government could come in, take over the bank, fire anyone they wanted, and run the bank themselves—or sell it.

Besides halting bond trading and writing off non-performing loans, the MOU instructed the bank to hire a new president with an extensive banking résumé. In addition, as a way of assuring that the demands were being met, the MOU insisted that the bank hire an independent consult-

ing firm to supervise the required changes. Siggi refused to let anyone replace him as president, and instead of hiring a consulting firm to be looking over his shoulder every minute, he offered to create an "outside compliance committee" comprising existing directors who did not work as employees of the bank.

FDIC regulators were furious with his refusal to step down as president or hire a consulting firm, and they judged his maneuvers as yet another typical Wilzig runaround.

When regulators with non-Jewish-sounding names came calling to check on progress with the MOU, Siggi let bank directors Don Brenner and Larry Codey deal with them. Better to have the non-Jews on his board and in senior management do the talking. Non-Jewish government bureaucrats, he figured, would be less harsh if dealing with their own kind. All he wanted was for them to leave so he could get back to work.

"He had come out of the camps with an ego twelve miles high," said attorney Joe Steinberg, "and a serious resistance to authority."

Letting gentiles deal with regulators didn't help, and in October 1994, their patience exhausted, the FDIC issued the dreaded Order to Cease and Desist.[89] The Order declared that TCNJ was engaged in "unsound banking practices and had committed violations of law and/or regulations." The bank was consequently ordered to stop all risky lending and collection practices, cease operating with inadequate internal routine and controls, and desist from functioning without qualified management.

Terms of the C&D were very specific and mirrored the terms of the MOU but in more strident language. TCNJ must hire a new president and follow standard accounting procedures. Siggi was to refrain from taking part in hiring or firing lower-level employees, and he was to refrain from personally signing off on smaller loans. Any non-performing loans were to be written down or written off. The bank was to sell its foreclosed properties and halt its bond trading. As well, TCNJ was to submit a writ-

ten plan of implementation for all the FDIC's demands, reevaluate all of the bank's loans and leases, improve earnings, develop a written ethics policy, cease extending additional credit to risky borrowers—the list went on for twenty pages.

According to the requirements of the C&D, Siggi now had no choice but to resign as president of TCNJ. To placate the FDIC's demand for "qualified management," he hired as the bank's new president Fred Moses, a former president of United Jersey Bank. To meet the C&D's requirement for verifiable outside supervision, Siggi was obliged to hire Furash and Company, a Washington, DC–based management agency. For the next two years, TCNJ would pay Furash millions of dollars to sit in loan meetings and oversee how the bank conducted its own business.

"It was like working for the government," Alan Wilzig commented. "Furash had eight to ten consultants taking shifts in the bank. They never left."

Siggi found two of the FDIC's biggest demands—that TCNJ halt bond trading and sell off its foreclosed properties—particularly offensive. He agreed to comply on the bond trading but flatly refused to sell off foreclosed properties and explained why to the bank's board.

"*Government schmucks!*" he yelled. "They've never had to run a business a day in their lives, and they don't know anything about real estate. The business is cyclical. You *expect* prices to go up and down. And *these* properties are less than five miles *from New York City*! They came back in value. *They wanted me to make some twenty-seven-year-old Wall Streeter rich by selling him my properties at a discount, just so he can sit on them and make a 50 percent profit two years later when the property value went up again? I WON'T DO IT!*"

By September 1996, the FDIC determined that nearly all of their demands had been met and lifted the Cease and Desist Order—despite Siggi's refusal to sell off TCNJ's foreclosed properties.

"The irony," recalled Alan Wilzig, "was that the FDIC had offered compelling arguments for the property selloff. They'd spelled out a down-

side to keeping the properties that, in the beginning, even had *me* convinced they were right."

The downside to retaining non-producing properties included taxes, insurance costs, maintenance costs, security costs, and the important time-value of money (cash that could have been reinvested elsewhere). Even if Siggi believed he could sell the properties later for a profit, examiners argued, he wouldn't realize anything on those sales after the carrying costs were factored in.

"What they hadn't taken into consideration," Alan explained, "was that when New York–area properties rebound, they can more than double in value, which would more than offset any carrying costs. And that's what happened. My father held onto the properties long after the C&D was lifted. The value of the properties finally went up, the carrying costs were covered, and TCNJ made millions on properties the FDIC had wanted us to sell. If we had followed their recommendation to sell, the consequences would have been disastrous. We would have depleted our cash reserves, and that would have forced us to raise new capital by issuing new shares—and that would have negatively impacted the underlying value of the bank stock and jeopardized the family's control."

Standing his ground on the properties issue had turned out to be the right thing for Siggi to do. On a subsequent visit to TCNJ, FDIC examiners slapped him on the back and laughed, "It's become quite a line of business for you, holding on to those old properties and then selling them. What are you going to do for an encore, eh, Siggi? Hah!"

The impeccably dressed bank president with a wavy head of hair laughed right along, showed them politely out the door, and turned to take the elevator back to his eleventh-floor office, mumbling under his breath, "*Schmucks.*"

Siggi fumed over having been forced to make so many changes, but these were the rules of banking and he had no choice but to comply. "I don't think there was ever a time when my father truly enjoyed banking for

banking's sake," Alan commented. "He loved making himself and others happy and rich, and banking was almost a necessary evil for doing that. Sometimes he would say, 'I should have had my head examined for picking the most regulated business in the world: state regulations, federal regulations, SEC regulations—what could be more stressful?' He hated taking orders from anyone."

"By the early 2000s," Alex Paul commented, "most of the BHC Act would be repealed and banks would be getting away with much riskier gambles than what Siggi was doing in 1972. He was just ahead of his time."

With the benefit of hindsight, officers of the Federal Reserve and the FDIC would have seen that Siggi's banking practices, while unorthodox, were nonetheless benign. By 2007, non-banking companies would be legally allowed to own banks, and America would witness the tragic consequences of truly malignant behavior inside the nation's financial industry as criminal investment strategies and brazen accounting fraud would force millions of working-class Americans to lose their jobs, their homes, and their retirement funds.

"Siggi had reason to be outraged," commented Dan Kaplan. "After being forced by the Fed to separate from Wilshire, he was on a winning streak with the bank and there was no valid reason for the FDIC to interfere except that they had a problem—not with Siggi making money, but with how he made it. Siggi never asked for clearance in advance. He preferred to make profits any way he could and then face the consequences later."

Casey Alexander was a special situations analyst for Gilford Securities, whose job included evaluating companies whose shaky performance might scare off other analysts. When introduced to Siggi by mutual friends at Kutsher's Country Club, at first Alexander was skeptical.

"I knew that Siggi had recently been 'sideways' with bank regulators," Alexander remembered, "but he came highly recommended by friends

1975: Siggi B. Wilzig, president, chairman of the board, and CEO of the Trust Company of New Jersey and Wilshire Oil Company of Texas.

June 29, 1975: More than eight hundred guests assembled in the grand ballroom of New York's Waldorf Astoria to attend the State of Israel Tribute Dinner for Siggi Wilzig, who was awarded the Prime Minister's Medal. That evening's dinner proved to be a fundraising milestone for Israel Bonds.

In 1977, along with his appointment to the US Holocaust Memorial Museum Council came an invitation to dine with President and First Lady Carter at the White House. From left to right: Siggi, First Lady Rosalynn Carter, President Jimmy Carter, and Naomi Wilzig.

Siggi in discussion with Vice President Walter Mondale.

In 1977, Speaker of the House of Representatives Tip O'Neill swears in Siggi as a founding member of the USHMM Council. Behind him is Council Chairman Elie Wiesel.

In April 1981, Siggi lights candles in a White House ceremony commemorating Holocaust Remembrance Day as Elie Wiesel (second from right), President Reagan (far right), Senator Ted Kennedy (third from left), and others look on.

Siggi holds a Nazi flag from Dachau concentration camp, part of a permanent exhibit in the US Holocaust Memorial Museum.

As a leader of New Jersey's Jewish community, Siggi was invited to meet President George H. W. Bush in 1990.

In 1996, Siggi and daughter Sherry meet with President Clinton.

Renowned comedian Jackie Mason joins Siggi for his seventieth birthday in 1996.

Siggi celebrates during the Solomon Schechter School's dinner held in his honor in 1996.

From left to right: Siggi, eldest son Ivan, daughter Sherry, and youngest child Alan.
Seated are wife Naomi and Sherry's two sons, Jesse and Jonathan.

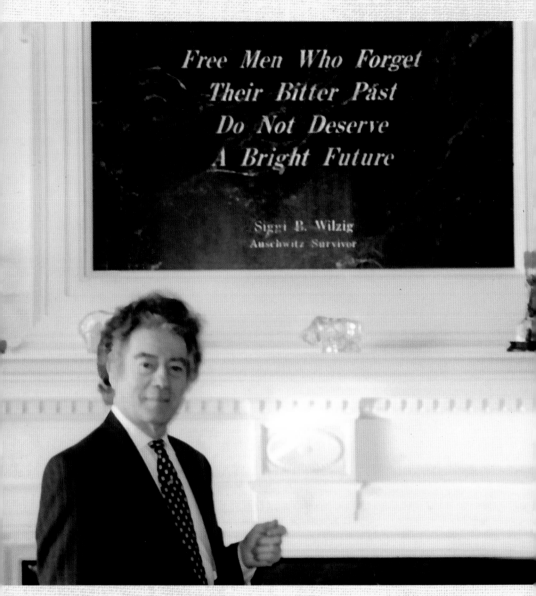

Siggi stands in his office at the bank, beneath a marble plaque displaying his motto for life.

at Kutsher's, so I went to meet him with an open mind. Normally at such first meetings, you spend maybe an hour with some senior executive. Siggi met me in person and we must have spent four hours talking, just the two of us. Naturally, he told me about his Holocaust background, and the impression after those four hours was that this guy's history was bigger than mine. He had such enthusiasm for life and accomplishment that you had to take him seriously. My conclusion was that this man would be extremely loyal to shareholders and borrowers. Listening to his side of the argument, I become convinced the bank had a high likelihood of success, and my firm agreed to recommend the stock as a good buy. I also told the press that I believed TCNJ was an attractive takeover target."[90]

His headaches with the FDIC finally resolved, Siggi turned his attention to more important matters. In particular, the time had come for his children to move up in the family business.

Tough Love

Alan Wilzig, born March 20, 1965, would grow up to be an outgoing, athletic, sharp-witted charmer with rugged good looks and a penchant for fast cars and beautiful women. In childhood, his older brother, Ivan, and sister, Sherry, often spent Saturdays with friends, and Alan relished having his father's undivided attention. Siggi gave him an old briefcase to play with, and Alan puzzled over the annual reports and press releases he found in it.

Occasionally, Siggi put Alan on his lap and read to him from the *Wall Street Journal*. Siggi's office manager, Lisa Roach, remembered Alan imitating his father's gestures and mannerisms, moistening his finger with his tongue before turning the pages of the newspaper, preparing to follow in his father's footsteps.

On Saturday morning, Siggi shed his suit and tie, put on white tennis shorts and an undershirt, and collapsed on a couch in front of the television. Alan knew the ritual well and joined his father to watch Mutual of Omaha's *Wild Kingdom* or a documentary that compensated somewhat for the education Siggi never had. "I may be president of an oil and gas

company, and I may be chairman of a bank," he admitted to Alan, "but I can't tell you what keeps my watch ticking."

When Alan was ready for college, at Siggi's insistence he attended the University of Pennsylvania's Wharton School, and Alan graduated with a bachelor of science degree in economics. Established in 1881, Wharton was considered the best business school in the world. Siggi, for whom the appearance of success was as important as success itself, insisted that Alan attend for the bragging rights: a bachelor's degree from Wharton carried as much prestige as a master's degree from any other business school, with the exception of maybe an MBA from Harvard.

"When someone asks where you went to school," Siggi told Alan, "and you say Wharton, they won't ask you anything else."

After graduating, Alan started work in TCNJ's facilities department, where he was responsible for seeing that snow-covered streets outside bank branches were shoveled, pigeons impeded from landing on the parapets of the roofs, and basements kept free of rats. Siggi had no intention of denying his son more prestigious positions in the bank, but those would come later, after Alan had mastered the requisite skills. Siggi told his son that starting at the bottom would earn respect from veteran employees, some of whom had been with the bank since before Alan was born.

Alan's next post was head of customer relations. "Customers won't know you're only in your twenties," Siggi said. "All you have to do is listen to their complaints and make them feel better so they'll keep doing business with us." Alan appreciated the strategy: disgruntled customers got to yell at the bank president's son.

Each of Alan's promotions came with an upgrade in automobile. First, he traded in his old Camaro for a newer model, then a Corvette. For his next promotion, Alan cashed in his savings bonds, emptied his bank account, and bought a bright yellow Ferrari. He parked the deluxe car under his father's window, hoping to impress him, and took the elevator to the eleventh floor.

Alan entered his father's office and found Siggi in discussion with Joe Bukiet, a major TCNJ customer and fellow Auschwitz survivor. The two friends were looking out the window and down at the Ferrari, which had drawn a crowd.

Siggi turned to his son. "Take it back!" he demanded.

"I'm not going to take it back," Alan said.

Siggi shook his head. "This is a terrible mistake, grabbing the brass ring so early. What are you going to do for an encore? Where will you find motivation to succeed in life if you have nothing to look forward to? What will you drive when you are forty if you have a Ferrari now, in your twenties?"

Alan left the office, dejected but realizing his father had a point. Halfway down the hallway, he remembered a business question he had forgotten to ask amid the scolding. He returned to his father's office and put his ear to the door. He could hear him laughing with Joe Bukiet like two schoolkids.

"Can you believe how crazy life is?" Siggi was saying. "Fifty years ago, we were worrying how we would die: by starvation or in the gas chamber. Today, my biggest problem is having to explain to young Prince Alan why buying a Ferrari at such a young age is a bad idea. Can you believe this?"

Dictating his children's choices in life was Siggi's way of protecting them. Whether it was their choice of cars or romantic partners, their preferences were subject to his approval, and his approval was not to be questioned.

"Father," son Alan once asked him, "why do you bust my chops so mercilessly over every single decision at the bank?"

"Because I'm not going to be around forever," Siggi replied, "and if you can tolerate me over and over, then you will be able to stand up to *anyone* after I'm gone. Never give up. Only death is permanent. Everything else can be fixed."

"For all his business success, my father was surprisingly down-to-earth," commented son Ivan. "He didn't care about designer clothing,

expensive cars, or fancy jewelry, and he didn't judge people by their level of education or what they did for a living—except when it came to his children. When it came to the people we dated, he was a bit of a snob. Without actually saying it in so few words, he made it clear to us that not only did our partners have to be Jewish, but he would prefer that they come from one of the most successful, philanthropic, and prestigious Jewish families in the country, such as the Tisches, Tishmans, or Bronfmans. And why not? In his mind, his three Ivy League–educated children were the offspring of a genius, so why shouldn't they marry the crème de la crème of Jewish high society? He had a saying: 'It's just as easy to fall in love with a rich person as a poor person.'

"My brother and sister and I forgave him for the strict rules he imposed on us," Ivan said, "because we knew he had been traumatized by his past. If we dared to question or disobey, he lashed out in cruel ways such as pretending to withhold his love. A parent's love is supposed to be unconditional, but he'd use this dramatic guilt trip to manipulate us into doing what he wanted. He always loved us, but it didn't always feel that way."

"I was seriously dating a man who was not from a prominent family," Sherry described, "and my father told me to stop seeing him. He said, 'He's not on your intelligence level. He's an idiot compared to you. In the long term it's not gonna work out.'

"When I told my father that this man made me happy," Sherry continued, "he said, 'Happy? What's happy? A dog is happy. You live, you survive, you have responsibilities—who cares about happy?' My happiness seemed irrelevant to him.

"The worst would have been to marry a non-Jew," Sherry said. "If we dared to do that, he would not only disown us, he threatened to literally sit shivah—meaning he would observe the Jewish mourning period. He would consider us dead. What child wants to live with the guilt of having caused a survivor father such suffering?"

Ivan remembered accompanying his father and mother on a business trip to Atlanta, Georgia. Ivan was sixteen at the time. He loved to dance

and told his parents he would be going to the hotel's disco while they had their dinner with business associates.

"No, you won't," Siggi told him. "Promise me you won't leave the hotel room."

"I'm not staying in the hotel room," Ivan snapped. "I'm going out."

"Don't you know," Siggi warned, "that the Ku Klux Klan headquarters are in Cummings, Georgia, less than one hour away from this hotel? Don't you know that two Jewish civil rights workers, Andrew Goodman and Michael Schwerner, were murdered in Mississippi—not that far away—in 1964? I'm not going to come home and find that you've been kidnapped or murdered. *YOU'RE STAYING IN THE ROOM!*"

And with that, he locked Ivan in his connecting room, put a chair under the doorknob, took Naomi by the hand, and left for dinner.

"He didn't have to lock me in," Ivan commented. "He'd already scared me half to death by telling me that violent antisemites were out there waiting to kill me."

"Do you know how the world sees us?" Siggi asked his sons when they were young. "They see us as the people who killed Jesus. They say the Jews crucified their God."

He pointed to Ivan and said, "They think you brought the wood."

He pointed to Alan and said, "They think you brought the nails."

Then he pointed to himself. "And they think I brought the hammer."

As fearful as Siggi was of antisemites causing physical harm to Jews, he was just as fearful of Jews causing harm to themselves by intermarrying. If any of his children dared to marry outside the faith it would not merely be a personal disappointment for him but a betrayal of every victim of the Holocaust.

"If you ever marry a *shiksa*"—meaning a non-Jew woman—"everything I lived for," Siggi would tell his sons, "everything I fought for and everything good I have accomplished in my life will have been for nothing and meant nothing. I might as well have died in Auschwitz."

"He said those words to me when I was thirteen," Ivan said fifty years later, "and I'm still terrified of falling in love with a non-Jewish woman,

of breaking my father's heart and losing his love. And he's been dead a long time."

Despite the severity of Siggi's position on marriage outside the Jewish faith, his love for his children was limitless. When they were younger, each night before they went to sleep Siggi sat on the edge of their beds and kissed them three times. "I kiss you one time," he told them, "because you are my child. I kiss you a second time because I love you. And I kiss you a third time for the million and a half Jewish children who were murdered and never had a chance to be kissed again."

Cold weather revived dark memories for him of Jews who died from pneumonia on the death march from Auschwitz to Mauthausen, and out of love he could be overprotective of his children if the weather turned even slightly chilly. "You'll catch pneumonia," he cautioned Ivan one chilly fall day, and ordered Naomi to bundle their son up in warm socks, a sweatshirt, jacket, gloves, and a beanie hat. Suffocating under layers of winter clothes, young Ivan stood on the corner waiting for his school bus, avoiding the stares of classmates who wore light jackets and looked at him like he was crazy.

Siggi displayed his unending love for his children from morning till night. Ivan remembered him bursting into his children's bedrooms while they were sound asleep and belting out an old German nursery rhyme at the top of his lungs:

"Raus Klaus!"—"Out, Klaus!" he'd yell, calling his three children by a typical German boy's name.

"Aufstehen ruft der Fuchs zum Hasen! Hoerst du nicht die Jaeger blasen!"— "Get up, said the fox to the hare. Don't you hear the hunter's blast?"

Then Siggi would blow an imaginary bugle over and over, "Duh-DA-duh-DA-du-DAAAH! Duh-DA-duh-DA-du-DAAAH! Duh-DA-duh-DA-du-DAAAH!" driving his kids totally crazy.

"He was like an annoying alarm clock that you couldn't turn off," Ivan recalled, laughing, "screaming out this obnoxious military-style reveille.

It was crazy what he would do to wake us up."

Occasionally Siggi even stretched the rules of Orthodox Jewish behavior if it brought his children some joy. When Little League practice fell on weekends, for instance, Siggi walked Ivan three miles to the ballfield from their new home in Clifton, New Jersey, since observant Jews did not drive on the Sabbath. Technically, Ivan should not have been playing baseball on the Sabbath at all, but Siggi would not deny his young son that simple pleasure.

"It's okay to play on the Sabbath now, but when you become an adult," Siggi told his son, "then you must follow the example of the Jewish baseball star Sandy Koufax."

Considered the best pitcher in baseball, Koufax refused to play game one of the 1965 World Series because it fell on Yom Kippur, the holiest day of the year for Jews.

"Now there's an example of someone who respects our traditions," Siggi proudly declared.

Ivan recalled October 16, 1969, when Siggi took him to Shea Stadium for the final game of the World Series. On that day, memorable in the annals of baseball, the "Amazing Mets" prevailed over the Baltimore Orioles to achieve one of the greatest upsets in World Series history. In the eight years of their existence, the Mets had never finished higher than ninth place. When they won that final game, 57,000 fans went berserk, tearing up seats, storming the field, and ripping up bases and sod to take home as souvenirs. Ivan and his father watched the mayhem from box seats on the first base line, immediately behind the Mets dugout. The VIP seats came compliments of Thatcher Brown, whose investment brokerage firm, G. H. Walker and Sons, owned a piece of the Mets and did business with TCNJ. They were the best seats in the stadium for the most important ballgame in Mets history.

But then, nothing Ivan's father ever did was like other people. Before the game began, he stood up and mimicked the food vendors, yelling *"Beer here! Get your ice-cold beer here!"* prompting people around him to

pull out their wallets. Siggi looked at them like they were crazy. "Whaddya looking at me for?" he said. "I didn't say that," kicking Ivan's foot under the chair and sending his son into hysterics.

In 1971 Siggi brought Ivan to a closed-circuit screening of the first Mohammed Ali vs. Joe Frazier world heavyweight championship fight, considered by some to be the greatest fight of the century. Boxing was the one sport that interested Siggi, since dodging another guy's punches was a skill he understood. Still, he loved that his son Ivan played tennis, which Siggi judged to be a sport that required more brains then brawn and wasn't particularly dangerous.

Notwithstanding the rough patches his children endured, Siggi spent as much time with them as possible and marveled at how they'd become productive adults. In May 1996, he attended a talk given by Sherry at the Solomon Schechter School in honor of Holocaust survivors and their families. It must have been a moment of great pride for him, seeing his daughter, a mature businesswoman, at the podium. Gone were the days when he used to joke with his high-school-aged daughter about her math homework. Sherry, the most studious of his three children, would be working on a calculus or trigonometry problem and her father would look over her shoulder and say, "Oh, yes, just move that number over there," both of them knowing full well he knew nothing about what he was talking about. Sherry was a straight-A student and Siggi had never gone past grade school. His math skills were as sharp as anyone's but limited to the basics—addition, subtraction, multiplication, and division—and the comic banter created a loving moment between them.

Sherry took the Solomon Schechter event as an occasion to express just how much she admired her father. The school was one of a network of religious day schools named after the rabbi who founded twentieth-century Conservative Judaism. At first, Sherry had been uncertain about sending her children there, since she and her brothers had only attended public school, not a Jewish day school, and she questioned whether her children would fit in. Then she realized that doing so would increase her

children's bond to their Jewish identity. There could be no better gift to offer her father.

"It is now, in my role as a mother," Sherry told the audience, "that my role as daughter of a survivor comes to the forefront. For now, I too must pass the responsibility of bearing witness from generation to generation."

She described the day her young son asked her, "Mommy, why did the Nazis kill Grandpa's parents?" and how lost she felt without a ready answer. She was grateful, she said, that the Schechter education was recreating the rich circle of Jewish family life that the Nazis had destroyed. How sad, she added, that while the number of survivors was diminishing, the number of Holocaust deniers was growing. "It is our duty," she reminded attendees, "to ensure that the world will never forget."

Siggi sat in the audience, mesmerized by her speech. At last one of his children had taken up the banner of Holocaust memory. He had lived to witness this moment, proof that he had fulfilled the promise made in those first frozen weeks in America: to have children, to raise them as good Jews, and ensure that the Holocaust and its victims would never be forgotten. Her speech was, he told Sherry later, the proudest moment of his war-torn, nightmare-filled life.

The next day, Siggi sent his daughter a thank-you gift of an elegant strand of pearls and had several hundred copies of her speech printed. Anyone coming to see him in his office to discuss business had to first read it before he would agree to talk about anything else.

For Siggi's seventieth birthday, Ivan proposed to his mother and siblings that they get front-row seats to the opening night of Jackie Mason's one-man Broadway show *Love Thy Neighbor*. Siggi adored the sixty-five-year-old Jewish comedian and his brazen social and political parodies— "a fiesta of defamation," as the *New York Times* once described his performances.[91] Mason slurred every imaginable group, most often Jews ("I

went to a reformed service the other day, it was so reformed the rabbi was a gentile") and Italians.

Siggi delighted in Mason's outspoken politics, no matter how controversial. Mason slashed at humanity's follies, earning him the sobriquet "equal opportunity offender" as well as an honorary degree from the Oxford University Debating Society, an honor previously bestowed on only three individuals: Mahatma Gandhi, John F. Kennedy, and Jimmy Carter. Siggi was so enamored of Jackie Mason that he took time out of board of directors meetings to repeat his latest jokes.

"The directors were important businessmen who had gone out of their way to attend these meetings," Ivan said, "and here's my father spending twenty minutes doing Jackie Mason routines." Hardly a day went by that Siggi didn't entertain someone in his office by imitating Mason's gestures and vocal intonations or paraphrasing his latest witticisms.

Ivan made some calls and eventually managed to find someone with connections to the renowned comic.

On opening night, the Wilzigs sat in the front row of the Booth Theatre alongside New York Mayor Rudy Giuliani and other VIPs. Mason was in fine form, riffing on different ethnic groups, poking fun at the quirky behavior of Jews and gentiles, offering political commentaries that skewered conservatives and liberals alike, and deconstructing the Starbucks coffee chain with such bravado that quotes from his routine made headlines in the New York press the following day. After opening night's show, Siggi and his family were ushered backstage for a personal meeting with the star, followed by admission to the producer's party at the nearby Marriott Marquis Hotel. Siggi was elated.

"Dad, don't make any plans for tomorrow night either," Ivan told him on the drive home.

"Why not?" Siggi asked. "We already celebrated my birthday."

"You'll see."

The following evening, the Wilzigs drove Siggi to Le Marais, New York's finest kosher steakhouse. As soon as they sat down to order, in walked Jackie Mason. The iconic comedian held out his arms and whooped, "Happy birthday, Siggi!" and over dinner for nearly three hours, Mason and his biggest fan jokingly insulted each other, traded one-liners, and competed to see who could be the funniest Jew at the table.

Determining who would run his empire after he died, on the other hand, was no joking matter. Siggi had ambitious plans for his eldest son, Ivan, whom he'd always wanted to be a doctor, lawyer, or businessman. That would earn him financial security and respect. If Ivan chose the law, Siggi would set him up as the bank's well-paid in-house legal counsel—and that was that. End of discussion.

Ivan graduated from Benjamin N. Cardozo School of Law in New York in 1980. Siggi had a surprise graduation gift waiting for him on the street outside their Clifton home: a metallic gold and black, ten-year anniversary limited-edition Datsun 280ZX. Attached to the rear window of the car was a huge cardboard sign displaying a poem about how wonderful a son Ivan was, ending with MAZEL TOV—Hebrew for congratulations—in big bright letters. The whole car was wrapped with an oversized red ribbon.

After Ivan earned his law degree, Siggi arranged for him to intern at the bank's main law firm in New Jersey, Lowenstein Sandler, to get a sense of what his future role at TCNJ would require of him. Ivan could not bear to disappoint his father, but he truly had no interest in law and failed twice to pass the bar exam, the second time by getting just two multiple-choice questions wrong. Ivan took it as a sign that becoming a licensed lawyer was not meant to be, and he announced that he would not take the exam for a third time. Siggi was furious.

"It was the biggest fight we ever had," Ivan reflected. "Up till then, I'd done everything he asked of me, and I'd agreed thinking maybe some aspect of entertainment law would interest me, but I had no interest at

all in becoming the middleman between rich people suing each other. I went to law school just to make my father happy. After sacrificing two summers in a row cramming for the bar, and giving it my best shot, twice, I was done."

Siggi dismissed the first two exams with a wave of his hand. "It took one of the Kennedy kids three tries before passing the bar," he said, referring to John Kennedy Jr. *"Take it again!* If you quit now, you'll be a quitter all your life!"

"No more," Ivan told him. "I'm done. Passing an exam doesn't make someone smart or happy. I've been interning at Lowenstein Sandler for more than a year and I'm miserable. You want a lawyer in the family? *You* take the bar! Loan documentation? Foreclosures? I'd never enjoy my life doing that."

Ever since attending Broadway musicals as a boy, singing had been Ivan's passion, and he told his father he planned to pursue a career in music—an image Siggi found unbearable and something he tried desperately to make Ivan abandon. At first, Siggi used logical arguments to convince his son to give up such folly.

"You're not from a showbiz family," he said. "You have no connections in the music business. You don't live in Hollywood, so you can't make those connections. Besides, it's a sleazy business and a low-paying career. Your average singer is starving to death, singing on street corners and in parks. On the other hand, your average lawyer is earning $75,000 first year out of law school, enough to support a wife and kids, buy a beautiful home, two cars, and join a fancy country club—and that's your *average* lawyer. You are much smarter than average."

The flattery didn't move Ivan, so Siggi tried bribing him by offering a carrot—many carrots.

"If you agree to put your music interests aside," Siggi said, "I'll buy you a beautiful home. I'll hire you a butler and a maid. You can join any two country clubs you like. You can have any sports car you want. I'll pay you a hefty salary with an unlimited expense account. You'll have your own limo and driver, and you'll be the youngest person in the history of

the 21 Club to have his own table," referring to the legendary New York restaurant, preferred by powerbrokers and celebrities.

"That's all very nice," Ivan said. "I'm not against material things. I love cars and clothes and being treated like a celebrity. But I don't want everything handed to me just because I'm Siggi Wilzig's son. I want to earn people's respect on my own. I never want to look back and regret that I didn't at least try to be a singer. Maybe I'll fail, but I have to give it a shot. Sorry. You can keep all those expensive perks. I want to sing and dance."

"OUT OF THE QUESTION!" Siggi yelled. He had no respect for artists. They were dreamers. Maybe one in a million ever made money. After Ivan rejected his bribes, Siggi tried threats.

"If you refuse to put aside this foolishness, you won't get a penny from me. You'll have no place to sleep. You'll have no money for food or rent. And if you defy me, there will be no bank job waiting for you when you fall on your ass as a singer. *I have no use for an aspiring singer in my bank! If you don't take a job at the bank now, I'M THROUGH WITH YOU.*"

"Don't worry," Naomi told Ivan. "As long as I'm your mother, you'll have a home and a place to eat and sleep."

From the start of their marriage, Naomi had been a traditional wife, obedient and loving, but she would not allow Siggi to intimidate their son with these threats. Ironically, if Siggi's wife and children dared defy him, it was in large measure because he himself had inspired them to never take no for an answer. He never backed away from fighting for what he believed, and neither did they.

His wife's defiance exasperated Siggi, but at this point in their long marriage it was not a surprise: in the past few years they had grown distant. The bigger Siggi became in business, the less attention he paid to Naomi's needs and to enjoying a life together. They never divorced, but eventually theirs became a marriage in name only, with Siggi in the New Jersey spotlight and his wife spending most of her time in Florida without him. Now it was more often Sherry who attended public events with her father. "If anyone asks why your mother isn't here," he told her, "just say

she's taking care of a sick relative." He was still president, chairman, and CEO of a major New Jersey commercial bank, and it would not do to have people speculating about trouble in his marriage. That would be bad for his reputation. Someone might think him less than perfect, less than the genius his customers thought him to be.

For years, Naomi had reconciled herself to life with a man who not only tried to control every aspect of his children's lives as well as her own, but who also suffered from hellish flashbacks and chronic nightmares brought on by seemingly insignificant triggers. For instance, Siggi forbade Naomi from cooking "mixed" foods: no casseroles or other combined dishes that would remind him of the scraps he ate in Auschwitz. Having lived in extreme dirt and filth in the camps, he meticulously washed his hands and cleaned his silverware before eating in a restaurant, scrubbing every surface until the slightest stain disappeared and the cutlery was sufficiently sanitized. Naomi said nothing and never complained about his habits.

She reminded their children not to buy anything that would upset their father. For instance, an innocuous pewter-mug souvenir of their trip to Colonial Williamsburg would remind Siggi of prisoners' cups in Auschwitz and trigger another nightmare. When black leather trench coats became fashionable, Naomi forbade her children from wearing them. They looked too much like the coats worn by the Gestapo.

But now her husband's iron will had led to a stalemate with their son over his career choice. By 1982 Ivan had had enough of the internship at the bank's law firm and quit. To pay his bills while trying to make his way in the music industry, Ivan got a job as a waiter in a New York City restaurant. Siggi could not bear the embarrassing thought of his highly educated son waiting tables. What would he tell people when they asked him what Ivan was doing these days? Neither bribes nor threats had worked with Ivan. Siggi's screaming no longer had the same effect it did when his children were younger. Something more was needed to win Ivan back.

He and Naomi were not speaking much, but he knew how close she was with their son and asked her to broker a deal.

"Your father wants to make you an offer," Naomi told Ivan. "Work at the bank and he'll let you pursue your music. Just do it on the side. No one needs to know where you are but your father. As long as your secretary can get ahold of you in case of emergencies, you can have the best of both worlds."

Ivan had no interest in working even part-time at the bank, but how could he deny a father who had suffered so much? How could he refuse the man who worked obsessively so that his family could live in comfort and who worried constantly about their safety? How could Ivan let this man down? He could not, so he agreed to start working at the bank while continuing to discreetly pursue a musical career. For the next twenty years, he contented himself with whatever creative assignments he could find at TCNJ: designing ads, coming up with marketing ideas, scouting locations for additional branches, planning grand openings, and providing tickets to sporting events and concerts to the bank's biggest customers. Ivan's big coup came when he cut a deal to open forty TCNJ mini-banks in major supermarkets across New Jersey, including Shop Rite, A&P, Pathmark, and Stop & Shop. That impressed Siggi. "The most important event in the bank's history," he told the press.[92]

Years rolled by and Ivan finally admitted to himself that there was no way he could pursue a career in music part-time. He had sacrificed his own dream for his father's dream of seeing him work in the bank. Nonetheless, Ivan still had his sights set on a music career, inspired in part by the Broadway musicals his parents had taken him to see as a child. He remembered vividly the magic of *The Wizard of Oz*, the tension of *West Side Story*, the celebration of *Fiddler on the Roof*, the romance of *Milk and Honey*, the youthful exuberance of the rock musical *Hair*, and the stirring idealism of *Man of La Mancha*. Just maybe, Ivan thought, it wouldn't be too late to pursue his own dream.

———

In the fall of 2000, Siggi looked out from the balcony of his new apartment in Fort Lee, New Jersey, and admired New York City on the other side of the Hudson River. The ultramodern apartment had originally been Ivan's before he moved into a smaller space in New York City. It wasn't Siggi's style, but now that Siggi was seeing less of Naomi and his children had moved into their own places, an apartment with a balcony view of Manhattan was quite sufficient.

Siggi's apartment was on the seventeenth floor of The Plaza, a prestigious New Jersey co-op. Many of the tenants were customers of TCNJ, "and whoever isn't yet," Siggi told himself, "will be soon." He sat down at the kitchen table and put finishing touches on a year-end letter to shareholders. "Without question," he wrote, "2000 was the best year in the history of the Trust Company of New Jersey." As he had done annually for the bank's financial reports over the past thirty years, he detailed TCNJ's many successes: net income up from the year before; new and enhanced products, services, and locations. Siggi had grown his bank from $180 million in assets to more than $4 billion by the year 2000—all without mergers or acquisitions. "We look forward to a successful and profitable future," he concluded and signed his name.

But he had not been feeling well lately, and the kitchen table was littered with prescriptions and receipts for medications to treat dizziness and nausea.

"A few pills and I'll be like new," he told himself.

It was a Thursday, and the next day he would drive to Kutsher's. A nice drive on the parkway would clear his mind. Maybe he would stop at the Quints' home on the way up. Since he first met them at the Saxony Hotel more than thirty years before, Jerry Quint, his wife, Terry, and daughter, Kelly, had become his surrogate family. Now, with Naomi in Florida and the kids off on their own, the Quints were a big slice of whatever social life Siggi had left.

"When Siggi first asked me to join the board," Jerry recalled, "I told him I was a doctor and had nothing to offer. Siggi said, 'We've already got

the Wharton Business School types—they have answers for everything. I need somebody like you who knows how to ask questions.'

"Going into that world of banking and finance was an eye-opener," Quint elaborated. "Everybody who worked for Siggi hemmed and hawed. The way I got along with Siggi was by always telling him the truth."

Jerry Quint was the kind of doctor who was always straightforward with his patients, and so, upon joining TCNJ's board, to Siggi he spoke his mind without hesitation. "I'm probably the only one who ever told Siggi Wilzig to go screw himself. Siggi's reaction was, *'What did you say? You can't say that to me!'* 'Well, I just did.' He had everybody else terrified, but not me."

Siggi and the Quints worked together on various charitable projects. Jerry was a supporter of Winslow, a not-for-profit that arranged for children with disabilities to go horseback riding. Jerry and other sponsors wanted to help build Winslow a better facility. Three banks agreed at first to share the mortgage, but one by one they backed out. Banks rarely financed a nonprofit on their own. Too risky. Siggi and TCNJ came to the rescue, and the bank loaned them all the money they needed. That registered as righteous with the Quints.

Siggi called the Quints. Come over to our place, they suggested, and we'll go out to dinner. The Quints knew what to expect. Siggi would be wearing a suit and tie, and when they were seated he would tell the waiter what everyone wanted to eat. "Chicken all around—but only the dark meat." The Quints loved a good time and always enjoyed their evenings with their autocratic friend, but when Siggi arrived at the Quints' home, Jerry was worried about the way he looked.

"For some time, I'd been on his case to get a checkup," Quint recalled, "but it was obvious he had not done it. He said he was driving to Kutsher's the next day, so I told him to stay with us. Our place was closer to Kutsher's and we had a spare room on the second floor."

During the night, the Quints heard Siggi throwing up. They ran upstairs and found the bathroom covered with blood and Siggi sprawled on the floor. They put him in their car and raced to Jerry's hospital, where X-rays and blood work revealed that stage four advanced multiple myeloma, an incurable blood cancer, had ravaged Siggi's body.

"The first time he learned he had cancer," Sherry said, "he called me and said, 'Baby, I'm a survivor. I'm going to fight and beat this thing. Don't you worry.' He knew he'd die eventually, but he'd escaped death so many times during the Holocaust that he stayed firm in his conviction that he was a survivor and could beat anything. There was a total lack of self-pity throughout every procedure. He used to say that in the camps, those prisoners who thought they would die in a sense were already dead. If you think you will die, it's over. He never did."

He refused to give the doctors' reports any credence. Over the weeks to come, if the numbers on his blood tests happened to show slight improvement, he ignored the rest of the report and announced to his family, "You see? I'm better." Fighting was simply Siggi's way of living, the way some people have brown eyes or some other permanent trait. He had fought Nazis, he had fought the Fed and the FDIC, and now he would fight cancer. It didn't matter which foe attacked him. He would fight back. It had always been that way, taking on battles lesser men would have found impossible, ignoring the pain, enduring whatever treatment was needed so that the real work—remembering the past and building a bright future—could go on.

When his family came to visit at his Fort Lee apartment, Siggi camouflaged his condition behind a neatly coiffed head of hair and words of reassurance. "I appreciate your coming to visit," he told his children, "but now go to the bank and tell them we're looking at acquiring another bank. Say that I have outside meetings and that's why they don't see me much. I don't want anyone thinking I'm sick." Rumors of a sick bank president might undermine the confidence of customers or shareholders in the health of the bank. That was more difficult for Siggi to contemplate than cancer.

He couldn't leave his apartment for long—his bones were too frail—but in early 2001 the bank board said there was an important topic to discuss and they needed him there. He dressed in suit and tie and coiffed his head of wavy hair, which luckily chemotherapy had not taken from him. His driver arrived at 7:00 a.m., eased him gently into the backseat, and drove to Journal Square in Jersey City. The sky was clear. It was a crisp winter day.

"He walked into the bank, dressed to kill," recalled bank officer Bob McCarthy. "He hadn't been around for quite a while, and stories were circulating. But here he was, hair done up perfectly, suit and tie immaculate. He walked through the lobby waving, 'Hi, how are you,' his normal old self. It sent a ripple through the building: The boss is back!"

Siggi rode up the private elevator reserved for the chairman and CEO, entered his expansive boardroom, and once again sat at the head of the twenty-five-foot mahogany table. Already seated were Rodgin Cohen, his legal guru; Ed Davin and Ray Catlaw, two senior bank officers; and Larry Codey, the bank's most prestigious director. Siggi touched his fingertips together as if in prayer and gazed up at the painted fresco ceiling. He already knew what was coming.

"We're appointing Alan the acting president," Codey said. Codey, who had been a TCNJ Director since 1988, was the only one capable of delivering such a pronouncement to Siggi. Codey was the former vice chairman of New Jersey's largest utility company, Public Service Electric and Gas, and had no qualms about being blunt. He got the message out fast and straight. If the bank was going to weather this transition, Siggi needed to step down now and let Alan take over.

Siggi sat silently. As far as he was concerned, the board was taking the cancer too seriously. He was on the road to recovery and would be back at work any day. Did they not understand that he was a natural fighter who knew how to handle such things, how to bob and weave and sidestep sucker punches? On what grounds were they making such a monumental decision? *A blood test?* He hadn't let Nazis slow him down and he wouldn't let cancer do so either. The cancer was irrelevant: the alternate reality was

the operative one. He could deny the reality of his condition because he had become a master of alternate realities.

"The doctors say I'm doing great," he said. "I had a good week."

The board knew better and could not afford to remain passive. The king had to be separated from his kingdom.

"Now is the time, Siggi," Cohen said softly.

Siggi rose and walked out of the conference room to the elevator, passing displays of plaques and awards that decorated the hallway walls: a Key to the City of Jersey City; a Certificate of Merit from the Union of Orthodox Congregations of America; a framed Ellis Island Award, bestowed on immigrants who had made a significant impact on American history; two honorary doctorates, one from Hofstra University School of Law and the other from Benjamin N. Cardozo School of Law, where he was a founder and board member. He rode the elevator down to the lobby and returned to his apartment in Fort Lee. As far as any of the participants at the meeting could recall, Siggi never returned to the bank again.

Back in Fort Lee, Ivan offered his father words of reassurance. "Dad, everybody agreed you have to step down," he said. "You should just concentrate on getting better."

"*Step down? What are you talking about?*" Siggi yelled. "*I'm not going anywhere.* Relinquish control of the bank? Who would take charge?" Then after a moment's reflection, he added, "Maybe you and Alan together. Two heads are better than one."

"Dad," Ivan said, "you can't have two captains running the ship. People want one person in control. Let Alan run the bank. He studied business at Wharton, I didn't. He's the right guy for the job. I'd rather spend this time with you. Everything will be fine. You won't have to worry. You have people on the board you can trust."

Daughter Sherry brought Rodgin Cohen to the Fort Lee apartment. He and Siggi had worked together for thirty years and were friends. Cohen knew how painful this was for him.

"We don't need to make an announcement just yet," Cohen said gently. "It's fine to say you have taken a leave of absence and Alan is in charge.

The message to the public is that Alan has been with the bank since 1987, and things are better than ever."

The family hired a nurse to care for him in his Fort Lee apartment, where he resumed his Monday night card games. If weekly get-togethers like this went on, things had at least the semblance of normalcy. Gin rummy had been Siggi's game of choice for years. He loved the one-on-one competition and the chance to "blitz" his opponents, blocking them from winning even a single hand, and he would *kibbitz*—the Yiddish word for joke—with the loser all week about how completely he had devastated him in the game. Card games became a dependable way of distracting Siggi from his medical condition.

Most other nights Siggi telephoned the Quints to talk about whatever came to mind, rehash memories, discuss items in the news, or comment on a documentary he'd seen on television.

"I'd be on one phone," Jerry recalled, "my wife, Terry, would be on an extension, and we'd talk with Siggi for hours. Even sick, he was the smartest guy I knew. Every time he'd make a statement about history or politics that struck me as wrong, I'd check it out and he was always right. He was also hilarious and saw humor in the strangest things. He could be talking about the Russian Revolution and turn it into a stand-up routine."

Jerry Quint had a pilot's license and flew planes as a hobby. To rally Siggi's spirits, he came up with an unusual idea. He called LaGuardia Airport to say he was on a photoshoot and needed permission to fly over the Palisades, on the Jersey side of the Hudson. Then he borrowed a four-seat helicopter, took off, and headed north over the river. He connected a phone to his headset and called the apartment. Siggi picked up.

"Go out on your balcony!" Quint yelled.

Siggi walked out, looked up, and couldn't believe it—Quint! Up in the air, in a helicopter! Quint dipped the copter left then right, looped around the building, circled, smiled and waved at Siggi from high above his building. Siggi jumped up and down, sick as he was, up and down,

waving his arms, dancing in circles like a ten-year-old—Quint! That *shmuck* who couldn't play cards to save his life. Look at him up there! *That's my air force! What's an army without an air force!* And for a brief moment, the fire burned bright again as Siggi remembered the sensation of waging war against tyrants, soaring high against the odds. Quint! That maniac! *Look at him!*

"We laughed over that one for a long time. He was his old self for a while," Jerry said. "But the current was against him."

CHAPTER 25

To Bear Witness

At Columbia Presbyterian Hospital, doctors first treated Siggi's cancer with thalidomide, a drug that had had success reducing cancer in trials on animals but which in humans sometimes induced vomiting, pulmonary embolisms, and heart failure. The doctors studied his declining numbers and recommended dexamethasone, also called Decadron, which attacked cancer with twenty-five times greater potency than other steroids. Veterinarians used it as an anti-inflammatory when treating horses for bruises, although in humans, the drug could bring on serious side effects: amnesia, confusion, dizziness, nausea, insomnia, and hallucinations. Siggi's doctor friend, Jerry Quint, warned the Wilzigs that resorting to Decadron carried risks. "I get calls from the police," he told them. "They find patients on Decadron walking down highways naked. It makes you insane." Siggi had no choice: he was deteriorating and gave doctors permission to begin the aggressive treatment.

At times, under the drug's influence, Siggi imagined he was not in a New York City hospital but in a concentration camp. He found a pencil and drew maps of the hallways, nursing stations, and laundry chutes. He

memorized routes and noted obstacles between his hospital room and the outside world, then showed the drawings to Sherry, who was always by his side, and whispered that this was how he planned to escape. The memories of Auschwitz were so vivid that he sensed the SS were lurking in closets and peering around the edges of corridors. Sherry recalled that when doctors wanted to position him inside a Magnetic Resonance Imaging (MRI) scanner, he refused, saying it looked like a crematorium.

A nurse wheeled Siggi past a room where children were hooked up to tubes and monitors while they received chemotherapy, and he wept at their plight. A nurse pointed out one of the children. "It's his birthday today," she said. From the pocket of his hospital gown, Siggi pulled out eleven dollars and gave them to the child. All the way back to his room, he moaned over not having had more to give.

Eventually the doctors allowed him to stay at home, since chemotherapy could be administered just as well in his Fort Lee apartment. He was adamant that no one in his building know he was sick. Nurses were obliged to sign confidentiality agreements and arrive in street clothes. Siggi's pain from the cancer was so severe that his nurses provided him with a self-administering morphine drip to get through the night. The morphine had him imagining there were meetings to attend, and each morning he dressed in freshly pressed khaki pants and a button-down shirt, then sat at his dining room table and waited for calls while shouting orders.

"Sherry! Where are you! Get me ready," he would yell. "I have an appointment with car dealers about their loans." Sherry played along. On one occasion he called Ivan to say he would attend a new branch opening and reminded his son to say nothing to anyone about his health. There was no new branch opening, but Ivan also played along.

In 2000, Ivan hired a music producer to help him record a techno high-energy dance version of John Lennon's hit song "Imagine." The recording was released on September 4, 2001, on the Tommy Boy label, ironically

one week before the tragedy of 9/11. Quickly, the record reached the Top 40 on the *Billboard Dance Chart*.

A few weeks later, a German film crew from Channel ProSieben arrived in New York, looking to shoot a documentary that would capture the mood of the city in the aftermath of the collapse of the Twin Towers. Ivan, now known by his stage name Sir Ivan, was prominently featured in the documentary for having recorded his own version of "Imagine," one of the world's most recognizable songs about peace.

A year later, a Japanese film crew called. They had heard Sir Ivan's remake of "Imagine" and wanted to interview him for a documentary exploring how the famous Lennon song had affected the world. The finished film featured archival footage of Yoko Ono and John Lennon, plus performances of "Imagine" by Neil Young, Stevie Wonder, and Sir Ivan. The program aired on NHK, Japan's oldest television network, and was voted by viewers Best Documentary of the Year.

Siggi watched a DVD of the Japanese film with his son in the Fort Lee apartment. The filmmakers had been moved by Ivan's description of his father's history and included photos of Siggi along with archival images of Auschwitz. If Siggi still harbored resentment over his son's interest in music, it was outweighed by seeing Ivan's talent serve as a vehicle for Holocaust memory.

"You inspired me to record a song about a better world," Ivan told his father.

Siggi's nurse, Mary Fahy, was reading the *Billboard* chart that Ivan had handed her.

"You should be proud of your son," she said. "He's in *Billboard*."

"What's *Billboard*?" Siggi asked.

Mary wondered how to convey the importance of the music industry magazine. "*Billboard* is to the music industry what the *Wall Street Journal* is to the banking industry," she said. That registered. Siggi raised his arms toward his son.

"Mazel tov!" he exclaimed. "Ivan, how much was the advance? I'll double it as my gift to you for your success."

If Siggi had not been facing imminent death, his reaction to Ivan's name on the *Billboard* charts might have been more critical, more Siggi-like. *"A waste of time!"* he might have yelled. *"You'll never make any money!"* Those days were gone. Even a small piece of good news was a breath of fresh air, and he bragged about his son's success to everyone who visited him. When anyone asked how Ivan got started as a singer, Siggi took the credit and answered, "Are you kidding? *I was the one who convinced him to take singing lessons!"*

With her father no longer able to travel, Sherry had to chair Wilshire's annual shareholders' meeting on her own. Siggi sent her a note of encouragement. "You're as good as three men," he wrote. When, as head of Wilshire Oil Company, Sherry was invited to ring the opening bell of the American Stock Exchange,[93] Siggi watched her interview on television, as proud as any father could be. He sent her word the next day: "Perfect! Wonderful!"

Siggi had fulfilled his vows to never starve again, to raise healthy productive Jewish children, and to help preserve Holocaust memory. There was still one project unfinished. He had not yet recorded his own experiences for posterity. There were things he had not yet shared, not even with his children, and little time remained for him to add his story to the expanding archives of survivor testimonies.

Holocaust witness testimony began in the fall of 1945 when David Boder, a forty-nine-year-old psychologist, spent two months touring France, Switzerland, Italy, and Germany, making audio recordings with a state-of-the-art tape recorder. This was at a time when tens of thousands of people, liberated from concentration camps but with no place to call home, were living in displaced persons camps across Europe. Boder

recorded 130 interviews with Jewish and non-Jewish survivors, as well as with perpetrators and so-called bystanders who had resided in the proximity of concentration camps.[94]

Other testimony projects followed. In 1979, Israel opened Yad Vashem, to this day the nation's leading Holocaust museum, research, and documentation center. That same year, a grassroots organization began videotaping Holocaust survivors in New Haven, Connecticut. In 1981, the survivors deposited the video collection at Yale University, and the following year, with funding from the Fortunoff jewelry family, Yale inaugurated the Fortunoff Video Archive for Holocaust Testimonies. In 1994, Steven Spielberg founded the Survivors of the Shoah Visual History Foundation, known as the Shoah Foundation. Between 1994 and 1999, the Foundation conducted 51,000 interviews in fifty-six countries and thirty-two languages, eventually becoming the largest repository of Holocaust eyewitness accounts in the world.

For years, Siggi had declined offers from the Shoah Foundation to videotape his memories, claiming he would tell his story in his own way one day in a book. He declined as well because entrusting his memories to such a big archive would mean relinquishing control over his life story. The Shoah Foundation had so many testimonies, he calculated, that his might just sit in storage somewhere, one more survivor's account among tens of thousands waiting for scholars to stumble onto it. Still, with cancer eating away at his life, Siggi's hopes of publishing his memories were rapidly fading.

Ivan wondered whether there might still be time to convince Steven Spielberg to videotape his father's testimony. In the summer of 2001, Ivan read in a Long Island newspaper that Spielberg would be attending a charity fundraiser in East Hampton. By making a two-thousand-dollar donation to the cause, Ivan secured an invitation to the event for his brother Alan and himself, and was prepared to stalk Spielberg all night if necessary to secure an agreement to videotape their father. Ivan and Siggi may have had their share of ups and downs, but their love for one another had never been a question. To get Siggi's memories on tape, preserved for

posterity by the most prestigious Holocaust archive in the world, would be a last good deed, a last gesture of Ivan's devotion to the man who had sacrificed so much for his family's security and comfort.

Ivan and Alan arrived at the Hamptons event and spotted the renowned director in conversation with other attendees. Ivan strode across the backyard with Alan at his side.

"Excuse me, Mr. Spielberg," Ivan said. "Can I speak with you? It's very important. Years ago, people from your organization approached my father about recording his testimony, but my father was a workaholic and passed on the opportunity. Now he's dying from multiple myeloma, and we don't know how long he has to live. You *must* tape him. He's extremely articulate, perhaps one of the most articulate Auschwitz survivors in the world. He lectured at your friend Elie Wiesel's class at Boston University. They served together on the council of the US Holocaust Memorial Museum. Our father came here after Auschwitz with nothing and took over companies in the two most antisemitic industries in America, oil and banking. It would be a tragedy if your foundation did not get his testimony on tape." Ivan had prepared his pitch well.

Spielberg was sympathetic but shook his head. "I'm sorry," he said, "but the interview phase of the project is completed. We're onto phase two, which is cataloging and translating. We're not doing any more interviews."

"That may be the case," Ivan argued, "but you *must* make an exception." Ivan had inherited his father's skill at never taking no for an answer.

"He's not like other survivors," Ivan pleaded, "and you won't regret it. Our family will show our appreciation with a substantial contribution. Please reconsider—and please check out who we are. Our rabbi's son, Shimon, is married to your sister, Nancy . . ." Ivan was not going to leave without getting Spielberg to agree. Guests at the fundraiser looked on curiously.

Spielberg took his time replying. "Occasionally," he said, "we do make exceptions. I'll try to set it up. Give me your card. You'll hear from me."

That was good enough for Ivan, who couldn't wait to tell Siggi.

When Ivan arrived at the Fort Lee apartment and announced that Spielberg had agreed to tape his testimony, Siggi's eyes opened wide and teared up.

"When?" he asked quietly.

"They're going to call us to set it up," Ivan said, "and they will tape for as long as it takes. They know you're getting chemo and that your voice might be . . ."

Siggi took Ivan's hand and planted a kiss on it. "That's terrific, son," he said, beaming with tears of joy for the first time in months. "I love you very much."

"We were finally on the same page," Ivan said of the moment.

From a father who did not often approve of his children's choices in life, Siggi's words were a soothing balm for Ivan, who felt in that moment that every mistake he had ever made in his father's eyes had been forgiven and every disappointment forgotten.

The video crew arrived at the Fort Lee apartment for the first time on August 29, 2002. The young staff introduced themselves and set about positioning lights, tripod, camera, and microphone. Siggi had done his best to prepare for the interview. His hair was freshly washed and styled, and he had dressed in a fine cotton shirt and pressed pants. Yet the aggressive weekly treatments had taken their toll and his speech was slower and his thoughts wandered.

"His body was saturated with cancer and all these powerful drugs," Ivan described. "Nothing was going to save him, but knowing that he was finally going to get his story out did more to keep him alive than any team of doctors or experimental medications. There was no way he would die before he told his story."

"He spent hundreds of hours in treatments," added Sherry, "and he was thoroughly depleted, but he found the strength to tape hour after hour with the interviewers. And he never complained. It says a lot that, no matter how lousy he felt, there was nothing more important than recounting his memories. The more I look back as an adult, the less I understand how anyone could survive what he went through. He lived all his

life as a survivor, and he fought to stay alive long enough to tell his story on camera. Then and only then, he could die as a survivor. That was the crux of his final chapter."

The Shoah Foundation film crew made multiple trips to Fort Lee to complete their videotaping of Siggi's testimony. Between August and November 2002, camera crews taped ten and a half hours of Siggi's testimony at the Fort Lee apartment. The transcripts filled more than three hundred pages, making his one of the longest entries in the Shoah Foundation's archive of 51,000 testimonies. In the final sessions, recorded in October and November 2002, he offered a candid appraisal of his life.

"When people ask me this question," Siggi said, "how did you survive? I leave out a small thing, which isn't really small. Namely, any survivor who has a heart and brains lives with guilt, that they survived and others didn't. My mother was sent straight to the gas chamber, my father was beaten to death, my sister Martha was murdered, my brothers Willie and Martin and Louie were murdered—and here I am, and they're all dead. Why them and not me? It was as if the Almighty had his hand on my shoulders to lead and guide me when I was all alone and in mortal danger.

"I remember everything since I was three and a half years old," he continued. "I can tell you the color of the stripes on my mother's sweater from when I was a little boy. It's good and bad, such a memory, because everything stays with you and you can't shut it off. I remember where we went fishing as boys, but I also remember what the barracks looked like in Auschwitz and the *kapo* with a stick in his hand and everything he did, and that memory is very, very bad. It never goes away."

He reached down and rolled up a leg of his pants. "Look. See? Since the day of my liberation, I wear two pairs of socks. For the past fifty years, I've never left the house without two pairs of socks. That, and a safety pin. Two pairs of socks because in the camps a pair of socks could make the difference between living and dying. The deficiency of the body, the dirt, the filth—from a splinter you would develop rotting flesh. One splinter

from a wooden shoe, and you would die. And why a safety pin? A little pin could save your life in the camps if you needed to hold a piece of cloth as a bandage around your leg, or to keep your pants up.

"How did I remain alive for almost two years in Auschwitz?" he said at the end of one interview session with the Shoah Foundation. "It wasn't by education. I didn't have any. It wasn't brains. I didn't have much of that either. It was the hand of the Almighty."

"I'm going to tell you something that I don't think I ever said," he told the interviewer. "As terrible as it sounds, I don't think I could live without the nightmares. It gives me a very ultrarealistic difference between life and death. It shows me what life is now, particularly as a Jew—and I would never give that up. Never, never, never."

A cold winter wind blew across the Hudson and rattled the bay windows of Siggi's river-view apartment on January 6, 2003. Mary Fahy, his nurse, prepared lunch. She put out placemats and silverware, careful not to disturb the surprise birthday cake he'd purchased for Ivan. Siggi no longer had the strength to go anywhere, and he spent much of his time looking out across the river or sitting in front of the television watching documentaries. Most of his life now was lived in solitude, his epic battles behind him. The calamities and triumphs had become things of the past, fading into memory.

Now, at seventy-six years of age, the most his days had to offer were lunch and an occasional visitor. Naomi still loved him and flew up from Florida to be by his bedside. She knew there was no reviving what no longer existed between them, but the man with whom she had shared so much of her life was dying, and she came to do whatever possible to make him comfortable.

Ivan flew back from a vacation in Miami on learning his father had taken a turn for the worse. It was Ivan's forty-seventh birthday. When he arrived at his father's apartment, he found him sitting at the dining room table. Siggi pointed with glee at the cake with candles and colored sugar swirls and snow-white frosting.

"Happy birthday!" Siggi called out weakly, his thin arms raised in delight.

The nurse lit the candles and with whatever strength he could muster, Siggi sang in a slow trembling voice, *"Happy . . . birthday to you, happy . . . birthday to you, happy . . . bbbb . . . birthday, dear I . . . Ivan, happy birthday to . . . you,"* gesturing as best he could. He ended the song and pointed for his son to blow out the candles, which he did.

Siggi was rushed to the hospital the next morning. He died that night.

Impossible Dreams

Siggi was buried on January 9, 2003, in King Solomon Cemetery, a memorial park owned by Naomi's late father that had served the Jewish community since 1942. Siggi's plot was located next to an obelisk donated by the Jewish Veterans Agency, a ten-foot-tall marble monument commemorating the six million Jews who perished in the Holocaust. Under the monument, sponsors had buried an urn of ashes collected from Auschwitz.

"My father and I were there in the 1970s when the Veterans Agency buried that urn," Sherry recalled. "We watched them dig the hole. He didn't know if any of his parents' ashes were actually in the urn, but he wanted to believe they were. That was the first time I ever saw tears running down my father's face. Now, standing here, I realize he chose a fitting place to be buried, next to the remains of other Auschwitz victims. His life had come full circle."

Announcements of Siggi's death appeared in newspapers, magazines, and Jewish journals nationwide, and the Wilzig family had no way of know-

ing how big the turnout would be for the memorial service they were planning. What they did know was that TCNJ had more than a thousand employees plus tens of thousands of customers and stockholders, and that no synagogue or Jewish funeral home in New Jersey could accommodate such a crowd. Since they could not predict the actual turnout, the Wilzigs had no choice but to lease the massive New Jersey Performing Arts Center (NJPAC) in downtown Newark.

The morning of the memorial service, a line began forming outside the NJPAC doors. By noon, the line was more than a thousand people long and growing.

"I'd never seen anything like it," said family friend Phil Kupperman. "The largest venue in New Jersey was filled to overflowing." An arena of well-wishers had come to offer respect.

When the program began, Ivan, Sherry, and Alan walked up to the stage and looked out onto an auditorium that held nearly three thousand attendees. Alan spoke first, candidly describing the challenges of working for their father. A family business was problematic, he said, since you never knew where to draw the line between personal affection and professional necessity. The challenge became even more complicated, he said, when the CEO was also an Auschwitz survivor.

Sherry spoke next, describing her late father's commitment to philanthropy and pledging to continue in his footsteps.

Then Ivan approached the microphone. *"The third tower has fallen!"* he cried out, his voice loud and strong, the way his father's used to be. "But one day the Trade Towers will be replaced with something even more important and long-lasting, and so, too, will we build something important and long-lasting from my father's death. Holocaust education was his most vital mission: to preserve the memory so that future genocides would never occur. I ask you, instead of sending flowers, please donate to the Shoah Foundation and my family will match it."

Ultimately, $150,000 dollars was donated by attendees, and another $150,000 was donated by the family for a combined donation to the Spielberg organization of $300,000.

———

In the years leading up to Siggi's death, the business of banking had undergone an unprecedented transformation that led to a reduction in the number of small- and mid-sized commercial banks. At the end of 1984 there were 15,084 banking and thrift organizations in the US. By the end of 2003, that number had fallen by nearly 50 percent, due primarily to mergers and acquisitions among the nation's largest financial institutions.[95] The enormous cost of rapidly changing technology was making it harder for small banks to keep up with the bigger banks. In addition, all banks faced pressures from a wider and more diverse range of competitors such as money market funds and life assurance companies. Consumers had more choices than ever for where to put their money, often at higher interest rates than commercial banks.

To compete and survive, America's top banks were attempting to grow bigger as quickly as possible through mergers and acquisitions. As early as 1993, Siggi had sensed that the time was coming to sell TCNJ.[96] He had looked for a buyer but had never found one who would pay a high price, agree to share power with him, and to whom he could entrust his family's fortune.

The TCNJ franchise had become extremely valuable, as all of its nearly one hundred branches were within a one-hour drive of midtown Manhattan and all were in northern New Jersey, with high concentrations of wealth and industry. Now with their father gone, it was finally time for the family to sell. To negotiate the deal, they hired Olivier Sarkozy, global co-head of the Financial Institutions Group at UBS Investment Bank.

In December 2003, the *New York Times* announced that North Fork Bancorporation of Long Island had agreed to acquire TCNJ for $753 million in stock. For anyone who had held onto their TCNJ stock from the time of the spin-off in 1983 until the acquisition of TCNJ by North Fork Bank in 2004, the gains were breathtaking. Adjusting for stock splits, the stock increased in value from $0.63 to $42.22 per share—an increase of 6,755 percent. Thanks to the rare occurrence of the acquiring

bank and the acquired bank's stocks both going up with the announcement of the merger—and staying up during the entire period up to the actual merger—many on Wall Street considered it to be the bank merger of the year.[97]

Siggi had always been the largest shareholder of the bank by far. Less than a year after his death, his estate was consequently worth hundreds of millions of dollars. Not bad for an immigrant who had arrived in America with $240 in his pocket.

EPILOGUE

In 2017, when Siggi's grandson, Jesse, aged thirty-one, arrived to be in-
terviewed for this book, it was startling to meet someone who so closely
resembled photos of Siggi at that age: the same handsome face, chiseled
chin, and shock of dark hair. Jesse had also acquired his grandfather's
devotion to the continuation of Judaism and Holocaust memory: he co-
chaired the University of Pennsylvania Holocaust education committee
and after graduating Wharton School of Business joined the Next Gen-
eration Board of the US Holocaust Memorial Museum. Jesse credited
Siggi for inspiring him to support the Jewish community, marry a deeply
religious Jewish woman, and wear a yarmulke. Jesse and I chuckled that
Siggi must be gazing down, arms outstretched, yelling "Mazel Tov!" loud
enough to be heard by every Jew in America.

When Jesse was born, Siggi organized the *bris*, the ritual circumcision
for Jewish males, and included the unusual step of having his eight-day-
old grandson passed around the room, from one Holocaust survivor in
attendance to another. Elie Wiesel was given the honor of passing the
infant child to Siggi, who acted as *sandak*, the person who holds the

newborn on his knees as the *mohel*, the specially trained rabbi or doctor, performs the act of circumcision.

"That continuity of the generations was what my grandfather lived for," Jesse reflected. "He was convinced that he had survived the Holocaust in order to help secure a future for the Jewish people, and that conviction was implicit in everything he did."

Beginning in the 1990s, Siggi spent every Sunday afternoon with his grandsons. The man who rarely had time for anything outside business let nothing interfere with attending the boys' school events and holiday meals. Almost every Sunday afternoon he arrived punctually at daughter Sherry's house, bearing boxes of chocolates and ready for card games with Jesse and Jonathan.

"On warm days," Jesse described, "he might say something like, 'You know, it was never sunny in Auschwitz.' If it was winter, he'd massage the arthritis in his hands and say, 'It was always bitter cold in Mauthausen.' I think he saw us as his primary audience, so Sundays always meant chocolates, cards, and a Holocaust lecture. I can't help but think I inherited my personality from him. These days, someone will say something, anything, and just like my grandfather I'll take it as my cue to launch into a lecture on the Holocaust."

Sherry's younger son, Jonathan, also shared his grandfather's legacy. He had been named after two young family members killed in the Holocaust, and when he turned thirteen, Sherry provided each guest at the bar mitzvah with a copy of "The Last Butterfly," a poem written by twenty-one-year-old Pavel Friedmann in concentration camp Terezin. Freidmann died two years later in Auschwitz. Other Jewish boys celebrated reaching manhood with sports or Hollywood-movie-themed Bar Mitzvahs. The gift of Pavel's poem conveyed to Jonathan's guests that this was not a typical American bar mitzvah but a recognition of his grandfather's Holocaust past.

Jonathan went on to study computer science and founded a software company that created educational programs for young people with au-

tism. "My father had deep appreciation for Jonathan's kind, compassionate nature," Sherry said. "He looked at him with an expression of awe, which was so different from his usual preoccupation with high grades and success measured in dollars and cents. Maybe it was a reflection of his past, but my father was moved by Jonathan's decency, by his kindness and compassion.

"Siggi would have been incredibly proud of a grandson whose goal in life is to help those in need," she said.

Like his older brother, Jonathan would also marry a Jewish woman, standing under the *chuppah*, the traditional Jewish marriage canopy, and wrapped in Siggi's *talis*, the prayer shawl Siggi had used for more than thirty years.

By 2001, Siggi could no longer travel because of the cancer, and Sherry drove her sons to the Ft. Lee apartment for Sundays with their grandfather. "To see the tears in his eyes when they visited him—the boys were the most important thing in his life," she said. "When he knew they were coming to visit, he'd dress up, pretending for their benefit that he wasn't so sick."

"He put on this whole show for us, wearing a suit and tie which he probably hadn't worn all week," Jesse said. These were precious hours for Siggi, more important than any financial victory or public acclaim.

"There are pictures of us dancing at my bar mitzvah," Jesse said. "He's hugging me and crying, and my brother and I realized he saw us as proof that Judaism would continue, that Jews had a future."

In letters to his grandsons, Siggi referred to them as his "partners" in Holocaust memory and shared experiences from his childhood. In one such letter from October 1997, he described an event that took place on his eighth birthday in 1934. His brother Joseph, two male coworkers, and two young ladies had arrived in Krojanke by train for his birthday party. As they left the station, five Nazi SS men attacked them. They trampled Joseph with their spiked riding boots and beat the others with such force that they ended up in the hospital.

"For me as an eight-year-old," Siggi wrote his grandsons, "that was the beginning of eleven years of suffering to come. But I survived, just to look at the two of you."

During my interview with Jesse, he described having recently attended a wedding reception. Guests from New Jersey regaled him with stories of his grandfather financing Jewish learning centers in Passaic in the 1970s. "The goal for him wasn't lighting candles or preserving historical artifacts," Jesse said. "As much as he talked about the importance of remembering the past, it was a future for the Jewish people that concerned him most, and education played a central role."

Hearing about Jesse and Jonathan's commitment to building a future for the Jewish people, it was evident to me that in his grandchildren Siggi had posthumously achieved his most enduring triumph.

Siggi's final words to Sherry, who held his hand as she sat by his bedside in the hospital just hours before his death, had been "Go home to the children," his thoughts in those last hours focused on what was most important in the world to him. He gave no thought to business any longer, but the future of his grandchildren and the entirety of the Jewish people remained sharp and clear in his mind.

Had he lived to see his legacy transmitted through the generations, Siggi would have celebrated by singing "The Impossible Dream" from the Broadway hit musical *Man of La Mancha*. The song was his favorite, a lyrical summary of the life of the unstoppable Siggi B. Wilzig, the Auschwitz survivor and penniless immigrant who never stopped fighting unbeatable foes or reaching for unreachable stars.

POSTSCRIPT

In the years following the sale of the bank, Ivan continued to pursue his music career and became a *Billboard* Top Ten recording artist. He also created The Peaceman Foundation to help battle post-traumatic stress disorder (PTSD), inspired by his late father's recurring nightmares. "I never escaped Auschwitz," Siggi often told his audiences. "I'm still there."

Sherry became a philanthropist and created the Blue Card's Siggi B. Wilzig Fighting Cancer Together Program, which provides services nationwide to indigent Holocaust survivors with cancer. She also became the first woman to be honored for her philanthropic achievements by the Rabbinical College of America in Morristown, New Jersey.

Alan had an Orthodox wedding; raised two children, Siggi and Winni; became a semi-professional racecar driver; and built his own racetrack, the largest privately held track in the country. He has served as director on numerous charitable boards and as vice chairman of Wilzig Hospital.

Naomi achieved acclaim in her own right as a generous supporter of many worthy charities. She was, among many other achievements, founder and a lifetime member of Hadassah Hospital in Jerusalem, Israel; a member of the Israel Bonds President's Club; and founder of Wilzig

Hospital in Jersey City, NJ. Naomi was a life member and director of the Daughters of Miriam Center for the Aged and served on the board of directors of the Holocaust Memorial of the Greater Miami Jewish Federation. In Miami Beach in 2005, Naomi opened the Wilzig Erotic Art Museum (WEAM), which continues to flourish. She passed away in April 2015.

In honor of their late mother and father, each year the three Wilzig children sponsor the Greater Miami Jewish Federation's annual Holocaust Remembrance Week.

THE BLUE CARD'S SIGGI B. WILZIG FIGHTING CANCER TOGETHER PROGRAM

Studies have shown that Holocaust survivors are three times more likely to suffer from cancer than members of the same age group and are also more likely to die from the disease.

"Imagine how sad and terrifying it must be for elderly Holocaust survivors with cancer," Sherry Wilzig described, "people in their eighties or nineties, poor and alone without family or friends to help them or provide their most basic needs."

The Blue Card is the only organization in the United States with the sole mission of aiding needy Holocaust survivors. Currently, the Blue Card supports more than three thousand Holocaust survivor households in thirty-five states. Sherry established the Blue Card's Siggi B. Wilzig Fighting Cancer Together Program, a critical initiative that offers additional assistance to Holocaust survivors battling cancer, including medical care, funds for co-pays and transportation, clothing, rent subsidies, food, and other basic necessities.

For more information and to make a donation in Siggi's memory, visit www.bluecardfund.org.

ACKNOWLEDGMENTS

Many people helped shape Siggi's story for print: family and friends; former employees and executives; lawyers and stockbrokers, some who knew him from the earliest days in oil and banking; customers and associates; friends from vacations in Miami and holidays at Kutsher's; congregants at synagogues where Siggi was the guest speaker; and a wide community of fans. Collectively, there were more than one hundred interviews conducted for this work.

Adding to these many interviews was a mountain of material from which to draw details of Siggi's journey from Auschwitz to the boardrooms of postwar American business. One day, not long into the initial research, a van pulled up in front of my home on Long Island. The driver, sent by Siggi's son Alan, unloaded three bathtub-size rubber bins filled with newspaper and magazine clippings, photo albums, wartime identity cards, awards, citations, and honorary doctorates from Hofstra University School of Law, where the Siggi B. Wilzig Center for Banking Law—at the time the only such center in the nation—had been established; and the Benjamin N. Cardozo School of Law. The bins contained dozens of plaques and certificates of appreciation from civic and government orga-

nizations, all testifying to his achievements and philanthropy. Some of the older documents, such as birth certificates and identity cards, dated back to the early 1900s.

Writing the biography of a deceased Holocaust survivor poses a challenge. With no opportunity to directly question my subject, I was obliged to rely on explanations offered through the subjective lens of those who knew him. There were ample accounts to verify his many astonishing achievements in business. Eyewitness verification was not available for the first section of the book, which describes Siggi's years in forced labor and concentration camps. These pages are consequently based on his videotaped testimonies and transcripts of speeches. To achieve as accurate a portrait as possible, details were compared with scholarly sources, educators, and websites of the US Holocaust Memorial Museum, Yad Vashem (Israel's preeminent Holocaust museum), and other archives.

Siggi's widow, Naomi (of blessed memory), was most gracious. She sat through several interviews in person and via phone and email and answered my unending questions with honesty and candor.

Sherry Wilzig deserves special mention. First, she spent days wading through stacks of boxes sitting in dusty warehouses, researching the collective history of Wilshire Oil Company of Texas and the Trust Company of New Jersey. Then she spent countless additional hours reviewing every line of the manuscript—several times—to make sure the story accurately reflected Siggi's true noble character. Her relentless attention to detail assured that his story would be told with integrity. Her father's heart is no doubt filled with pride and gratitude for the care, persistence, time, and effort she invested into this project.

Alan Wilzig offered personal and professional insights, without which the story would not have had such full personal detail. My thanks to him as well.

I discovered a kindred spirit in Siggi's niece, Sophie Wilzig, who worked for years compiling a history of the Wilzig family, and I'm indebted to her for her assistance.

For allowing me to interview them, I am grateful to Casey Alexander, Michael Berenbaum, Norman Bickoff, Lenny Boxer, Ira Braun, Michael Bukiet, Rodgin Cohen, Irving Cyzner, Charles Damian, Edward Davin, Herbert Dobrinsky, Milton Donnenberg, B. J. Douek, Libby Ekre, Mary Fahy, Barry Farber, Rich Fracaro, Paul Fried, Kelly Gersh, Batsheva Goldberg, Lisa Goldstein, Bret Harwood, Rabbi Heshie Hirth, Richard Kanter, Dan Kaplan, Shimon and Rivka Katz, Tosca Kempler, Mark Kutsher, Steve Landau, Martha Lester, Robert and Jean Margulies, Erik Mayer, Perry McAnally, Marty Meyerson, Ted Moskowitz, Maria Nocosia, Peter O'Brien, Larry Pantirer, Alex Paul, Eli Pfefferkorn, Terry and Jerry Quint (of blessed memory), Menachem Rosensaft, Dave Rowitt, Dr. Billy Schwartz, Tom Sellaro, Bruce Shoulson, Joe Steinberg, Ernie and Rose Wachtel, Peter Weidhorn, Martin Willschick, Arnie Young, Frank Van Grofski, Irving Watchman, Sharon Wiener, and Ehab Zied. Dozens of other interviewees chose to remain anonymous.

For their editorial expertise and guidance in bringing out the many nuances of Siggi's story, I'm grateful to David Groff, Kyra Ryan, and Dan Gerstein at Gotham Ghostwriters, with special thanks to Susan Leon for her meticulous and insightful analysis of the text. If ever there was a publisher who deserved acknowledgement for dreaming impossible dreams, it is Raoul Goff, the visionary founder of Insight Editions. My heartfelt thanks to him, along with Vanessa Lopez, Jennifer Smith, Michelle Dotter, and Pat Walsh. I'm deeply grateful as well to Alicia Gough for her detailed research and careful cataloging of seven years of material.

For having given the manuscript a close reading, I'm grateful to Martha Lester and Esther Fortunoff-Greene. For his thoughts on free will, which offer a provocative counterpoint to Langer's "choiceless choice" inside the camps, I had the privilege of input from my brother, physicist Brian Greene.

Thanks as well to Professor Herbert Reginbogin, who spent time in Krojanke and Złotów, Poland, researching conditions there in the early part of the twentieth century. His work was facilitated by Zofia Jelonkowa, director of the Muzeum Ziemi Zlotowskiej, and her hus-

band Jerzy Jalonik; Janusz Justyna, editor of the newspaper *Panorama Złotowska*; and translator Alicja Heimann. Professor Reginbogin spoke with many people who remembered the stories about the times prior to World War II, including Dr. Przemysław Matusik, science director at the History Institute of the Adam Mickiewicz's University in Poznan; and Professor Rafal Witkowski, deputy dean of the Faculty of History, Adam Mickiewicz University. His work benefitted as well from the help of historian Joachim Zahrenka and Constanze Krause, assistant to the director of the Preussisches Geheimes Staatsarchiv. Many documents pertaining to the history of Krojanke had been either destroyed at the end of the war or else confiscated by the Russian army and sent to Moscow. Help in finding whatever documentation was currently available came from Dr. Sabine Dumschat of the Bundesarchiv, as well as the staff of the Staatsbibliothek. Dr. Ulrich Baumann, deputy director of the Foundation Memorial to the Murdered Jews of Europe, offered his expertise, as did Dr. Torsten Lorenz and Professor Mathias Niendorf.

Help also came from people in the oil and banking industries. Among them, Dan Kaplan from Ernst & Young and legendary banking lawyer Rodgin Cohen of Sullivan and Cromwell deserve special mention for making themselves available for frequent clarifications on banking practices. Renowned radio celebrity Barry Farber was generous with his remembrances. I'm grateful for input from Bruce Wells, executive director of the American Oil & Gas Historical Society, and Tim Beims, editor of *The American Oil & Gas Reporter*.

For their help in locating documents and contacting museum advisors and staff who knew Siggi, my thanks to Arthur Berger and Jeffrey Carter of the US Holocaust Memorial Museum in Washington, DC. I am indebted to Anna Patton at The Peaceman Foundation for her constant help throughout the production of this book.

Above all others who deserve my thanks and recognition is Ivan Wilzig. It's awkward thanking someone for loving his father as much as Ivan loved Siggi, but only love can explain why he would read every word with such care and every draft with such impeccable attention to detail

dozens of times. Ivan served as more than an editor on this book. He is its heart and soul. The first time I met Ivan, he showed me a box containing six hundred pages of transcripts of Siggi's interviews and talks, many recorded in the 1990s when he was an in-demand speaker for Holocaust memorial gatherings in synagogues and schools. The bulk of Siggi's video testimony was recorded between August and November 2002, ending only a few weeks before he passed away. For the sake of clarity, some liberties were taken in adapting Siggi's English for this book, and some of his memories as recounted here were composited from more than one transcript. Ivan deserved credit for having been integral to this process from its inception.

Finally, let us acknowledge the millions of men, women, and children who perished in the Holocaust and whose stories will never be told. I hope Siggi's story has stimulated in you, as it has in me, challenging insights into "history's darkest hour" and a lasting admiration for Siggi's efforts to assure that the world will never forget.

Chronology of Events in Siggi's Life

1926 Born Krojanke, West Prussia
1936 Family flees to Berlin
1941 Begins forced labor in army-run munitions factory
1943 Deported to Auschwitz
1945 Death march from Auschwitz to Mauthausen
1945 Second death march from factory in Melk back to Mauthausen
1945 Liberated by US Army forces
1946 Begins work for US Counter Intelligence Corps
1947 Arrives in New York on SS *Marine Fletcher*
 Various jobs: shoveling snow, bowtie-manufacturing sweatshop,

gluing leather bags, traveling sales (leather goods, household catalog items)

1953 Marries Naomi Sisselman

1956 Birth of son, Ivan

1958 Birth of daughter, Sherry

1961 Begins purchasing shares of Wilshire Oil and Gas

1962 Meets Sol Diamond, plans takeover of Wilshire Oil and Gas

1964 Siggi and friends have acquired 20 percent of Wilshire

1965 Birth of son, Alan

1965 Wilshire board appoints Siggi president, chairman, and CEO

1966 Wilshire purchases Brooklyn Tire & Oil and Eastern Radio Corps.

1968 Wilshire begins purchasing shares of Trust Company of New Jersey

1969 Wilshire purchases Electrical Supplies Corps.

1969 Wilshire has acquired 25 percent of TCNJ

1970 Wilshire has acquired 50 percent of TCNJ

1971 TCNJ board appoints Siggi chairman and CEO

1972 Federal Reserve announces "regularizing" of holding companies

1973 Wilshire acquires control (87 percent) of TCNJ

1974 Wilshire board appoints Siggi president

1974 Federal Reserve demands that Wilshire divest ownership of TCNJ

1975 State of Israel honors Siggi with the Prime Minister's Medal

1975 West Point invites Siggi to be first survivor to address cadets

1975 Siggi becomes first person to sue the Federal Reserve

1978 Siggi meets Elie Wiesel at dinner, Saxony Hotel, Miami

1979 Speaker of the House Tip O'Neill swears in Siggi as member of the US Holocaust Memorial Museum Council

1979 Siggi and Naomi dine in the White House with President and Mrs. Carter

1981 Wilshire sells Wilshire Electronics for $13 million

1982 Federal Reserve forces Wilshire to divest its banking interests

1982 Siggi takes part in Holocaust Remembrance candle lighting in White House

1983 Siggi positions twenty-three-year-old daughter Sherry as new head of Wilshire

1983 *Forbes* magazine publishes glowing profile of Siggi

1985 Hofstra University awards Siggi honorary doctorate of law

1985 Congressman Frank Guarini enters Siggi into Congressional Record

1985 On Barry Farber's nationwide radio show, Siggi denounces President Reagan's plans to visit SS cemetery Bitburg

1985 Dedication of Liberator's Monument, Liberty State Park, NJ

1992 Troubled by the rise of Holocaust denial, Siggi resumes lecturing (Kean University)

1993 Opening of US Holocaust Memorial Museum

1995 Sale of Wilshire's stock in Jacobs Engineering nets $48 million

1998 Receives Ellis Island Medal of Honor

2000 TCNJ surpasses $4 billion in assets

2001 Siggi is diagnosed with multiple myeloma

2002 Shoah Foundation videotapes Siggi's testimony

2003 Siggi passes away

BIBLIOGRAPHY

Bauer, Yehuda. *The Holocaust in Historical Perspective*. Seattle: University of Washington Press, 1978.

Berenbaum, Michael and Yisrael Gutman, eds. *Anatomy of the Auschwitz Death Camp*. Bloomington, IN: Indiana University Press, 1994.

Bukiet, Melvin, ed. *Nothing Makes You Free*. New York: W. W. Norton & Company, 2002.

Dinnerstein, Leonard. *Antisemitism in America*. New York: Oxford University Press, 1995.

Dochuk, Darren. "Blessed by Oil, Cursed with Crude: God and Black Gold in the American Southwest." *Journal of American History* 99, no. 1 (2012): 51-61.

Epstein, Helen. *Children of the Holocaust*. New York: G. P. Putnam, 1979.

Felzenberg, Alvin S. *Governor Tom Kean: From the New Jersey Statehouse to the 9-11 Commission*. Piscataway, NJ: Rutgers University Press, 2006.

Frankel, Bruce. *What Should I Do with the Rest of My Life? True Stories of Finding Success, Passion and New Meaning in the Second Half of Life.* New York: The Penguin Group, 2010.

Fulbrook, Mary. *A History of Germany 1918—2014: The Divided Nation.* Chichester, West Sussex: Wiley Blackwell, 2015.

Goldschmidt, Hermann Levin. *The Legacy of German Jewry.* New York: Fordham University Press, 2007.

Hakes, Jay. "Introduction: A Decidedly Valuable and Dangerous Fuel." *Journal of American History* 99, no. 1 (2012): 19-23.

Helmreich, William B. *Against All Odds: Holocaust Survivors and the Successful Lives They Made in America.* New Brunswick, NJ: Transaction Publishers, 1996.

Langbein, Hermann. *People in Auschwitz.* Chapel Hill, NC: The University of North Carolina Press, 2004.

Langer, Lawrence. *Using and Abusing the Holocaust.* Bloomington, IN: Indiana University Press, 2006.

Levi, Primo. *The Drowned and the Saved.* New York: Summit Books, 1988.

Linenthal, Edward T. *Preserving Memory: The Struggle to Create America's Holocaust Museum.* New York: Columbia University Press, 1995.

Pfefferkorn, Eli. *The Muselmann at the Water Cooler.* Boston, MA: Academic Studies Press, 2011.

Slavin, Stephen L. and Mary A. Pradt. "Corporate Antisemitism: A Self-Perpetuating Pattern." *Jewish Currents*, February 1979.

Yergin, Daniel. *The Prize: The Epic Quest for Oil, Money & Power.* New York: Simon & Schuster, 1991.

Wiesel, Elie. *And the Sea Is Never Full.* New York: Alfred A. Knopf, 1999.

Wright, William. *The Oil Regions of Pennsylvania.* Charleston, SC: BiblioBazaar, 2008. First published 1865 by Harper & Brothers.

NOTES

1 Known today as Krajenka, Poland.

2 Prisoners in Auschwitz chosen to be murdered were forced to strip naked, locked in the gas chambers, and asphyxiated with Zyklon B gas. After they were killed, prisoner orderlies dragged the corpses out of the gas chambers, cut off the women's hair for use as mattress stuffing, wrenched out any gold teeth from the bodies with pliers, and burned the corpses in pits and crematorium furnaces. Ashes from the burned bodies were used as fertilizer and landfill.

3 Helmreich, 29–31.

4 *Shoah*: the Hebrew word for the Holocaust. Originally founded in 1994, the Steven Spielberg Shoah Foundation was initially known by its full title, Survivors of the Shoah Visual History Foundation, a nonprofit organization dedicated to making audiovisual interviews with survivors and witnesses of the Holocaust. Today, the organization is housed at the University of Southern California and is known as the USC Shoah Foundation.

5 Goldschmidt, 207.

6 Johannes Erwin Eugen Rommel (1891–1944) was a German general and military theorist. Popularly known as the Desert Fox, he served as field marshal in the Wehrmacht of Nazi Germany during World War II.

7 Researchers have calculated that the Nazis established about 42,500 camps and ghettoes between 1933 and 1945, including 30,000 slave labor camps; 1,150 Jewish ghettoes; 980 concentration camps; 1,000 prisoner of war camps; 500 brothels filled with sex slaves; and thousands of other camps used for euthanizing the elderly and infirm (https://www.jewishvirtuallibrary.org/how-many-concentration-camps).

8 Postwar records reveal that of the 1.3 million people taken to Auschwitz, about 400,000 had serial numbers tattooed on their arm. In order to avoid excessively high numbers, in May 1944 the SS authorities introduced new sequences of numbers. This series, prefaced by the letter "A," began with "1" and ended at "20,000." Once the number 20,000 was reached, a new series beginning with "B" was introduced. Siggi's relatively low number 104732 signaled that he had been there a long time. There are stories in his testimony that suggest this earned him a degree of respect from other inmates.

9 Siegbert not only spoke German and Yiddish but also had an ear for languages, and during nearly two years in Auschwitz he learned to communicate in Polish, Russian, Romanian, Greek, and Ladino. In his later years, he conjectured that his language skills may have been the reason he survived.

10 The hatred of guards toward inmates of the concentration camps was fueled by two "facts" of Nazi propaganda. One held that Germans were racially superior to Jews, and that Germans were a "pure" people destined to rule the world. The other held that Jews were not truly human and more like a disease that must be purged from human society. Germans, by these standards, had a moral obligation to take part in the purging. Called by historian Saul Friedlander "redemptive antisemitism," this po-

larizing of humans—Germans at the upper extreme of civilization, Jews at the extreme bottom—and the government-sponsored imperative to eliminate Jews from the world fueled the antipathy and violence against prisoners in the camps. Accelerating the abuse was one further factor. Postwar records confirm that career criminals released from German prisons were given positions of authority in the concentration camps, a power many used to extreme lengths. "Hoess is silent about something that his deputy Hans Aumeier freely admitted in captivity—namely, that in Auschwitz block elders were selected for their positions because of their sadistic temperament. He testified that most of them were career criminals" (Langbein, 144).

11 www.ushmm.org/research/publications/encyclopedia-camps-ghettos.

12 Josef Mengele (1911–1979) was known as the Angel of Death for his deadly human experiments on Auschwitz prisoners and his part in selecting victims to be murdered in the gas chambers. In January 1945, Mengele transferred to the Gross-Rosen concentration camp just ten days before the arrival of the Soviet forces at Auschwitz. After the war, he fled to South America where he evaded capture for the rest of his life.

13 The Nazi regime viewed the extermination of Jews as a top political priority to be achieved at all costs. Still, laborers were needed, and the camp system permitted certain Jews, the *Arbeitsfaehige* (those capable of work), to be temporarily spared from murder in the gas chambers. Yet, even serviceable skills did not exempt Jews from retribution for even a tiny infraction. According to one Auschwitz survivor, author Tadeusz Borowski, there was an inmate functionary named Sepp—"the terror of all roofers"—who would throw inmates from the roof because of a badly hammered-on nail (Langbein, 161).

14 Langbein, 161.

15 Some of Siggi's stories stretch the boundaries of credibility, and research was needed to determine whether or not to include them. There are very few accounts of murder by poisoned potatoes in Auschwitz, and this ac-

count on first consideration didn't make sense. Why would guards not just send the sick prisoners to the gas chamber? Why waste time and potatoes? There is the following statement in *The Holocaust: An Encyclopedia and Document Collection* (Santa Barbara: ABC-CLIO, edited by Paul R. Bartrop and Michael Dickerman, 597): "In the last days before liberation, the Germans poisoned storehouses of potatoes so that many Jews died eating the food, the only food to be found." In *Two Rings: A Story of Love and War* (Philadelphia: Public Affairs, a member of the Perseus Books Group, Millie Werber and Eve Keller, 2012), one of the two authors describes, "One time we were moved to another area of the [Auschwitz] camp. . . . In our new barracks we saw in the middle of the room a barrel filled with boiled potatoes. The women were all excited—food! An unexpected Godsend. . . . Everyone ran to a barrel, reaching in to grab a potato. But then, just after a bite, everyone spit it out, coughing, gnashing [their] teeth. There was something wrong with the potatoes; they were rotten or poisoned in some way." Neither of these accounts described poisoned potatoes distributed inside a prisoner infirmary, but they offered sufficient parallel cases that we allowed Siggi's account to stand.

16 Primo Levi writes that in Auschwitz thirst was even more debilitating than hunger. The water was contaminated with so many impurities that SS staff were instructed not to drink it, a warning which did not apply to prisoners (Levi, 79).

17 By August 1944, Auschwitz I, the main camp, housed about 17,000 prisoners (roughly 10,000 Jews, 4,000 Poles, and 3,000 prisoners from other ethnic groups). This was the location of the SS garrison administration, the commander of the local garrison, and the offices of the Auschwitz I commandant. Auschwitz I also contained offices of the political department and the prisoner labor department, the main supply stores, workshops, and SS companies. Work in these administrative and economic units and companies was the main labor assignment for the prisoners in this camp.

18 Regarding the impossibility for Siegbert to know which truck was the better choice, Langer comments, "Victims [of the concentration camps] were plunged into a crisis of what we might call 'choiceless choice,' where critical decisions did not reflect options between life and death, but between one form of 'abnormal' response and another, both imposed by a situation that was in no way of the victim's own choosing" (Lawrence Langer, "The Dilemma of Choice in the Death Camps," *Centerpoint: The Holocaust* 4, no. 1, [Fall 1980]: 54).

19 Clothes were not often washed, but the SS developed a fear of typhus and periodically called for clothes to be disinfected.

20 Prisoners in the satellite camps were not as isolated from the outside world and frequently came in contact with civilians in their workplaces.

21 In 1939, Kaduk volunteered to serve in the Waffen-SS, and in the spring of 1940, he was transferred to Auschwitz where he became a Roll Call Leader (*Rapportfuehrer*). At the Auschwitz war crimes trials that took place in Frankfurt between 1963–65, former Auschwitz victim Milton Buky testified that he witnessed Kaduk use vicious guard dogs to force prisoners into the gas chambers. "At first it was difficult to watch this," Buky said, "but later I got used to the sight." Buky also testified to seeing Kaduk murder a ten-year-old boy because he was crying. "Kaduk took him by the hand, calmed him down, led him to a ditch, and shot him." A fellow officer described Kaduk as someone for whom "schnapps was everything." Kaduk himself testified that by ten o'clock in the morning, he "was already loaded" (Langbein, 392).

22 An estimated 1.2 million men were homosexuals in Germany in 1928. Between 1933–45, an estimated 100,000 of them were arrested, and of these, some 50,000 officially defined homosexuals were sentenced. Most of these men spent time in regular prisons, and an estimated 5,000 to 15,000 of the total sentenced were incarcerated in concentration camps. How many of these 5,000 to 15,000 "175ers" (borrowed from paragraph 175 of the German criminal code, which made homosexuality a crime) perished in the concentration camps will probably never be known. His-

torical research to date has been very limited. One leading scholar, Rü-diger Lautmann, believes that the death rate for "175ers" in the camps may have been as high as 60 percent (cited in www.ushmm.org/infor-mation/exhibitions/online-exhibitions/special-focus/nazi-persecution-of-homosexuals, accessed October 21, 2020).

23 In the 1990s a woman survivor of Auschwitz described hiding the corpse of her five-year-old child under the straw of her bunk for five weeks, to collect his rations. "We had to behave like animals," she told an interviewer. "There was no other way to behave." (Testimony of Myra L., Fortunoff Video Archive for Holocaust Testimonies, Yale University, testimony mssa.hvt.0299, recorded November 5, 1984.)

24 Not all prisoners shared Siggi's ability to talk about food and "feel like you ate something." Martin S., who was twelve years old in Buchen-wald, described, "I remember the hunger. The wrenching, twisting pain that lived with you on a daily basis. All you could ever think of is to get something to eat. You could never fill your belly. It used to be uppermost in your mind. You used to dream of a feast. Just one day you kept hoping you could get through the day without this twisting pain that you felt. That is an indescribable feeling." (Fortunoff Video Archive for Holo-caust Testimonies, Yale University, testimony mssa.hvt.0330, recorded October 11, 1984.)

25 The late Holocaust scholar Terrence des Pres drew from descriptions given by survivors to portray the consequences of stealing bread in Aus-chwitz. "Hunger tormented us all incessantly and transformed men into irresponsible beasts. Even those who had formerly passed for honorable men stole from their comrades the bits of bread that many had laid by from their evening rations for the next day. . . . We knew that the thieves did not realize the crime they were committing, for hunger had driven them nearly out of their senses. But we knew also that these bits of bread were the life-preserver by which we might keep ourselves afloat until the longed-for moment of freedom. And when we caught a bread thief, we punished him so severely that he lost his taste for stealing." (*The Survi-*

vor: An Anatomy of Life in the Death Camps [New York: Oxford University Press, 1976], 140–41).

26 By May 1944, Auschwitz and the rail lines that led to it from Hungary were within striking range of Allied bombers. That same month, Rabbi Michael Weissmandel and Mrs. Gisi Fleischmann, leaders of the Slovak Jewish underground, smuggled a letter out of Slovakia describing deportations and the fate of deportees and pleading to the outside world to "bombard the death halls in Auschwitz." Others such as Jacob Rosenheim of the New York office of the Agudath Israel World Organization appealed as well. When their pleas reached the War Refugee Board, the board proposed to Assistant Secretary of War John J. McCloy that the War Department instruct war theater commanders to do whatever possible to support rescue efforts. McCloy jotted his reply on their dispatch: "I am very chary of getting the Army involved in this while the war is on." The War Department subsequently turned down all proposals to bomb Auschwitz and the rail lines leading to it, claiming such proposals were "impracticable" because they required the "diversion of considerable air support essential to the success of our forces now engaged in decisive operations elsewhere." This proved false. For a detailed explanation of the failure of the Allies to destroy Auschwitz, see Gutman and Berenbaum, 567–87.

27 Gutman and Berenbaum, 32.

28 According to the USHMM encyclopedia, in January 1944, a Mauthausen subcamp was established in the abandoned Wehrmacht Freiherr-von-Birago pioneer barracks in the lower Austrian city of Melk about sixty-two miles east of Linz. Altogether there were 14,390 prisoners from at least twenty-six countries held in Melk. Around 30 percent of the prisoners in Melk were Jews (https://encyclopedia.ushmm.org/content/en/article/melk-1, accessed March 22, 2020).

29 According to the Mauthausen Memorial Organization archives, "Mr. Wilzig was committed to concentration camp Mauthausen on January 25, 1945 (Sign. AMM/Y36b), where he was deported to after the evacu-

ation of Auschwitz concentration camp. According to the documents in our collection, Mr. Wilzig was transferred to 'WS' (abbreviation for the subcamp Wien Saurerwerke). The subcamp Saurerwerke was closed on April 2, 1945, and its prisoners were evacuated to subcamp Steyr-Münichholz and from there to the branch camp Gusen where they finally were liberated on May 5." (Information provided by Sherry Wilzig's son, Jesse, based on his research at the Mauthausen memorial site.)

30 Siggi always remembered and honored the armed forces that liberated him. One of the commemorative projects he supported was the installation of a fifteen-foot-tall statue titled *Liberation*, a bronze memorial to the American soldiers who helped liberate Nazi concentration camps. The statue, depicting a soldier carrying a death-camp victim to freedom, was created by the renowned Polish sculptor Nathan Rapoport and dedicated in New Jersey's Liberty State Park on May 30, 1985.

31 After the war, the United States, Great Britain, France, and the Soviet Union each occupied a part of Germany, and each occupier went about "denazifying" its zone differently. In October 1946, the Allies began classifying former Nazis into five categories, intending to punish those in the first four: Major Offenders; Offenders; Lesser Offenders; Followers; and Persons Exonerated. Nazis were made to fill out a questionnaire and classify themselves; most true major offenders lied about their participation in Nazi actions and were not punished at all (www.yadvashem. org/odot_pdf/Microsoft Word - 6265.pdf, accessed March 22, 2020).

32 The doors of the United States, Canada, and the rest of the countries of the West remained closed to refugees for quite some time despite humanitarian and political efforts to the contrary. Only 12,000 Jewish refugees succeeded in immigrating to the United States before 1948, and Israel became the preferred destination for many displaced Jews (www. yadvashem.org/articles/general/liberation-and-the-return-to-life.html).

33 From September 1944 through September 1946, the *Aufbau* printed lists of Jewish Holocaust survivors located in Europe.

34 At the time, "melancholic depression" was seen as a distinct disorder. The American Psychiatric Association (APA) no longer recognizes it as a separate mental illness and categorizes melancholia as a subtype of major depressive disorder.

35 Ashkenazi Jews are members of the Jewish faith whose ancestors lived in the Rhineland valley and in neighboring France before migrating eastward to Poland, Lithuania, and Russia after the Crusades of the eleventh to thirteenth centuries. Ashkenazi Jews have the custom of naming a child after a relative who has passed away.

36 Dinnerstein, 162.

37 Dinnerstein, 163.

38 Dinnerstein, 155.

39 Slavin and Pradt, 29.

40 In 1965, the Second Vatican Council issued *Nostra Aetate*, "In Our Times," one of the most radical documents in Church history. *Nostra Aetate* repudiated antisemitism and the longstanding propaganda that Jews were collectively guilty for the crucifixion of Jesus Christ. The "Christ killer" charge had been a common Church teaching for centuries and a major incitement to violence against Jews, reaching its apogee in the Holocaust.

41 Field Marshal Bernard Law Montgomery (1887–1976), nicknamed "Monty" and "The Spartan General," was a senior British Army officer who fought in both the First World War and the Second World War.

42 Wright, 57.

43 Dochuk, 56.

44 *Moody's 1981 Manual* spells out some of this complex history, although questions are left unanswered. According to the 1981 *Manual*, Wilshire

Oil Company of Texas was incorporated in Delaware in 1951. In 1960, Wilshire merged with Riffe Petroleum Company of Tulsa. *Moody's* goes on to state that in October 1962, Wilshire then became a subsidiary of Britalta Petroleum Limited. This needs to be reconciled with a statement by Robert L. Reed, who was Wilshire's president at the time, in support of a plan to reorganize the company in January 1964. According to Reed's statement, Wilshire had acquired "substantially all of the properties of Britalta" on August 1, 1962, in exchange for common stock of Wilshire. (Siggi B. Wilzig Archives.)

45 Tyrone Edmund Power Jr. (1914–1958) was an American film and stage actor. From the 1930s to the 1950s, Power appeared in dozens of films, often in swashbuckler roles or romantic leads. His better-known films include *The Mark of Zorro, Blood and Sand, The Black Swan, Prince of Foxes, Witness for the Prosecution, The Black Rose,* and *Captain from Castile.*

46 Quoted by Roger D. Friedman in "From Auschwitz to a Castle in the Hamptons: The Wilzig Story" (Observer.com, February 1, 1999).

47 Securities and Exchange Commission regulations stipulate that when a person or group of persons acquires beneficial ownership of more than 5 percent of a voting class of a company's equity securities registered under Section 12 of the Securities Exchange Act of 1934, they are required to file a Schedule 13-D with the SEC.

48 "A Drive Shaped on a Deadly Lathe," *Herald News,* January 19, 1971.

49 *New York Post,* November 14, 1974, as quoted in "Corporate Antisemitism: A Self-Perpetuating Pattern" by Stephen L. Slavin and Mary A. Pradt, *Jewish Currents* (February 1978): 30.

50 Dinnerstein, 238.

51 As reported in the *New York Observer,* January 1999.

52 By way of quantifying the value of this consolidated reporting proce-

dure, for the twenty-six months ending February 1983, tax payments from TCNJ to Wilshire amounted to $9,389,000. Other benefits to the Wilshire-TCNJ relationship included the power to raise capital based on their combined financial statement. In the difficult banking period prior to 1982, TCNJ had lost its ability to raise capital, except through Wilshire, which added $3 million to the bank's capital by investing in 30,000 shares of TCNJ's preferred stock. (See letter from William Goldberg, Wilshire's senior vice president and treasurer, to Burton Ahrens, Esq., dated December 23, 1985, Siggi B. Wilzig Archives.)

53 Noted in Appendix B of the Wilshire Oil Company of Texas By-Laws dated July 25, 1969, Exhibit C – Subsidiary Banks (Siggi B. Wilzig Archives).

54 *Electronic Buyers' News*, issue 029, October 16, 1972.

55 NASDAQ was initially an acronym for the National Association of Securities Dealers Automated Quotations. It was founded in 1971 by the National Association of Securities Dealers (NASD), which divested itself of NASDAQ in a series of sales in 2000 and 2001.

56 *New York Observer Online*, profile by Roger D. Friedman, February 10, 1999.

57 "The bank has not forgotten the 'little people,'" described *New Jersey Business* magazine. "Its customer base includes 40 per cent individuals with checking and savings accounts and mortgages, 40 per cent small businesses and 20 per cent medium- to large-sized firms. While the bank routinely handles $20-million loans to corporations, it has not abandoned those whom Wilzig calls 'the working people.' 'It is not by accident that in the more than 20 years I have headed the bank we've only had 20 residential foreclosures. We work it out,' he described. 'On commercial [mortgages] we're tough. But we work it out with [homeowners] and have never been a loser for it.'" (Quoted in James T. Prior, *New Jersey Business* 38, no. 4 [April 1992]: 18.)

58 "$2,550,000 For Israel's Economy Raised at Siggi Wilzig Tribute," *The Jewish Standard*, July 4, 1975.

59 Felzenberg, chapter 1.

60 As far as published information about the destruction of Europe's Jews was concerned, reports had appeared in early 1942 in London's *Jewish Chronicle and Zionist Review*. An article appeared in the *New York Times*, March 1, 1942, quoting Jewish community representative Dr. Henry Shoske that, based on reliable information, "there will be no more Jews in Poland in five or six years." (Quoted in Bauer, 20.)

61 *The World at War* is a British television documentary series chronicling the events of the Second World War. At the time of its completion in 1973, it was the most expensive series ever made. The twenty-six-episode series was produced by Jeremy Isaacs, narrated by Laurence Olivier, and first shown in the US in syndication on various PBS stations in 1975, shortly before Siggi's talk at West Point.

62 "West Pointers Hear of Holocaust From a Survivor," James Feron, the *New York Times*, December 14, 1975.

63 The Jewish vote had played a decisive role in many major elections, including that of President Kennedy. "If the Jewish vote had split," wrote one historian, "Nixon would have been elected." (Arthur Hertzberg, *Jewish Polemics* [New York: Columbia University Press, 1992], 113.)

64 "Appointments by Governor Confirmed," *Herald-News* Trenton Bureau, February 4, 1976.

65 By April 1970, Wilshire owned 7.03 percent of Selas Corporation's outstanding Common Stock. (Noted in Appendix B of the Wilshire Oil Company of Texas By-Laws dated July 25, 1969, Exhibit F – Non-Banking Companies Other than Subsidiaries. Siggi B. Wilzig Archives.)

66 The bid and ask prices are stock market terms representing the supply and demand for a stock. The bid price represents the highest price an

investor is willing to pay for a share. The ask price represents the lowest price at which a shareholder is willing to part with shares. The listed closing price is the last price anyone paid for a share of that stock during the business hours of the exchange where the stock trades.

67 James T. Prior, *New Jersey Business* 38 no. 4 (April 1992): 18.

68 A grandfather clause is a provision in which an old rule continues to apply to some existing situations while a new rule will apply to all future cases. Those exempt from the new rule are said to have grandfather rights or acquired rights, or to have been grandfathered in.

69 As early as 1972, the Fed had argued against TCNJ's position. "The Board announced its determination that Wilshire is not entitled to 'grandfather rights' under the Bank Holding Company Act since, in the Board's judgment, Wilshire did not exercise a 'controlling influence' over Trust Company on June 30, 1968" (press release from the Federal Reserve dated July 27, 1972, Siggi B. Wilzig Archive). In the Board's Order, the Fed argued: "It does appear that on June 30, 1968, Wilshire was capable of exerting some influence on the bank through its share holdings, representation on the board and its presence primarily through its president. . . . However, that 'influence,' in the Board's opinion did not amount to a 'controlling influence' over Trust Company. . . . These conclusions are founded upon a number of observations on the character of Wilshire's relationship with Trust Company on June 30, 1968, including the following. . . . Wilshire's ownership of 8 per cent of the outstanding voting share of Trust company . . . without the existence of other factors, appears inadequate to establish a 'controlling influence' . . . [and] the very brief interval of eight months between Wilshire's first contact with Trust Company and its alleged assumption of a 'controlling influence', and the fact that only two Wilshire representatives became 'insiders' (two of 16 Trust Company directors) just two months prior to June 30, 1968, indicates that strong historical ties between Wilshire and Trust Company had not developed." Based on these and other findings, "the Board is unable to conclude that Wilshire exercised or possessed

the power to exercise a controlling influence over the management or policies of Trust Company on June 30, 1968. Accordingly, the Board has determined that Wilshire is not a 'company covered in 1970' within the meaning of section 2(b) of the Bank Holding Company Act" (Federal Reserve System "Determination of Status of Wilshire Oil Company of Texas Under Bank Holding Company Act," 10–13, effective July 27, 1972).

70 Ben Weberman and Robert McGough, "The Battles Lost, the War Won," *Forbes*, January 31, 1983.

71 Ultimately, the Supreme Court declined to review the case.

72 A correspondent bank is a bank authorized to receive deposits from, make payments on behalf of, or handle other financial transactions for another bank.

73 Hubert P. Janicki and Edward Simpson Prescott, "Changes in the Size Distribution of U.S. Banks: 1960–2005," Federal Reserve Bank of Richmond *Economic Quarterly* vol. 92, no. 4 (Fall 2006): 291.

74 Masha Leon, "A Gleaming Night at the Jewelers' Gala; Siggi Memories," *The Jewish Forward*, January 24, 2003.

75 Pfefferkorn, 25.

76 Wiesel, 10.

77 Wiesel, 221.

78 Fulbrook, 235.

79 Konrad Hermann Joseph Adenauer (1876–1967) was a German statesman who served as the first chancellor of the Federal Republic of Germany from 1949 to 1963.

80 The first White House ceremony for the Day of Holocaust Remem-

brance was held on April 30, 1981.

81 "In his innermost thoughts," wrote journalist Eric Trager while a doctoral student in political science at the University of Pennsylvania, "Ronald Reagan was genuinely friendly toward American Jews." He quotes the Anti-Defamation League's National Director Abraham Foxman as saying, "I think it was an episode—a sad episode. The Jewish community's attitude toward Reagan was that he was a friend, and certainly a friend of Israel. . . . [The Bitburg visit] did not tarnish him significantly" (Forward.com, October 12, 2007).

82 David Irving, *Hitler's War* (New York: Viking Press, 1977). Until the 1980s, Irving was regarded by the academic world as a decent historian who had written several well-received books including *The Destruction of Dresden* (1963) and *Hitler's War* (1977). He marginalized himself in 1988 when he began espousing Holocaust denial, and his remaining credibility was forfeit altogether in 1996 when, in the course of an unsuccessful libel case against American historian Deborah Lipstadt and her British publisher Penguin Books, the defense proved that Irving had deliberately misrepresented historical evidence to promote Holocaust denial. Not only did Irving lose the case, but in light of the evidence presented at the trial, a number of his works that had previously escaped serious scrutiny were discredited.

83 "First they came . . ." is Pastor Martin Niemöller's (1892–1984) description of the cowardice of German intellectuals following the Nazis' rise to power and the subsequent purging of their chosen targets, group after group. There is some disagreement over the exact wording of the quotation and when it was created. According to historian Harold Marcuse, "In November 1945 Niemöller visited the former Dachau concentration camp, where he had been imprisoned from 1941 to April 1945. His diary entry about that visit and some subsequent speeches he gave imply that that visit triggered the thought that became this famous quotation" (www.history.ucsb.edu/faculty/marcuse/niem.htm).

84 Financial liquidity refers to how easily a business's assets can be converted into cash. While other Garden State bankers rushed headlong into real estate ventures and questionable loans and investments, TCNJ eschewed junk bonds, foreign loans, joint ventures, leveraged buyouts, long-term bonds, and fixed-rate long-term mortgages. Thus it rode out the real estate debacle and the area's economic downturn by investing in short-term US Treasury Notes, a virtually risk-free medium, which returned a profit to the bank, rendering TCNJ extremely liquid.

85 James T. Prior, *New Jersey Business* 38, no. 4 (April 1992): 18. A bank's health is measured by its capital. In 1992, under federal guidelines, a commercial bank had to maintain a Tier 1 risk-based capital ratio of 4 percent. The Trust Company in 1991 had an 11.97 percent ratio.

86 Bukiet, 13–14.

87 Helen Epstein, *Children of the Holocaust: Conversations with Sons and Daughters of Survivors* (New York: Penguin Books, 1979).

88 "Stock Fight on at Jacobs Engineering: Former Director Urges Founder to Sell Shares," *Star-News* Business, July 23, 1992.

89 Order to Cease and Desist, FDIC-94-129b, October 12, 1994 (Siggi B. Wilzig Archives).

90 "Trust Co. earnings up 25%: Increases Change of Bank's Takeover," *The Record*, Business Section, October 22, 1997.

91 Glenn Collins, "Jackie Mason, Top Banana at Last," *New York Times*, July 24, 1988.

92 Quoted by Roger D. Friedman in "From Auschwitz to a Castle in the Hamptons: The Wilzig Story" (Observer.com, February 1, 1999).

93 The New York Stock Exchange judged a company's qualifications for membership based on volume of shares traded, the value of all shares combined, and the price per share. Wilshire's assets had shrunk to the

point where the company no longer met the requirements of the New York Stock Exchange and moved to the American Stock Exchange.

94 In 1949, a selection of transcripts from the Boder recordings was published under the title *I Did Not Interview the Dead*. A biography of David Boder is available from Alan Rosen, *The Wonder of Their Voices: The 1946 Holocaust Interviews of David Boder* (New York: Oxford University Press, 2010).

95 Kenneth D. Jones and Tim Critchfield, "Consolidation in the U.S. Banking Industry: Is the 'Long, Strange Trip' About to End?" *FDIC Banking Review* 17, no. 4 (2005).

96 "Trustcompany Open to Buyout Offers," *The State-Ledger*, April 26, 1993.

97 The market typically assumes a buyer overpays since there are usually "skeletons in the closet" that aren't discovered until after the deal closes. This was particularly true in the hot bank-merger mania of the early 2000s. In the case of the NFBC-TCNJ merger, the market reacted with atypical enthusiasm. Since the deal was share-for-share rather than a fixed dollar value, both TCNJ and NFBC's shares traded up, making it arguably the bank merger of the year—an accolade Alan Wilzig recalled reading in *Bank Mergers and Acquisitions Monthly*.